W9-BFR-899

Slow Dance to
Pearl Harbor

Also by William J. Ruhe

War in the Boats: My World War II Submarine Battles

Slow Dance to Pearl Harbor

A Tin Can Ensign in Prewar America

Capt. William J. Ruhe, USN (RET.)

BRASSEY'S
Washington • London

Copyright © 1995 by Brassey's, Inc.

All rights reserved. No part of this book may be reproduced, stored in a retrieval system, or transmitted in any form or by any means—electronic, electrostatic, magnetic tape, mechanical, photocopying, recording, or otherwise—without permission in writing from the publisher.

Library of Congress Cataloging-in-Publication Data

Ruhe, William J.
    Slow dance to Pearl Harbor: a tin can ensign in prewar America/
Capt. William J. Ruhe.
     p. cm.
    ISBN 1-57488-020-9
    1. Ruhe, William J. 2. World War, 1939–1945—Naval operations—
Destroyer. 3. World War, 1939–1945—Naval operations, American. 4. World
War, 1939–1945—Personal naratives, American. 5. World War, 1939–1945—
Campaigns— Pacific Ocean. 6. United States. Navy—Biography. 7. Sailors
—United States—Biography. I. Title.
D783.R83 1995
940.54'51—dc20   95-8906
                                                     CIP

10 9 8 7 6 5 4 3 2 1

Printed in the United States of America

Contents

Preface

PEOPLE AROUND THE WORLD have been both fascinated and amused by books, movies, and television programs about life on a U.S. Navy ship. Frequently, tyrannical captains play a major role in these stories. Some involve the personal traumas experienced during the start-up of a big war. The best known of these fictitious tales include Thomas Heggen's *Mister Roberts*, Marcus Goodrich's *Delilah*, and Herman Wouk's *Winds of War*.

I was always struck by how well these interesting stories reflected what I experienced as a young U.S. Naval Academy graduate before World War II. I lived the life depicted in these recreations of shipboard experiences. I saw how Americans were slowly awakening to the dark clouds of war gathering around the globe. What you will read in this volume is not fiction—the events happened to me and to my friends, colleagues, senior officers, and shipmates described in this book.

My story is derived from a copious journal that I kept between September 1940 and June 1941 of my existence on a destroyer. Fortunately, it has the added spice of describing a period when U.S. naval officers enjoyed an elite—though badly underpaid—lifestyle and when the Pacific war was approaching. The book also lets the reader inside the personal affairs of an ensign whose loves and infatuations were affected by ship movements, regulations, the threat of war, and war itself.

In using my journal to write this book, I slowly realized that it contained a unique social history of a period in which the Navy prepared for war while society seemed to ignore the dangers of the future. The world I describe is painted in the sepia tones of an old movie, often set in the pleasurable social environment of some of the best homes in the areas that hosted Navy ships. You'll share my memories of slow dancing in Newport, Halifax, Norfolk, San Diego, and Honolulu. You will join with me on visits to numerous colorful Caribbean and Pacific islands. You'll experience my joys and disappointments, as I meet many wonderful, beautiful young women and fall deeply in love in Holland and in New York City.

All of these events were seen through the eyes of a newly minted ensign, only a year out of Annapolis. It's now been more than fifty years since I first served on a "tin can." (Destroyers were so named because of their fragile one-quarter-inch steel hull. The ten months I spent on the destroyer *Roe* as a young, gung-ho Navy ensign, had a major effect on my naval career: I established the professional discipline necessary to make me a good naval officer and to stay alive through the tough war that shortly followed.

This story is much more than just a story of America and of the professional development of an ensign. It's a universal story of how a young man in a conservative organization runs afoul of an autocratic and abusive boss. The youth's offense is that he won't knuckle under to his boss—while trying to improve his organization and himself. With the resilience of youth, he takes his hard knocks like water off a duck's back, yet he is scarred by his low fitness ratings. He is able to weather the psychological storm because of the sympathy he gets from his shipmates. They not only approve of the young man's attempts to get results, but they join him in fighting the boss's tyranny in order to produce a higher level of teamwork and effectiveness in their business. Good results despite bad methods is the basic story.

After graduating from the Naval Academy in 1939, I served a year in the cruiser *Trenton*—as a "fresh-caught" ensign. My duties on this big warship were inconsequential, giving me little preparation for the rigorous professional training that I encountered after being transferred to the destroyer *Roe* (DD-418) in August 1940.

Within the U.S. Navy, destroyers were considered the finest training ground for aspiring top-notch line officers. The Navy rewarded tin-can skippers who ran taut, spit-and-polish ships—even if they created "hell ships" in doing so. Whether the *Roe*'s skipper was among the worst of the martinets of such ships is debatable, since many of my peers thought that their captains were also too demanding.

In comparing notes with my Naval Academy classmates regarding how to react to overzealous skippers, I discovered that I was far more confrontational with Lieutenant Commander Richard M. Scruggs, the commanding officer of the *Roe*, than my classmates were with their ships' captains. They felt that rolling with the punches provided smoother sailing in the Navy than bucking the system. It seemed that I was learning to be a competent naval officer the hard way and being battered in the process. Perhaps my difficulties flowed from the combative experiences I had learned in varsity sports competition at the Naval Academy. Another explanation came from the fact that in the peacetime Navy, the captains of destroyers were generally very ambitious, insecure, and scared as hell of hazarding their careers through ship mishaps or security violations. It was no wonder that they were tough on the men who crewed their destroyers. Perhaps my assignment was not that unusual. Indeed, truth often seems to emulate fiction.

Fortunately, the Navy in its wisdom often assigned a "good guy" as executive officer on a destroyer where there was a "bad guy" skipper. The balance achieved resulted in a barely livable but efficient man-of-war. Such seemed to be the case with the *Roe*. Whether Captain Scruggs helped shape me into a competent naval officer in the ten months I was aboard the *Roe* is the heart (and guts) of this account.

The lingo used in this account reflects the language used by a greenhorn ensign just before World War II—as faithfully recorded in my journal. It imitates the way old seagoing men of the '30s talked. Their words and expressions are colorful but they are for the most part self-explanatory.

Destroyer life and duties were (and still are) interesting, adventurous, and a challenging business.

Acknowledgments

To my father, Percy B. Ruhe, who made me an astute observer and comprehensive recorder of my experiences in the unique society that I enjoyed, to the many Naval Academy '39 classmates who were destroyermen and who commented usefully on my manuscript, and to Susan Megee and my son Edward, who computerized my writings.

Slow Dance to
Pearl Harbor

1

Welcome Aboard

A YEAR AFTER GRADUATION from the Naval Academy, I was ordered to the destroyer *Roe* (DD-418). Lieutenant Commander Speed Rogers, the first lieutenant of the cruiser *Trenton* from which I was being detached, remarked to me, "You're lucky to be assigned to a tin can, because you've already lost a year in the Navy through your playing around in Europe." Lucky? Well, perhaps, since a tin can was generally thought to be the best place to learn how to be a top-grade surface ship operator. What Speed Rogers had considered to be playing around I felt was creating good will among the people of Europe. At least that was the advertised purpose of European Squadron 40 T, of which the USS *Trenton* was the flagship.

After detachment from the *Trenton* in late August 1940, I took seven days of "proceed time." Thus, I arrived late in the evening of 30 August at the destroyer *Roe*, which was tied up in the Brooklyn Navy Yard. It was the start of the Labor Day weekend, so there was just a skeleton crew on the *Roe* and only a duty officer to provide the traditional, "Welcome aboard."

Lieutenant (junior grade) Burris D. ("B.D.") Wood, the duty officer, was called topside to meet me as I marched up the gangway carrying a single suitcase and my guitar. The cruise box that I'd left in my fifty-dollar Chevrolet car was hauled aboard by two enlisted men whom B.D. ordered to "bring it to the quarterdeck, for Ensign Ruhe." After studying my orders to the *Roe*, B.D. had me "logged in" by the quartermaster of the watch. I was alarmed that B.D. kept shaking his head from side to side as he studied me closely. "You've come to a tough ship, Mr. Ruhe," he gloomily ventured.

1

"It's 'Bill,'" I corrected.

"Okay, Bill. You might as well know from the start that this isn't the happiest of tin cans. Captain Scruggs likes to describe it as a 'taut' ship." I'd been in the Navy long enough to learn that those commanding officers who ran taut ships were considered to be "sundowners"—strict disciplinarians with a mean streak. In the very old navy, a "sundowner" was one who sadistically had all of his crew return to their ship by sundown so they would have to spend the night aboard. Was Captain Scruggs actually a sundowner? Or was B.D. exaggerating?

"The skipper is a rough taskmaster," B.D. continued, "He's a stickler for details and a bit erratic. Part of the time he's the nicest, most congenial senior officer you'll ever know. Then he's stamping all over you for some piddling thing. He thinks he's either trying to get your attention or he's trying to make you a better naval officer." B.D. paused to let this sink in. Then he continued, "Stay rigged in for awhile—that means saying, 'Yes, sir' to everything. And don't let him see you wasting time while you're on this ship. He keeps quoting, 'life is real and life is earnest,' which means, 'act serious and dedicated to your job,'—at least while he's watching you."

"Job?" I asked.

"You're going to relieve Ozzie Wiseman out of '38 Naval Academy as communications officer. So get together with him as soon as he comes back to the ship. Ozzie is leaving for flight school at Pensacola soon, and is eager as hell to get off this ship as fast as possible. Ozzie is no fun to work with. But stick close to him and learn all about how to stay out of the Captain's hair, while carrying out your communication duties. Unfortunately, the Captain is more bugged by communications problems than by anything else. So you've got a tough row to hoe ahead."

"How does Ozzie get along with the skipper?" I innocently asked.

B.D.'s frowning response was not optimistic: "Captain Scruggs thinks that Ozzie is the best officer aboard because he keeps claiming that he's spending hundreds of hours keeping his publications corrected, while working hard to train his men. And he is. But he's as slow as molasses in whatever he does. So he's working at his job without letup and acting never caught up. When the skipper is watching, Ozzie puts on a great act of being exhausted from overwork. He'll be a tough act for you to follow. And you don't look like the type who'll be overwhelmed by a communications job."

B.D. was right on. I wasn't going to lose my liberty time just to impress the Old Man. There'd be no act of keeping my nose to a grindstone when work was finished. I believed in enjoying activities ashore. Perhaps things might change, however, while I was on the *Roe*.

"Am I now 'George' on this ship?" I asked. As the lowest-ranked officer on the ship I'd be handed a host of menial, no-account jobs. And this would really complicate a swift reduction of my workload—which I was counting on, so I could pursue my many interests on the beach.

"Well, perhaps your classmate, Blatz Helm, who's aboard, is lower than you in class standing."

Remembering that Blatz claimed to be the anchorman (the graduate with the lowest academic standing) in the Naval Academy's class of '39, I strongly—and with great relief—stated, "He is. He's several hundred numbers below me, so he continues to be 'George.' Right?"

B.D. chuckled and pleasantly nodded. His round, boyish, open face made me feel that he would be a good shipmate and ally on this "taut" ship. Then I noted a look of concern on B.D.'s face when I glanced around the topside. "The *Roe*'s in refit right now," he explained, "and doesn't look shipshape. It's my job as first lieutenant to get her cleaned up. In fact, we'll all be working hard as hell to avoid the Captain's wrath for having a dirty ship. His threats can't be taken lightly because he doesn't mind giving unsatisfactory fitness reports. Or even restricting us for almost anything he doesn't like."

At this point, B.D. remembered that there was mail for me on his desk. He sent a messenger, who returned with three letters, one of which was an airmail letter from Holland. The address on it in Lucrece's stylish handwriting made my heart beat faster and I felt a little light-headed. It was the first letter from my girl in Holland since the Lowlands were invaded by the Germans on 10 May 1940. I wanted to tear it open then and there. But with B.D. watching, I resisted the great urge to find out what had happened to my Lucrece. So I crammed it into my pocket until I was alone. Then, I could properly savor the contents of this agonizingly delayed letter. It should show whether our love affair was still strong or whether it had been wiped out by the Nazi invasion of Lucrece's harmless country.

Thus, as soon as B.D. left me alone for a moment, I ripped open the envelope and read the first few lines to be sure that Lucrece was still healthy and uninjured. She was. And I noted that under the date of the letter, 28 July 1940, she'd penned, "your birthday." Since something good always seemed to happen on my birthday, I expected that her written words would be favorable:

> My darling Bill,
> The German invasion was a nightmare. But the occupation troops have strict orders not to harm Dutch women. So, I've been able to carry out my Red Cross duties without fear of being molested. Unfortunately, young, handsome German soldiers are always by my side trying to help me in my work with the injured. I hate them when they're so close to me. They are trying to gain my favor and my affections...."

I read no further and put the letter back in my pocket. It was evident that my Lucrece was not a victim of the war. Nor did she seem too unhappy about the German occupation of the Netherlands. Moreover, she was apparently resigned to her fate, as well she might be, since the Dutch had lost all hope of being liberated quickly after the evacuation of Allied troops from Dunkirk in late May.

Later, after I pleaded a need for sleep, B.D. assigned me to an officer's stateroom. Again alone, I continued to read the letter from Lucrece:

> When the air raid sirens began howling about nine in the morning, everyone rushed around wondering what was going to happen. Was Rotterdam going to be bombed? And why would the Germans want to bomb our poor old port city—an "open city"? I quickly put on my Auxiliary Red Cross outfit and rushed into the Oostplein to see where help might be needed. But then the sky was filled with parachutes near the airfields and many German soldiers came floating down. Most of our people were in the air raid shelters expecting bombs to drop— not heavily armed enemy soldiers. A few of our young men were at the airfields and had old rifles, shotguns, and pistols to kill the descending paratroopers. But the Germans shot the men who were in the open. The enemy's fast-firing weapons were too much for our brave Dutch boys. So not too many of the Nazis were killed before they landed. Soon there were so many Germans on the ground that our armed men had to flee for safety. But they were killed under the bridges or pulled from homes and shot. The Germans paid no attention to me because I was wearing my Red Cross uniform and was a woman. The fighting was all over so rapidly that I felt terribly ashamed because we Dutch were so badly prepared for this

unexpected kind of invasion and could be conquered so easily. Later I heard that the Germans had expected to have 65 percent casualties on their first drop of paratroopers at Rotterdam. But it was laughable at how few Germans were either injured or killed. Soon after, the Germans bombed Rotterdam, killing fifty thousand citizens. It appears that the Germans enjoyed the same quick takeover of all the large cities of Holland while suffering few casualties of their paratroops.

When I rushed to provide first aid to a wounded Dutch soldier there was always a young German soldier beside me, acting protective. Their attitude, that they were the very considerate conquerors who you'll come to appreciate and soon cooperate fully with, was unbearable to me. I've never liked Germans and these Nazis are the worst. Their occupation of Holland will be a dreadful thing. Already they've rounded up all the Jews and have shipped them to Germany to work in the munitions industries.

Perhaps I should leave the above out of this letter if there is any hope for its reaching you. Still, an International Red Cross worker here feels that she can smuggle this letter out of the country without it being seen by any Germans.

My love, we might have to wait until this war is over to get married. But I'll keep loving you devotedly every moment that we are separated.

Your Lucrece

That night, after finishing Lucrece's letter, I lay awake for several hours remembering and reliving the very few days we had spent together in July 1939. That's all we had to build on, but it had produced a love that robbed me of my sleep on many nights. Lucrece had become a main part of my future.

I recalled spending the early afternoon of my previous birthday with most of the *Trenton*'s officers touring the docks of Rotterdam in the burgomaster's boat. It was very boring stuff, but considered necessary to emphasize our "good will" toward Holland. Then, at the Town Hall, the burgomaster gave a tiresome, long-winded welcoming speech, which was followed by an equally flowery, dull speech, by Admiral Charley Courtney, who was the head of European Squadron 40 T. His command consisted of a single cruiser and two destroyers and was a simple force to carry out a modest task. His speech, both wordy and almost meaningless, had to be suffered through.

I was falling asleep at the back of the crowd of forced attendees when there was a slight stir at the rear of the hall. A glance over my shoulder showed the most beautiful girl in all of Holland. She was cautiously entering so as not to disturb the distinguished admiral's speech. How did I recognize her as the most beautiful girl in her country? It was easy.

The *Trenton* had arrived in Rotterdam on 22 July 1939, and for the next four days Maxie Berns and I had ridden our bicycles around the city of Rotterdam looking for attractive girls. Finding none, we had put our bikes on a train to Amsterdam the next day. Once there, we joined the thousands of pedalers who thronged the city's wide streets. The bicycle traffic moved so fast that our inexperienced, weak-legged low speeds caused many of the cyclers to yell, "Hurry up!" or "Get out of the way!"

The rapid flow of women and men on their simple, one-speed bikes—additional gears were unnecessary on the flat surfaces of the Lowlands—caused me to focus only on the bare legs of the girls gliding by. Most appeared muscular and a bit heavy. However, when I spotted a slim leg pumping away, I'd speed up to examine her body and to get a good look at her face. But failing to concentrate on the traffic flow brought me more curses and bicycle bell-ringing, which I ignored as I studied one after another pretty Amsterdam girl.

It was while I was zeroing in on a blonde with a shapely leg, nice body, and pink cheeks, that I observed that other Dutch fellows were ogling the same girl. One particular male who wanted to show his especial interest in the girl rang his bicycle bell twice and the girl answered with two rings and took off as though in a drag race. Evidently the two rings meant, "I like what I see and I'm going to catch you." Her answering two rings meant, "Come ahead, but I'm not easy to catch." It was a game of courtship being played out. The furiously pedaling girl was acting coy and hard to get, while the fellow had to prove that he really wanted to make a conquest. After initially widening the gap between herself and the chasing boy, she eased up on her pedaling, as if she wanted to be friendly. This let her pursuer catch up and grab her bicycle seat. At this, the two would drop out of the traffic, move to the sidewalk, and mumble words of introduction. It was an easily understood charade. I also noticed several other chases where the fellow never overtook the girl bicyclist by the time both had disappeared from view far out ahead of Maxie and me.

Understanding the game and recognizing that Amsterdam had a considerable supply of good-looking girls, Maxie and I pulled out of the moving traffic pattern and stopped on the sidewalk to discuss how two cyclists in poor shape could be successful in this girl-boy game. Maxie suggested: "Let's just pedal close to a likely prospect and let her look us over. Then we ring our bells twice. Since we're clean and decent-looking American guys, the girl might be persuaded to slow up after she's initially raced away at a great speed." This plan left out our first having to hear her two rings of assent—if she wanted to be chased.

Why not give this idea a try?

So, when back in the traffic, on spotting an exciting, clean-limbed girl with flowing blond hair, I rang my bell twice. At this, the girl rang her bell twice and took off like a bat out of hell. Shortly, she glanced back and a look of disgust spread across her face as she noted that I was not closing the gap. In fact, our separation was widening. Consequently, she sped off and got lost in a dense crowd of bicyclers. I made several more unsuccessful attempts to get acquainted with a beautiful creature. But no luck. Maxie did no better. So we decided that the Amsterdam girls felt that the two of us were not worth slowing down for. Dejected, we put our bicycles back on a train for Rotterdam and returned to the *Trenton*.

Thus, when this truly stunning young woman appeared in the doorway at the back of the hall, I moved swiftly toward her to preempt her attention. Her loveliness was like a rare and beautiful landscape. The looks of awe and the gaping jaws of other officers who had turned at the interrupting noise made me realize that she was worth risking the fury of the admiral by furtively shuffling across the parquet hardwood floor of the hall. Even so, the immediate pause in the admiral's speech, when he heard my footsteps, struck my back like a well-directed arrow.

But when the swarthy-tanned girl, who had sparkling dark-brown eyes and wavy bronze sun-bleached hair, smiled warmly at me, my impulsiveness seemed justified. It was love at first sight! Compared to the blond, blue-eyed, plain beauties bicycling around Amsterdam, this new arrival resembled a movie starlet who could charm males everywhere.

Soon, I was to learn that she actually was starring in Dutch films. She revealed this as we walked back to the *Trenton* for dinner. Also, that her name was Lucrece Dolée. She pronounced it "Lew-cress Dolay" in such a melodious way that I felt she must be very good in musicals. Her last name, "Dolée," didn't seem to fit her volatile, yet fluid gestures. She resembled a hula dancer interpreting a Hawaiian song. Evidently, she was of Italian heritage. I also noted that she walked beside me discreetly and shyly, keeping a considerable separation between the two of us. There was no touching of shoulders or grasping of hands. Lucrece was undoubtedly feeling out our relationship. And that was good, because overly aggressive girls usually turned me off.

In the *Trenton*'s wardroom I smugly introduced Lucrece to ogling junior officers, who seemed enchanted by her presence. Maxie Berns had also brought a girl with him for the evening meal —Lucrece's friend, Lillian. Thus, after the meal, Maxie suggested that the four of us go dancing somewhere. Lillian felt that we'd do best at Scheveningen—the Atlantic City of Holland, located on the North Sea. I was all for dancing with Lucrece since it would bring us closer together. So, we borrowed the wardroom's automobile and Maxie drove us fifteen miles to the Casino at Scheveningen.

On the way there I held hands with Lucrece, discovering with a rude shock that her palms were heavily callused. "I row almost every day for exercise," she admitted. "In the early morning I do a few miles around the canals in my scull— when I'm not on location for a movie." Her rough, muscular hands had me worried. But her nice, dimpled knees and smooth, soft thighs, displayed when she accidentally repositioned herself on the backseat, allayed my concerns.

The movie business intrigued me. So I asked about her roles and their importance in the films she was in. She dodged these questions but was emphatic about the work. "I hate it. I have to get up at five-thirty in the morning and work until the mid-afternoon. The shooting goes on for only a few weeks and I get no more than a hundred dollars a day when I'm working. I'm not getting rich like your Hollywood movie stars." A hundred dollars a day? That was really big money to an ensign who was being paid only $125 a month!

When asked about her travels, she said that she and Lillian had just returned from Germany, where they'd been wined and dined by some of Hitler's aides—Goering, Hess, Himmler. Apparently, the Nazi party leaders doted on having beautiful women at their social gatherings. What that meant about Lucrece I could only guess, but it suggested that she might admire top-dog Nazis.

The following afternoon, Lucrece and I rode bicycles to her swimming club. When I rang my bell twice, she laughingly answered with two rings and took off like a sprinter coming out of the starting blocks. Then she slowed down and let me overtake her and grab her bicycle seat. At this, she giggled in such a silly fashion that I knew she was embarrassed at her too-easy acceptance of my courtship.

At the pool she devastated me with her breathtaking, shapely body. She was truly a thoroughbred. Her swimming was strong and graceful. So I had to show off on the diving board, doing difficult trick dives. My double-twist corkscrew dive was new to her and she clapped for it enthusiastically. Lillian, who'd come with Maxie on bicycles to join us, added to the applause.

Again we returned to the ship for dinner. But this time I insisted upon first meeting her parents and her sister, Manon. Her mother proved to be an effervescent, plump, black-haired woman who was always short of breath as she enthused about "her Lucrece." The father, on the other hand, was a low-key, taciturn, wiry Dutchman who ran a jewelry store. Only the hint of a smile showed on his face when he shook my hand when I was introduced.

Then there was Manon, the younger sister, who was much like her mother, bright-eyed and dark, but slim. She told of being a dress designer who created dresses for Lucrece to wear in her movies. When we took her back to the *Trenton* for dinner, she was well impressed by the watercolors I'd painted and said that they were "very good for a naval officer who did such things." Manon was definitely the kid sister, not too attractive, but likeable and clever. And evidently not jealous of her exceptional sister.

Only three more days of swimming, dancing, and walking together beside the windy North Sea remained before the *Trenton* departed for Saint-Nazaire, France, for another good will visit.

On our last night together, Lucrece and I went to Scheveningen to hear a symphony, played by the National Symphonic Orchestra and directed by Ernest Ansermet. He was one of Europe's best conductors, according to Lucrece. The guest piano soloist, Mary Barrett Dew, was "world renowned," and the music was powerful and enchanting, Lucrece was ecstatic during the Debussy *Chanson du Mer* suite and transmitted her deep feelings through her hand, which I held throughout the concert. Her shivers of delight at a beautiful passage of music produced in me a strong emotional reaction, which generated a heightened interest in classical music—and Lucrece.

Coming back late at night in a taxi, we kissed passionately. But Lucrece said, "You shouldn't kiss me as though you love me when you're actually only fooling with my affections." She said this so sadly that I felt a little guilty. "And I am deeply hurt since I have begun to love you and you aren't serious about our relationship," she added. What Lucrece was saying was that my lovemaking was mere flirting. She protested, "For me, this is a great tragedy in my life. I feel that it would be much better if we never see each other again." Give up this perfect liaison with this wonderful woman? Didn't she realize how smitten I'd become?

Then she told me of some of her unhappy, short-lived love affairs with overly aggressive movie people—handsome but shallow macho men who were anything but considerate of her deep feelings in their relationships. She told me these things so woefully that it made me love her more tenderly. Her reproach for my sexual desire, however, was disturbing, and this tragic side of her personality was most puzzling. How could a person who was so beautiful and outgoing not hold the world by its tail and be fully able to enjoy her destiny? Finally she said, "At least let's continue through the years to be good friends." She sounded like a member of the gloom-and-doom crowd who were groaning that war was coming soon to spoil their easy lives.

Walking hand in hand on the beach at Scheveningen in a strong gale on our last night together, I felt a supreme sort of happiness. Lucrece, on the other hand, acted very depressed. She said that I was withholding from her my involvement with some other girl who obviously had intentions of marrying me. So I told her about my hometown girl, Polly, who for the preceding three years had been my main love. But that had all ended when I had reported to the *Trenton* as an ensign just out of the Naval Academy. Polly had flatly stated that she wouldn't accept the two-year waiting period required before ensigns could get married. She said she couldn't picture herself following a naval officer from port to port as a service wife. So she'd given me a good-riddance talk before I sailed to Europe. I had remained firm on not leaving the Navy. Marrying her and then settling down somewhere to raise a family weren't my cup of tea. That's the way it was for me. At this, Polly had flippantly given me an "it's-best-that-we-part" talk and gone home to Allentown, Pennsylvania. Our parting was cool and final. Lucrece accepted this explanation, but it didn't dissipate the dark cloud that she was brooding under.

Thus, Lucrece's letter, which I reread a fifth time, only heightened my desire to get her out of Holland before things got much worse. If she stayed, the opportunity to have a long life together would evaporate. So I had to start calculating how she might be extricated from Holland and delivered to the United States, there to wait for me. Work through the Red Cross? Use political pull with a Pennsylvania senator? Get her to escape in a fishing boat and go over to England, as they had done at Dunkirk? It could be done, and I had to find a way to do it.

Instead of clearing my mind of the past, I tossed around in my bunk most of the night, cluttering my thoughts with things unrelated to the tough business of becoming a good destroyer-man. Hence, bleary-eyed from lack of sleep, I went to the eight in the morning quarters for the few hands who had to man the *Roe* during the holiday weekend. Ozzie Wiseman, a sharp-faced, dour person with pale white skin, was there. He was the man I was relieving and the tutor for my first few days on board the *Roe*. Charley King, another '38er, signified, "Here" when his name was called. Charley was a tall, hand-some, well-browned man with a slow, amused smile for every-thing except when the skipper was berating the officers. Blatz Helm, my classmate, had also answered, "Here." Round-faced, semibald, and with a broad toothy smile, he looked like he should be in a beer ad. In fact, he was called "Blatz" because of the large amounts of Blatz beer he consumed while at the Naval Academy. Then, of course, there was B.D., who was relieved as duty officer and who later departed for the St. George Hotel to join his wife for the remainder of the week-end. The early morning quarters were a required, meaningless routine since there were no special instructions to be promul-gated, but the duty watch would rapidly report any of their relievers who didn't show up. And the grimy, soot-stained Navy Yard buildings beyond the dock where the *Roe* was tied up made the dockside environment depressing.

When dismissed from quarters by B.D., Blatz, who smelled strongly of stale liquor, dragged himself to his bunk to sleep off "a hard night." Ozzie had to drone on about his mix-up with his wife. Looking haggard, Ozzie explained that he had gone to Wilmington, Delaware, the day before so he and his wife could be together for the weekend. But she had come to Brooklyn to be with him. "Fouled-up communications," Charley loudly whispered "You can expect that from a com-munications officer." Ozzie winced at that and his jaw tightened. But nothing more. Evidently this was only mild criticism compared to what he normally got on board the *Roe*.

Then Ozzie took me around the ship, introducing me to a few men who were standing around doing nothing. It was obvious that with the Captain off the ship everything had slacked off. However, on his return Tuesday morning every-body would then be buzzing around—at least looking busy. When in the communication spaces, Ozzie tediously described

how each piece of equipment was used. This included searchlights, signal flags, tactical radios, sonars, etc. I kept muttering to myself, "Why don't you just shut up and join your lonely
wife at the St. George Hotel . . . and get out of my hair?" But
Ozzie took no hint from my evident lack of interest and kept
giving me even the most insignificant of facts about anything
he thought I should know in order to do my new job effective-
ly. "You'll be responsible for the cleanliness of all communications spaces, including the flag bags. And no dirt or dust in
equipment. You'll have to make sure your communication personnel are clean, have short haircuts, and their uniforms look
like new. And they will have to have full bags of the proper
clothing—stenciled. You'll have to draw and correct all classified publications and ensure their security at all times. You'll
have to . . ." Ozzie droned on and on, making me blank out on
what he was saying. Later I would ask him what additional
duties I had to worry about.

So the morning dragged on endlessly. I guessed that Ozzie
was showing me what a well-trained Scruggs man was like.

Saturday night, the *Roe* was too dismal for me to remain on
board reading publications—ones that Ozzie insisted needed
reading before I could relieve him. So I went to Lieutenant
DeMetropolis's quarters in the Navy Yard where Blatz hung
out, doing his drinking. Demo, a bachelor, had a refrigerator
full of beer and an open liquor cabinet. But of primary importance was a massive five-cent slot machine in the living room.
Demo's unfettered hospitality depended on all visitors literally
standing in line to pull the one-armed bandit's lever, trying for
the jackpot. The profits from this gambling device, according
to Demo, more than made up for all the free alcohol drunk by
his guests.

The rest of the weekend was a wash. It included a church
service at the Cathedral of St. John the Divine and a browse
around the Central Park Zoo that was highlighted by a badger
doing hilarious stunts and a black panther that looked like a
good pet for the *Roe*. Finally, I ambled slowly through the
Museum of Modern Art on Fifty-third Street. In between stops,
I bought a copy of Marjorie Kinnan Rawling's *The Yearling*—a
story about an orphaned fawn that was found by a very com-
passionate woman who lovingly raised it to adulthood. It was
the sort of thing Lucrece would enjoy reading. I'd have to get
it to her somehow.

At breakfast after Labor Day all the officers were back
aboard and seated at the wardroom table. They silently stared

into their plates as the Captain mapped out how all would have to get down to business, to get ready to sail to Newport on the 4th.

Captain Scruggs was a broad, fine-looking, graying man with a keen eye. He was, as he stated, "a rules and regulations man who goes by the book." And he insisted that all of his officers scrupulously carry out existing rules, no matter how foolish some of them might seem in practice. The rule put out by the district commandant to wear a coat and necktie when going on liberty—even to go bowling—was one such irrational rule.

Then, after the Captain had studied a slip of paper alongside his plate, similar to slips beside everyone's plate, he roared with a note of anguish, "A thirty-dollar mess bill for August! My God, B.D., don't you supervise the buying of food by your mess stewards? This is a scandal."

B.D., who was serving as mess treasurer since July, when Ozzie had relinquished the job, cringed at the Captain's words. Ozzie had fed the officers for only $23.90 in July. But that was a month, according to Charley King, when the officers spent very few hours on board because it was the start of the *Roe*'s refit. In August, however, the officers had to oversee the completion of work in their spaces and were on the *Roe* for most meals.

B.D., I noticed, was in a jittery state. He had the nervous shakes, perhaps sensing that the ax was about to fall on his neck. When the Captain snarled, "This is margarine you've got on my butter plate!" B.D. sprang from his seat and rushed to the pantry window to see who had dished out margarine instead of butter for the Captain's hot rolls. At least the hot rolls were tastefully served in a basket and wrapped inside a snow-white, clean napkin. Margarine instead of butter? That was a big deal? It sure was to the Captain!

A few months of this stuff and I'd be putting in for flight school and follow Ozzie to Pensacola.

2

First Steps to War

I DIDN'T GET BACK TO THE *ROE* until one o'clock in the morning on the 4th, having shot the bull with Jack Munson, a first-string lacrosse midfielder with me on Navy's national championship teams in 1938 and 1939. Thus, I was barely awake to act as junior officer of the deck under Ozzie, the officer of the deck (OOD), when the *Roe* finally went to sea. The Roe was headed for Newport, Rhode Island, where she would check out her torpedo-firing system. Acting as an understudy for the OOD job was a bit insulting, and I told Ozzie as much. He conveyed this to Mr. Parish, the executive officer, like a little tattletale. Hence, when I got off watch, Mr. Parish, a placid, portly, medium-size man, asked me about my underway deck-watch experience. I told him that I'd been qualified as a top watch stander on the *Trenton*'s bridge, while honestly admitting that the *Trenton* had rarely gone to sea while I was aboard her. Nevertheless, Mr. Parish assigned me to the afternoon watch as the OOD. I was from then on the OOD, without Ozzie around to make things confusing.

Mr. Parish, an imperturbable, fatherly man of considerable wisdom, was a passed-over senior-grade lieutenant of the Naval Academy class of 1926. When he'd failed to be promoted, he was not forced to resign from the Navy but was allowed to wait for future selection boards to pick him up and promote him. Moreover, he didn't consider himself an inferior officer. With a good sense of humor, he would quietly joke that once free of the *Roe*, he'd blossom into a superior destroyer skipper. His self-confidence and good judgment were so apparent that I liked him as a shipmate—one who made the *Roe* more livable.

During my afternoon watch on the bridge, the skipper went into a frenzy when he noted wisps of black smoke issuing from the *Roe*'s single smokestack. "We're smoking badly, Ruhe," he yelled from the wing of the bridge. "You're making this ship look sloppy, Ruhe. Do something." Then he loudly growled: "Get the fireroom to adjust the burners. Dammit, we're not running a tramp steamer."

At this, I called the fireroom and snapped, "You're making smoke. Get a clear stack . . . on the double." Grudgingly, the fireroom's reply was an apathetic, "Aye, aye, Sir." The boiler-tending gang seemed inured to gripes from the bridge about occasional lapses in the proper regulation of air supplied to the burners that heated the boilers. The *Roe* ran on super-heat-ed steam. Hence, occasional changes in speed to dodge the many fishing boats along the coast required rapidly adjusting the burners to eliminate shots of black smoke out of the stack. The ideal, actually, was a constant emission of an "economy" haze of slightly brown gas. This indicated that the boiler's burners were adjusted so as to provide a maximum amount of heat for a minimum amount of fuel burned.

In time, while studying the stack gases, I became aware of how grimy the outside of the stack looked. The *Roe* badly needed a washdown to remove the soot and dirt that she had acquired during her two months in the Navy Yard.

During all this flap about "making smoke," Bill Norvell was standing quietly beside me waiting to take over the deck. At one point he muttered, "The Captain acts as though we were steaming in the middle of the whole fleet. He thinks that puffs of black smoke make him look foolish to his seniors in accom-panying ships."

By sundown the *Roe* was tied up to a buoy in Narragansett Bay off the city of Newport. Ozzie, having read the pertinent mail concerning our visit to Newport, mentioned to the Captain that the *Roe* had usurped the buoy assigned to the destroyer *Hopewell*, which was still at sea on exercises.

"Get me the name of the *Hopewell*'s skipper," the Captain ordered. Ozzie frantically paged through a publication carried on the bridge that listed all Navy ships in the Atlantic Fleet along with their commanding officers. Soon, Ozzie read aloud the name of the *Hopewell*'s captain.

"Get his signal number out of the Naval Academy Register, Ozzie," the Captain ordered. At this, Ozzie dashed below. Quickly he was back on the bridge quoting a signal number many digits higher than that held by Captain Scruggs. With a sly, smug smile, the Captain turned to go below and said over his shoulder, "We won't bother about changing buoys. Secure the sea watch."

Being senior, if only by a few numbers, was of considerable importance in Scruggs's navy. As he frequently said: "Rank has its privileges."

After tying up to the buoy, I studied Newport, a few hundred yards away, for its potential as a watercolor painting. It was a quaint, clean town, built mostly on the side of a small hill. There were no disturbing ads posted on the sides of buildings nor any garish fluorescent lights marring the scene. Only a few automobiles slowly moved along the main street at the bottom of the town. A simple, snow-white, eighteenth-century wooden church, Trinity Episcopal, dominated the quiet seaport town with its peaked roof and sharp, tall, triangular tower. It was a powerful symbol of the Christian church's key role in the development of our country. The huge mansions of the extremely wealthy people, for which Newport was famous, were not visible from my vantage point on the bridge of the *Roe*. But the gleaming, light-gray stone, low-lying buildings of the Naval War College, on the edge of Narragansett Bay a mile north of Newport, reminded me that it was there that Alfred Thayer Mahan, a president of the War College, had developed the thesis that sea power was the major influence on the destiny of many maritime countries.

My going ashore in Newport was ruled out by the need to correct a mountain of classified publications that had been drawn in the Brooklyn Navy Yard just before we sailed. In addition, the washdown of the ship had been made an all-hands project. The Navy Yard dirt that had settled in the communication spaces was the first order of business for Ozzie and me; we spent the morning ensuring that the entire communications gang was busy cleaning up. During the afternoon we corrected page after page of far too many directives and instruction books. The sheer volume of papers, so many of which were stamped "Secret," made me wonder how a navy so encumbered could actually be ready for war. The time-consuming requirements to read everything and to safeguard each page every second that it was out of a three-combination locked safe not only had to handicap ship readiness but also established a priority of importance little related to the fighting functions of the ship. If the U.S. destroyer navy was going to war soon—and that seemed a good possibility with the Germans pounding Britain with heavy air raids—it had better deep-six a lot of secret stuff. Otherwise, the mass of paperwork would make for colossal inefficiency.

At the Friday afternoon inspection of the ship by the Captain I had to stand by for his scrutiny of the communication spaces. Ozzie had been excused to do more correcting of publications. He had moaned appealingly that he had at least fifty more hours of work to get caught up on. The Captain believed it. But Mr. Parish muttered, "Oh, yeah?" realizing how inefficient and badly organized Ozzie was. Without Ozzie beside me, I caught all the hell for specks of dirt that the Captain found under the radio transmitters and in the corners of the flag bags. The Captain wore white gloves while inspecting. Thus, when his gloves were soiled by dirt he became raging mad. What a way to be initiated into a "taut" ship! However, when nothing was said about reflecting these discrepancies in my fitness report, I decided that much of his criticism was meant to make me cringe with fear while he was steering me down a winning professional path.

I was up early on the following morning to prepare for a rugged personnel inspection by the Captain. My lack of a new cap and neatly pressed uniform had me worried. But the Captain unpredictably focused on two of my men who were wearing nonregulation shoes. On the spot, he had the men take off their shoes and throw them over the side into the bay. He ignored me as I stood in front of my communications gang.

After the inspection, with the help of a sonarman, I fired up the *Roe*'s active sonar to see what sort of sound-ranging capability the *Roe* might have. I tried pinging on the anchored lightship less than a mile away but had no luck receiving any returning echoes. I did pick up concrete piers along Newport's waterfront; this meant that the ship's sound gear would be lucky to pick up a submarine as close as a thousand yards. Later, I played tennis with Charley King, a charming and gentlemanly person in his game. Unfortunately, he was not very good. He had the sturdy build of an athlete, yet he bragged that his only sport was cribbage and that he'd spent his afternoons at the Naval Academy as "a member of the radiator squad keeping his backside warm."

On returning to the *Roe*, I contacted Mary Henriquez—an attractive girl with big, dark-brown eyes, whom I had met at a campfire singing party on a rocky beach near Newport during a midshipman cruise in 1937. She was staying at her grandma's mansion on Bellevue Avenue and, unfortunately, was tied up for the evening. But she shortly called back to say that "Grandma wants you and your destroyer officers to come to lunch tomorrow at one in the afternoon after church. She'll send her limousine to the ship to pick all of you up."

Within an hour I was able to confirm that the Captain, Bill Norvell, and Ozzie Wiseman could be picked up at the *Roe* while Blatz and I would first go to church and then hike up to her grandma's palatial home near the Vanderbilts'. (Mary had pointed it out to me in 1937 as she and I drove back from the beach party and I had not forgotten it.) These arrangements pleased Mary.

Thus, Blatz and I went to Trinity's Sunday morning service, enjoying the gaudy vestments of the three clergymen taking part in the service—their genuflecting in high Episcopal fashion and their chanting, some in Latin, in Catholic Church fashion. Enclosed pews with silver-inscribed plates attached to the doors identified the wealthy Newport family for which the pew was reserved. At the end of the service the reverend noted to me that this more than two-hundred-year-old church had a light-gray plaster coating inside made from finely pulverized clamshells. And why not? All that calcium should produce a tough-binding kind of cement. Moreover, at the beach party in 1937 I had noticed the great abundance of clams as we dug many of them up at low tide before the party and baked them over a fire.

When Blatz and I hiked up the hill through a narrow park to Bellevue Avenue, which ran along the top of the hill above the town, we passed a twenty-foot column of field rocks that was supposedly built by Vikings to mark their being there. Vague fourteenth-century writings about Viking explorations of "Vinland" in North America suggested that Viking longboats could have come as far south as Newport before they decided that colonizing such an area was not practical: The threat of "the ferocious red men" who inhabited Vinland seemed too great for Viking families to live there.

Once on Bellevue Avenue, we passed the Newport Lawn Tennis Club. There, pictures on the walls of the clubhouse showed the wealthy late-nineteenth-century citizens of Newport playing lawn tennis. The players in the pictures were dressed exclusively in white—the men wearing long white ducks and white golfing-type hats, while the women wore dresses that reached their ankles and big, wide-brimmed floppy hats. Pictures of the players volleying showed the balls being scooped up underhand, a foot or two above the obviously very spongy grass turf.

Grandma's mansion was a huge, three-story structure with much marble. The living room to which we were escorted by an old seedy butler, was ornate and crammed with Louis XV furniture. But it was in good turn-of-the-century taste. When

Blatz and I were introduced to the dowager by the butler,
Grandma immediately rang a bell and told her servant to
"notify Miss Mary that her ensign friends have arrived." When
shortly the three officers from the *Roe* arrived, Grandma
greeted them with: "You Navy men are always welcome in my
home. It's a privilege to entertain such attractive gentlemen
when they're occasionally in our port."

Then when Mary appeared, she asked her grandma if she
could take me up to her room to see the sketches she'd made
in the past few days. "Ensign Ruhe is an artist and was very
encouraging in his praise of my art the last time he was here,"
she shyly said.

Without hesitation, Grandma replied, "Certainly, my dear.
But don't be long because you have to help me entertain our
Navy guests." Me alone with Mary in her bedroom was okay?

Mary's bedroom was in a corner of the third floor. The paint
was peeling on the walls and there were cracks in the plaster
on the ceiling. Evidently, these mansions had seen better days.
But Mary's sketches showed nice improvement and I soon
reported this to Grandma—who was busy telling the Captain
about her life in great detail. I had observed during past visits
that the people of Bellevue Avenue favored a lot of small talk
and didn't actually listen to what one was saying. They only
wanted to talk about their own interests. But that seemed to
be the nature of a society that partied too frequently.
Moreover, the six additional Newport friends of Grandma,
who joined us at lunch, offered only conversation about local,
social matters. To the make-talk question, "What brings your
ship here to Newport, Captain?" the response of Captain
Scruggs, "We're checking out our torpedo-firing equipment
with the help of the Torpedo Station people," was seemingly
ignored. It failed to elicit any thought that with a war going on
in Europe, perhaps it was wise for the Captain to be readying
his destroyer for the possible entry of the United States into
that war. In fact, at Grandma's luncheon my attempts to determine how worried these rich people were about what might
happen if we went to war fell on deaf ears.

I also reflected that being U.S. Navy officers made us privileged persons—even to being allowed to go to Mary's bedroom without constraint. It was evidently taken for granted
that officers in the Navy were gentlemen.

Being privileged had been explained on my last day of "bull
class" at the Naval Academy. The professor, a commander
who taught First Class English, took time out to talk about
the Navy we would join shortly as ensigns: "In a few short

days, gentlemen," he began. He always wore brand-new gold stripes and beautifully crafted lightweight blues and drove a red convertible; his wife was gorgeous and sported a mink coat as she sat beside him most of the time. We knew this officer "had it made." Thus, when he continued, we were all ears. "You'll be joining the fleet as officers and will discover that you'll be accepted socially into all circles of our society. In fact, you can marry a movie star, the high school beauty queen, a street walker, a prominent woman lawyer—or even a very rich Palm Beach girl." Then after a long pause, "But mark my words, gentlemen, if you marry wealth you'll earn every cent of it!"

As for the "gentlemen" part of it, Grandma and the high society of Newport socially accepted U.S. naval officers without reservation.

After a beautifully served lunch at a long table with twenty-four place-settings, Grandma asked me if I'd escort Mary to "a neighbor's dinner party" on Saturday night. "He's a dear old White Russian friend who married one of our heiresses after World War I. He's entertaining several naval officers from the War College—amongst others. And he wanted me to bring Mary but I suggested she come with a young ensign escort who'd fit right into his formal dinner party. He said that was a lovely idea."

When I agreed to escort Mary, Grandma stared at me questioningly, "You do have formal dinner wear with you, don't you?" I assured her that I would wear my white mess jacket with gold buttons and shoulderboards, my stiff white shirt, gold cummerbund, and black dress pants and black shoes.

Mary's sparkling eyes smilingly confirmed her feelings about the date. So everything was "go."

On Monday at lunch, with Blatz Helm as the new wardroom mess treasurer who'd relieved B.D. of the job, the Captain had a new victim to berate for incompetence. The flies were buzzing around the Captain's food, and he yelled for Blatz to get a fly swatter and do something about it. Anger flashed from Captain Scruggs's eyes. He growled: "I'm not used to having flies all over my food." As if the rest of us were happy to eat out of garbage pails!

Blatz smilingly took the whole business in composed fashion and called for Weber, the stewardsmate, to "get the fly swatter going and get rid of all the flies in the wardroom." Within seconds, Weber was swatting and swatting and dead flies were littering the wardroom table. The Captain then put a halt to Weber's command performance and rose majestically from his chair to stalk off to his cabin. He sulked while the rest of us wardroom mess members ate without protest as a few remaining flies kept buzzing around.

On Tuesday, the *Roe* was under way at eight in the morning to shoot five experimental torpedoes that the Newport Naval Base people had put aboard. But before the *Roe* could leave Narragansett Bay, fog rolled in and hence the *Roe*'s anchor was dropped. By noon the fog was still so thick that the *Roe* was returned to her buoy.   However, the next morning at eight-thirty the *Roe* headed for the six-thousand-yard torpedo-firing range. When the two range-buoys were lined up, the five torpedoes were fired one by one. The first of the eleven-hundred-pound exercise-head "fish" leaped out of the water before settling down to a good run. The two fish I was allowed to shoot, using data from my torpedo director, missed the far buoy by about twenty feet on either side. One then sank and the other surfaced at the end of its run. My second torpedo had spurted large flames as it was launched, searing everyone close to the torpedo tubes. The fire must have come from ignited alcohol that had leaked from the afterbody of the torpedo.

All five firings proved successful and the Captain was well satisfied with his torpedo-firing team. The gunnery and torpedo officer, Bill Norvell, led the team. Bill was a simmering, unhappy officer from the Naval Academy's Class of '31. Earlier, when the Captain had ridden him too hard, he frankly told the skipper, "You're ruining the morale of this ship with your raising hell about everything." Bill had already gotten an unsatisfactory fitness report and felt that the Captain would find some excuse to give him another, on only a slight pretext. A few bad fitness reports and a man's chances for promotion would be just about nil.

On return to port, I received a letter from Lucrece, which, in essence, said, "Let's just be good friends." There was more about how she couldn't understand why I would prefer her to the many glamorous girls that I was meeting in America. Was she being tragically noble and making the ultimate gesture of sacrificing her great love for me in order to give me the freedom to find another girl to marry? Then in a postscript, she paradoxically wrote: "You know I'll never stop loving you."

For the evening, I was assigned the job of shore patrol officer in Newport. Since it was a foul night with heavy rain, business was slack. I looked in on a couple of miserable floor shows at some sleazy night clubs. The cabarets had only a few badly dressed floozies sitting around on bar stools. None looked enticing. After peering into a few bedrooms up above a cabaret's entertainment area and seeing little action, I observed to the owner that the rooms showed "good sanitary conditions," which I would record in my report of the evening's activities. I ended my duties by getting two men from the destroyer *Bancroft* out of jail and then putting them in a taxi with orders to the driver to take them back to their ship. The men had been held in jail for flirting and drunkenness. Flirting? U.S. sailors?

On Thursday, the *Roe* moved over to the Torpedo Station dock to reload the same five torpedoes that had been fired earlier. They were to be shot a second time . . . on Friday the 13th, a date that didn't bode well for the firing results. But things went well. I fired three of the fish this time. The first went bouncing along over the waves, although I had set it to run at four feet of depth. That torpedo sank at the end of its run. The other two fish ran "hot, straight, and normal" and passed close to their mark—the far buoy. All in all, the Captain again acted well satisfied with the firing performance of Bill Norvell's torpedo team.

Then, after returning to the Torpedo Station dock to on-load the *Roe*'s torpedoes—which we had left ashore while firing the experimental ones—the Captain held a thorough materiel inspection. He griped incessantly about the poor materiel condition of the *Roe* and especially the communication equipment. Yet, I had to admire how thoroughly he examined each item and spotted the beginning of rust, dust in motor windings, worn shoes on shock-mounted equipment, etc. He was the best man at this business whom I'd ever seen in action. But his criticism of those whom he thought were responsible for the discrepancies was too severe. He just made everyone mad at him.

At mast before the evening meal, he dished out fifteen days of restriction to a man for wearing his hat on the back of his head while on liberty. And later at dinner, he gave Ross, the duty wardroom steward, three weeks of restriction to the ship for mixing canned milk with fresh milk. Ross was a brash, burly black wiseguy who created problems that kept the mess treasurer in continual trouble.

As a result of the Captain's meanness, all officers, except me as duty officer, went ashore to get drunk. The Captain had left the *Roe* to join his wife.

By one o'clock in the morning, the officers returned to the *Roe* in an uproarious state. Charley King sprayed Ozzie with a fire hose. Then there was a soaked-washrag fight between the officers, with much laughter and lurching around. At this, I turned in for some sleep. But I was awakened periodically by somebody wanting to sit on the edge of my bunk and talk inanely to me about most anything.

At five forty-five, after I got some steady sleep, Blatz came into my room and announced, "We're getting under way right now for Norfolk. The Torpedo Station wants the *Roe* clear of its dock so that the destroyer *Bancroft* can come alongside at eight o'clock to take aboard torpedoes." The Captain, who didn't particularly like Newport and had gotten a good night's rest, said, "What the hell. Let's go," and ordered the underway detail called away. Poor Mr. Parish. He could scarcely stretch his bleary eyes open as he got to the bridge to navigate the *Roe* out of Narragansett Bay. On my part, I called Grandma's Bellevue home and left word with a half-asleep butler that I was unexpectedly leaving for Norfolk and couldn't escort Mary to her neighbor's dinner. The butler said he was sorry to hear this, but would "tell Miss Mary."

I had the morning deck watch, with the *Roe* rolling about ten degrees on a side. It was not enough to affect the officers, except for the Captain. He stayed in his bunk. This ensured a peaceful trip south. He was seasick as usual, enough to limit the loudness and number of his complaints. He left orders for the OOD to "plot a position of the *Roe* every ten minutes; watch the fathometer constantly for readings less than ten fathoms; challenge all vessels and record their identity."

Some ships, however, were smart enough not to answer the *Roe*'s intrusive challenges and I wondered why the Captain wanted to know the names of merchantmen sailing along the East Coast of the United States. Did he expect to find that one was a disguised German ship? Then what? The United States was still a neutral in the Atlantic War.

In the evening, my bridge watch was complicated by fishing boats littering the ocean. Their tiny, bobbing white lights were visible only relatively close at hand. This forced me to weave the *Roe* carefully past each small craft while shouting down the voice tube to the Captain's sea cabin each course change and why I was making it. His barely audible grunts of acknowledgment were worrisome. I wasn't sure how much he was absorbing about topside activities. Bill Norvell, who was beside me near the end of my watch, said, "The skipper gets this way with even the slightest bit of rough weather. And he'll want to get off the ship the moment we tie up. Thank God." Bill, who was a serious but volcanic man, was only too prophetic.

By midmorning the *Roe* was moored alongside the destroyer *Buck* at the Naval Operating Base, Norfolk, and the skipper precipitously hurried down the gangway—to "get his sea legs back" and to join his wife, who was faithfully waiting for him on the dock. She followed him everywhere.

Norfolk was an aging town with houses needing repair and painting due to the hard times of the '30s. No distinguishing landmarks rose above the skyline. But it had many friendly, well-bred Southern girls who welcomed young naval officers with open arms. We enjoyed this phenomenon to a lesser extent in other seaport towns—but, uniquely, in Norfolk the parents of the girls also seemed to have an enthusiasm for entertaining midshipmen and junior naval officers.

I recalled how on my Third Class Midshipman Cruise in 1936, the battleship *Wyoming* had put into Norfolk for a few days of recreation for the midshipmen. After tying up to a pier in downtown Norfolk, we were greeted by more than fifty hosts who were there to offer their hospitality to large groups of midshipmen. Dancing parties had been planned at the Cavalier and Surf Beach Clubs at Virginia Beach, outside of Norfolk, and many midshipmen in smaller groups went to ocean-front homes for beach parties. The whole idea was to get the daughters together with the midshipmen and let nature take its course.

I had met Louise Outland, the oldest of three daughters of an insurance executive, discovering in the process that the Norfolk girls were eager to attend Naval Academy hops. Consequently I'd "dragged" her to the Third Class Dance during June week and had an evening of sheer delight, what with her wearing a white evening gown that seemed plastered to her good figure and her following my dance steps flawlessly and smoothly. Hence, after logging in the confidential material received on arrival, I made my way with a borrowed car out to Louise's home on the beach near Cape McHenry. It struck me then to ask her why the upper-crust families of Norfolk (there being little distinction in Norfolk between the rich girls and those of the upper-middle class) treated the young U.S. naval officers and midshipmen so well.

Laughingly, she explained: "You fellows are men who have jobs—unlike our young men hereabouts who are idle because of the Depression. To our fathers and mothers you represent Academy people with secure jobs far into the future and would therefore make good husbands for their daughters." (There was never a thought that in the next year or so many of us might be dead ducks.) "Your four years of learning discipline and manners made all of you gentlemen. So promoting a match between one of us and one of you makes good sense to our parents. That's why my daddy literallly shanghaied you and some of your classmates off the *Wyoming* and brought you out to our beach home." This was much of the attraction of a Third Class cruise on a battleship.

Recalling how I'd visited and revisited the Outlands' home with each return to Norfolk, I slyly suggested: "There's still a chance, Louise, that your father's strategy will work."

Louise had a throaty chuckle for that.

"The girls at William and Mary envied me for my weekend dates at the Naval Academy," Louise continued. "That's a pretty glamorous place and you fellows looked so nice in your midshipmen uniforms. And then it was a good opportunity to meet more midshipmen—which was a break for me when you dumped me for that little hometown girl you'd taken a shine to."

Sitting with Louise out on the pebbly beach late at night, her drawling, musical Southern talk sounded like a siren's song enticing me to stop thinking about other loves, particularly "the one far across the seas." I'd brought the guitar along so I sang a few of the songs I'd composed since we'd last been together. She preferred "I'd Rather Be Dancing with You" and suggested we go to the Cavalier Beach Club Tuesday night to dance to Harry James's band.

In the first few days that the *Roe* was in Norfolk, Ozzie and I were busy inventorying publications and readying for the turnover to me of the communications department. Ozzie was so tardy in getting down to work and then so slow in methodically checking off each item that I thought I'd never make it ashore. Putting superseded things into a "burn" pile slowed Ozzie even more. Hence, I told Ozzie I'd take all of the stuff to be burned to the base incinerator and check off each page before consigning it to the flames. He approved of this.

On my first trip to the incinerator I found a page missing from a classified document. Its loss would have to be accounted for and I didn't relish telling the Captain about it. It would set him off like a sky rocket. So on my return to the *Roe* I spent several hours searching for the lost page. I found it in with some papers yet to be burned. What a relief! And what a loss of good partying time with the Norfolk girls!

On my next trip to the incinerator with more classified material to be burned, I observed an utter disaster— not for me but for my classmate, Frank Blaha.

Frank was the custodian of classified publications on another ship. While both of us were burning our piles of classified material page by page, Frank put his pile on the hood of a battered, old vacant truck that was parked close to the mouth of the incinerator. Perhaps both of us were too wrapped up recalling our football games together at the Academy, or perhaps we were both too intent on checking off each page being burned. At any rate, we were startled to hear the truck suddenly pulling away from the incinerator with Frank's pile of secret pages being scattered into the wind. When we last saw the truck, pages were fluttering off and being blown by the wind all over the Naval Operating Base.

Both Frank and I scurried about gathering up a page here and another there, for many minutes. But they were so widely dispersed that we knew we'd be all day trying to locate most of the missing pages. Frank should have called for help—anyone from anywhere—since losing classified material was a heinous offense in the peacetime Navy. The person guilty of such a deed would either get a Letter of Reprimand, a transfer off his ship—or both.

In the middle of our chasing after missing pages, the base general alarm started sounding. Someone had alerted the base commander to the crisis that was occurring. As it turned out, Captain Scruggs was driving back to the *Roe* through the base and some pieces of paper floated onto his windshield. He stopped his car and examined several of the papers. Horrified to find them stamped with a large "SECRET" in red letters, he immediately called the base duty officer to alert all personnel on the base to a "true emergency." Then, with the ringing of the base general alarm, bullhorns spread around the base instructed all available personnel regarding the recovery of classified papers scattered all over the base.

The base was in an uproar. People ran hither and yon, feeling like real heroes when they picked up a page stamped "SECRET." Frank and I, however, went sheepishly back to our ships to find out how bad things were—never mentioning our role in the fiasco.

The Captain met me at the gangway and roared, "Ruhe, why aren't you out there helping to recover the classified material?" Then he thought about the culprit who caused this emergency and yelled into space, "They ought to throw the book at the guy responsible for this!" Poor Blaha. I knew that eventually the authorities would identify whose documents had been involved by the identifying numbers on retrieved cover pages. So Blaha would get some gross type of punishment for his doping off.

But by keeping my mouth shut, I would not be identified as an accomplice. In this peacetime navy, getting ready to fight a war at sea was of far less importance than maintaining the security of its voluminous paperwork—which might easily be the Achilles' heel of the fleet.

I never did find out what happened to Frank. I was afraid to be connected with his crime because somehow Scruggs, if he knew I was involved, would blame me for the whole business and punish me severely. Acting chicken was certainly the better part of valor.

On Tuesday the *Roe* was degaussed after her degaussing belts were calibrated. These were cables forward, midships, and aft, which were wrapped around the inside of the *Roe's* hull below the waterline. When energized with electricity, they would remove the magnetism from the steel of the *Roe's* hull and equipment. This protected her from a magnetic influence mine—a mine triggered off by the magnetism of a ship passing overhead.

Unfortunately, the *Roe* stayed at sea after being degaussed in order to check her slight retained magnetic signature. We didn't return to the dock until ten o'clock—too late for me to pick up Louise and make the dance at the Cavalier.

At one lunch during this period, Captain Scruggs pleasantly asked that I paint "a portrait of the *Roe*" on the wardroom's forward bulkhead. Someone had probably told him how I had painted a watercolor of the Newport waterfront while we were there and he had realized that he had a captive "artist" in his wardroom. "Make it about four feet long and broadside too," he suggested sweetly. "I know you can do it well." His toothy, reassuring smile was used to con me into cooperating. Even though his proposal sounded like my cup of tea, my heart sank. Art on demand was never much fun. Did he want a silhouette of the *Roe*, I wondered, or a realistic image of how she looked at sea? I wouldn't ask, but would attempt the latter.

I was not sure whether the Captain would favor an artistic or an accurate rendition of the *Roe*. Was he art minded? Or was he like the senior officers of the cruiser *Trenton*, who were invariably irritated by my carrying a newly painted scene done in oils back to the ship in the officers' motorboat. Commander "Speed" Rogers, the first lieutenant of the *Trenton*, had in fact ordered me to use the crew's liberty launch if I was going painting or returning to the ship with a completed oil painting.

If Captain Scruggs had little or no sense of how to construct a picture, he would unquestionably interfere with my day-to-day and step-by-step development of the *Roe*'s portrait. He'd have useful suggestions to offer, such as: "The ship should be painted a lighter color than you're using." "You have to show more details in the things carried on the foremast." "You show only forty-six stars in the American flag being flown." "There's more red in Old Glory than you've used." A great help.

I thought long and hard about what I was getting myself into. My solution was to take a large piece of canvas and drape it over the picture after each day's work and to paint furtively only while the Captain was occupied on the bridge. And I never made any comments as to the progress achieved.

Using a large, colored snapshot of the *Roe*, I completed the *Roe*'s picture in eight days. Then after lunch in the wardroom, I announced to the Captain that the *Roe*'s picture was ready to be unveiled for his approval. He smiled in anticipation.

Cutting the strings that held the canvas covering, I let it drop to the floor, all the time closely watching the Captain's reaction. A broad smile and a slow, approving movement of his face from side to side as he examined "his" ship from bow to stern seemed promising. He appeared to be almost overcome with wonderment that I had portrayed his ship so well.

But then his face slowly darkened, and his smile was replaced with a disapproving frown, which deepened as his eyes studied first a single detail of the ship back aft and then moved to the fo'c'sle. There, his eyes steadied on something I had painted. His jaws tightened perceptibly and his teeth began to grind. Whatever it was brought a flushed color to his face.

Except for the five-inch gun, which I felt I'd shown correctly, there was little else forward on the main deck that he could criticize.

Suddenly, the Captain shifted his black look to the five-inch gun on the *Roe*'s stern. After long study of that gun, the Captain's gaze went back to the forward gun—his jaw now working with undisguised fury.

I waited to be bawled out.

"Dammit, Ruhe! I won't have it looking this way," the Captain snarled. "You've got the five-inch guns secured with their barrels at six degrees elevation. Four degrees is proper, NOT six degrees! Change it!" he roared while rising from his seat, "Then, I'll look at your silly destroyer again." At this, he stomped up the ladder to the bridge.

"Well, I like it," Bill Norvell observed. And Mr. Parish, with a pitying, weak smile said, "It's pretty good, Ruhe. But the

Captain won't let it stay on the bulkhead for more than a few days. That's the way things are on this ship."

Later, I got out a protractor and actually measured the elevations of the guns. Both were close to six degrees and that meant that the Old Man was correct as usual. But six degrees versus four? Big deal!

As predicted, although I repainted the guns with a four-degree elevation, the Captain at the next lunch gave the *Roe*'s portrait one last disapproving look and then ordered, "Get rid of that abortion, Ruhe. A blank wall is better than having that thing on it."

So the painting was scraped off and the bulkhead repainted. Thus, the officers had nothing to stare at as they listened to the Captain incessantly offering "good advice" on how their divisions should be run.

3

Improving the *Roe*'s Gunfire

WITHIN THE FIRST FEW DAYS in Norfolk, the word was passed that the *Roe* would go to Panama later in the month and be there for two months providing services to the S-boats based at Coco Solo while practicing antisubmarine operations. However, in the next few weeks plans were finalized for us to go to sea daily for short-range battle practice with the five-inch guns in order to fire for an "E"—for excellence in use of the guns. The scores made "for record" would be combined with other gun firings to determine the top gunnery destroyer in the Atlantic fleet. That destroyer would have a big white "E" painted on her stack.

Thus, early on 18 September, the *Roe* headed for the southern drill grounds, where she made practice gunnery runs in company with the destroyer *Buck*. Both ships towed six-foot-square white canvas targets mounted on sleds well astern. Each destroyer would alternate making a run on the other towed target, allowing the pointers and trainers on each five-inch gun practice in properly laying the gun on the target's bull's-eye.

B.D. and I constituted one of the pairs of officers to be used on the "officer's string" for the competitive firing. B.D. trained the gun in azimuth while I set a correction on my binoculars to account for range and then elevated the gun so that the shell would leave the gun several degrees above the target and then curve downward for a hit. I received my elevation correction over earphones from the man on the optical range finder in the turret above the bridge.

During these gun practices, I usually called B.D. "Burris." This followed the Captain's alternate use of several names for B.D. It was "Wood" when the Captain was angry. It was "Mr. Wood" when the Captain was critical but not too incensed by B.D.'s actions. When the Captain was feeling overly friendly, it was "Burris." And it was "B.D." when he thought the job being done was average. For the five-inch gun shoot, the Captain expressed high expectations for B.D.'s performance. He was silent about mine.

The runs were made at twenty-five knots, with the *Buck* and the *Roe* using speed flags to alert each other to speed changes. However, the *Buck* almost ran the *Roe* down when she failed to slow in response to an executed *Roe* speed flag that indicated that the *Roe*'s speed had been cut to ten knots. The Captain yelled loudly at me, as though the *Buck*'s mistake was my fault. But I didn't feel insulted. The Captain was just being the Captain.

At four in the afternoon, the anchor was dropped and "swim call" was announced. The Captain had been a water polo player at the Naval Academy and loved to swim. The water was warm, about seventy-two degrees, so the long swim was most enjoyable. I tried diving from the rail on the top of the pilothouse. It was forty-five feet to the water and caused a heavy shock to my head. So I tried a full gainer on my next dive, entering the water feet first. That was a snap.

The *Roe* remained at anchor through the night, then resumed the short-range battle practice runs with the *Buck*. Over and over we alternated runs. In between, I inventoried publications so Ozzie could break free and head for Pensacola. I saw that he wasn't working on corrections, and I pulled a sneaky ruse by suggesting that the Captain had asked, "Does Wiseman still have some publications left to correct?" I phrased this question to indicate to Ozzie that his leaving would be delayed if he thought he could just drop the bricks on me and take off for southern climes.

In the evening, I had another dreadful run-in with the Captain. My duty radioman had failed to copy a Fox schedule, which, unfortunately, had a *Roe* message in it. When the *Buck*'s skipper queried by signal light what Captain Scruggs intended to do about the message, our Captain became aware that his communication gang had missed something. I was called to his cabin and put on the pan. "Ruhe, you've got to do much better with your communicators," he snapped. He figuratively put a knife into my stomach and twisted it. Consequently, I studied *Communication Instructions* assiduously far into the night with the vow that I'd eliminate some of the pitfalls that kept appearing in my path. I didn't always have to learn from dumb mistakes.

At the end of the next day's practice runs, the *Roe* returned to Hampton Roads, and Ozzie left for Pensacola at eight that evening. Joyfully!

Stuck with the duty next day, I had to resign myself to remaining on board. I spent the afternoon having the roll and pitch and rake equipment prepared for the gun firings starting on Monday. A message to the *Roe* in the evening surprised me; it said that she would shortly report to Commander Destroyer Squadron (ComDesRon) 30 to be part of his squadron and fly his flag after he came aboard.

On Sunday night, Captain Scruggs returned aboard with his wife and little son, Dickie, for supper. Dickie fired crayons at me with a rubber-band slingshot and the Captain beamed at the "cuteness" of his little four-year-old. Cute? He was a little monster! Then, they went to watch the movies topside. But the regular movie operator of the *Roe* hadn't returned from liberty. It was just my luck. So I got a movie operator from the destroyer *Manley*, which was anchored close by. He showed the movie *LaConga Nights* starring Hugh Herbert, in six, film-ripped segments. My man from the *Manley* kept having to splice the film. Perhaps he wasn't a movie operator after all. And, of course, this cost me a few bucks with the Captain.

On Monday morning the 23d, the *Roe* was under way at eight o'clock for the drill grounds off the Virginia Capes. Twelve Marine Corps planes flew low over the *Roe* as she hurried to get to the firing area. They were practicing the delivery of mail to a ship from the air. But they didn't show much guts. They flew too high and, as a result, missed their drops. A few sacks of soaked mail, retrieved from the water, was all that their delivery method accomplished.

At the drill ground, I was assigned to the forward director as its gunnery officer. Bill Norvell, who seemed to have some faith in my improving "officer qualities," decided to make me his assistant gunnery officer. Blatz was then released from that job to take on the sole duties of assistant engineering officer under Hop Nolan. The joy-stick control of the five-inch guns in automatic, I found, was a neat development. It was probably the only satisfactory way to have all the five-inch guns efficiently pour out their shells at aircraft. Even for surface ship targets, the joy-stick control was best for ensuring hitting salvoes with a tight grouping at long ranges.

At the end of gun practice, I held a summary court martial for a man who was AWOL (away without leave) and he pleaded guilty to his offense. Because he lacked any remorse, I gave the man the maximum punishment allowed, since over the past year he'd already had three convictions on other hateful misdemeanors.

The *Roe* left early on Wednesday for firing runs. The wind, however, had picked up into a strong gale and the seas were running heavy—so heavy that it was difficult to transfer men between ships using the whaleboats. The boats would dive out of sight into the troughs of the sea, then teeter on the crests of oncoming waves. The firing observers had to climb Jacob's ladders to board the destroyers. The roll and pitch of the two firing destroyers were so great we experienced poor practice runs before we even started actually shooting. On the officers' string of firings, B.D. and I took fifty-five seconds to get off four rounds. That was not an "E" performance. But all four five-inch shells went through the target at the four-thousand-yard range. That was good shooting, considering the weather conditions. The Captain clapped for us when we looked up at him on the bridge.

A big storm was brewing, which temporarily canceled further gun shoots. And a sudden shift of wind brought a cold blast of wet air, heralding a northeaster—along with a big drop in temperature. The *Roe* and the *Buck* went back to anchorages in Hampton Roads. After dark, the *Roe*'s motorboat that was sent to the Amphibious Base to pick up mail finally beat its way back to the *Roe* through the raging storm. And all through the night a watch had to be kept on the bridge to check the bearings of navigation lights to ensure that the *Roe* was not dragging her anchor.

The storm didn't abate. So the *Roe* stayed at her anchorage all through the next day. That night, I went ashore as an errand boy for the Captain and then missed the last streetcar into town. So I walked to Norfolk, where I was half an hour early for the last boat back to the anchored ships. But then I went to sleep while waiting for my ride back, only to wake up as the last boat left without me. Consequently, I slept on the transom in the waiting room of a dockside hut until six in the morning, when I caught the market boat back to the *Roe*.

At seven on Friday, the *Roe* headed back to the drill grounds for her firing runs. While at anchor she had rolled so heavily that all through the night I'd slept fitfully, hearing many crashing noises from objects that were being hurled from bulkhead to bulkhead. Sleeping was also difficult because one had to lie flat on one's stomach with arms and legs wide apart to keep from thrashing around in one's bunk.

The seas were too rough for shooting, so the *Roe* was finally headed back to the Naval Operating Base, with the hope of shooting on Monday.

During the long hours at anchor I had tried to get the classified material into good shape. But one idea of the Captain's, to stamp all classified letters with a large, red-ink stamp, backfired on me. The big red warning letters, he felt, would prevent classified things from getting mixed in with unclassified things. That wasn't a bad idea. But in my wild stamping of certain pages with a red "CONFIDENTIAL" stamp, I'd inadvertently stamped an unclassified page. The Captain, I was certain, would consider this a terrible breach of "the rules," whatever they were. So I tried all sorts of ways to remove the red letters. I erased them, swabbed them with water and then tried to rub them off. That didn't do it. So I softly sandpapered them and tried using alcohol. Nothing worked. Bill Norvell, watching my attempts to remove the letters, said, "I'm glad that at times you aren't so damned efficient." The speed with which I made corrections, calculated gunnery scores, or drew up new department directives, bothered him. He happened to be a man who worked slowly and precisely. Yet he admired others who got things done rapidly.

With the red-stamped letters still visible, I had the pharmacist help me try all sorts of concoctions. But still no luck. So I finally took the inadvertently stamped page to the Captain, who signed his name over the letters without comment or even a twitch of his jaw. I breathed much easier.

Sadly, the final inventory of classified publications showed that five were missing. Four we soon discovered from my notations made at the incinerator were burned. Ozzie had apparently failed to record them as having been destroyed. The other was an error in the actual count of missing publications. This time, Mr. Parish commented: "You're working too fast, Ruhe." Normally Mr. Parish would just whistle as he watched me hastily doing these career-destroying things.

When the *Roe* was finally anchored in Hampton Roads, the wind promptly blew her around through more than 360 degrees. This caused the anchor chain to wrap itself around the extended sound dome. It then took three hours of twisting the *Roe* to make the anchor chain fall clear of the sound projector. Grimly, the sonarman said that the sound dome might be damaged and not work. But because there were no targets to test it on, there was no way of knowing whether it might be totally ruined until it was examined in dry dock. A failure to retract the sound head before anchoring had caused this mess. We had been using it after entering Hampton Roads and should have raised it before arriving at the designated anchoring spot. But short of the anchorage position, the Captain had suddenly ordered, "Let the hook go. This is good enough." And down the anchor went!

During the weekend we conducted exams for the crew and scored their papers to validate each man's fitness for his next higher rating. By late Sunday afternoon I was so fed up with work, work, work, that I decided to go ashore. I paused to wonder if that would be worthwhile, considering the soaking I'd get from the heavy seas while going to and fro in the ship's open motor whaleboat. Still, I went out to the Norfolk Yacht and Country Club, where I played piano for a loud gang-sing with the "country club crowd" of young Norfolk girls. Going ashore, however, seemed more of a catharsis than an escape from the *Roe*.

On Monday, with a small hurricane brewing, the *Roe* was brought into a pier at the Naval Operating Base (NOB). When we arrived, Captain Schuyler Heim, Naval Academy Class of '07, came aboard with his staff and made the *Roe* ComDesRon 33's flagship. This was a different squadron commander than the one designated for the two-month Panama stint.

The weather remained atrocious, so the *Roe* stayed in port until Friday. Then at eleven-thirty, she, with the *Buck* in company, headed for the drill grounds to compete in five-inch short-range battle firings. En route, the *Owl*, a tug for towing the target sled, joined up with these two destroyers. The seas had abated somewhat, so all was ready for firing runs on Saturday.

At six o'clock on the morning of 5 October, the *Roe*'s observing party was transferred to the *Buck* to score her firing runs. The Captain, noticing that I had stayed behind, quickly said, "If you've got nothing to do, Ruhe, you go to the *Owl* and act as target repair officer. The skipper of the tug, Colby Rucker, will tell you what he wants you to do." This proved a most interesting last-minute task because Lieutenant Commander Rucker philosophized about the U.S. Fleet's strategy in the Pacific and about destroyer life in general. As the *Owl* steamed on a steady course at ten knots and the *Buck* fired her five-inch guns on run after run, I estimated the *Buck*'s shots with my rake equipment and listened to Colby Rucker's ideas.

It was great to be with a senior officer who was worried about how destroyers would be used in a possible war with the Japanese—and in what needed doing to prepare U.S. warships to fight an efficient war. It was the first time I'd heard an older naval officer discuss these sorts of things in so much depth.

The *Buck*'s competitive officer's run got four hits for four shots fired. But the rest of her firing by the crew achieved only nineteen hits out of forty shots. That was close to an "unsat" performance. The *Roe* would do much better than that, I felt.

We returned to the *Roe* in a whaleboat, and all observers were transferred to the *Roe*. First, we conducted one rehearsal run. Then, with B.D. as trainer and me pointing the five-inch gun, we got a bull's-eye with the first round. But at that point the gun's antikick valve failed and slowed our firing. Thus, despite three more hits close to the bull's-eye, we failed to make an "E" score because of a time penalty. On the rest of the *Roe*'s firing runs only twenty-six hits out of forty shots were recorded. This was better than the *Buck* but a disappointment. However, the number three five-inch gun with an eight-for-eight string, earned an "E," which would be painted on the outside of its turret. My number two gun got only four out of eight hits. The smoke inside the turret had gotten so thick that I felt I was about to pass out from the pungent gases; this also affected the shooting.

All day Sunday, I helped Bill Norvell finish his gunnery reports. We were not congratulating each other, but Bill was happy to get through the whole business without being chewed out by the Captain and without any people being injured during the firing runs.

Personally, I felt exhilarated by the successful conclusion of three weeks of firing our big guns and fighting the very bad weather. It was truly a man's world of rugged life that I'd had a taste of. And it was the sort of life I didn't want to be deprived of by marrying some woman who didn't want to be a "Navy wife."

4

Help for the British: Lend-Lease Destroyers

WITH THE ARRIVAL OF Commander Destroyer Squadron 33 on board the *Roe*, it was soon evident that the *Roe* would play a major role in the turnover to the British of the final ten old-age U.S. destroyers. In September 1940, President Franklin D. Roosevelt had announced that the United States would provide all possible aid to the British short of war and would transfer to them fifty four-stack U.S. tin cans that had been laid up since 1919 and were only recently recommissioned. These destroyers were being lent to the British by the United States for a reciprocal U.S. leasing of base facilities in the West Indies, Bermuda, and Newfoundland. This was a Lend-Lease bargain between the two countries.

The fifty old destroyers had received little maintenance while they were laid up and remained unmodernized. They were known to be poor seakeepers. But they did have sufficient endurance to accompany Allied convoys all the way across the Atlantic. Moreover, the British had only enough escorts to adequately protect convoys in their last 450 miles across the Atlantic. Further west, only a single coverted antisubmarine merchant ship was providing some convoy protection.

The wisdom of President Roosevelt's emergency action was confirmed by the loss in September of 450,000 tons of Allied shipping to U-boats and German long-range aircraft. The fifty obsolete tin cans consequently provided additional and much-needed antisubmarine and antiair protection for the hundreds of Allied ships plying the north Atlantic each day in support of the British war effort. It was a critical time in the European war, and the *Roe* was to play a small part in ensuring England's survival.

Hence, for the next month our activities were dedicated to preparing to move into the periphery of an active sea war while coordinating the movement to Halifax of ten destroyers to be handed over to Great Britain.

At the same time, we made a frantic rush to fit in a great deal of social activity ashore. The looming threat of being enmeshed in the Neutrality Patrol of F.D.R.'s "phony war," after getting rid of the four-pipers in Halifax, made it seem certain that henceforth we wouldn't have much shore liberty.

The *Roe* went to sea on 4 October with a newly installed radio telephone in the pilot house. As she passed the Virginia Capes, I was officer of the deck and was able to use the telephone to tell the cruiser *Tuscaloosa* (which was out of visual range) my intentions to have the *Roe* increase speed and take a course to head for the drill grounds. Then, when the *Tuscaloosa* acknowledged receipt of this information on her radio telephone, my broadcast of "execute" told the *Tuscaloosa* that the *Roe*'s changes had been put into effect. It was most pleasing not to have to rely on flag hoists or the slow transmission of a message by semaphore for maneuvering actions. The radio telephone should almost totally eliminate the need for signals from the bridge—except when radio silence was necessary. This innovation should also reduce the hell-raising by the Captain for the occasional signal-gang glitches—of which there seemed to be quite a few since I'd taken over the communications department.

When I handed the Captain a new organization chart of the communications department, he gravely discussed the sad state of training of the *Roe*'s radio and signal gang. I told him that I had been holding daily training sessions for all my people. Yet he said, "Ruhe, you are not progressing at all decently. You've got to do better. Above all you have to show more force and initiative." My thoughts, hidden behind a blank face, were that I'd been using too much initiative without being sure of what I was doing. I'd been plunging right into problems and then trying to learn from my mistakes.

The next day, the Captain called Bill Norvell to his cabin and gave Bill the same song and dance. For Bill, the results of the short-range battle firings had shown that he was not doing well in the training of his gun crews. But worse, the Captain showed Bill his fitness report. The Captain had marked Bill, "Unsat," in several categories. Loyalty to his commanding officer was one of them. After Bill regarded his marks with growing anger, he exploded, "Captain, if I were like you there wouldn't be a man left in my gunnery department!" Bill also blurted, "And I'm putting in for transfer from this hell-ship."

The Captain just laughed at him and said, "I'm only doing this for your own good."

Bill never submitted a request for transfer.

Blatz Helm also reported getting a lecture from the Captain about what a rotten wardroom mess treasurer he'd been. The Captain cited several incidents that showed Blatz's poor supervision of "his wardroom stewards." One was: "Your boy, Ross, served canned peaches at lunch yesterday. But I ordered them taken away. Canned things are to be used only while we're on a long cruise. Then Ross chopped up those peaches and put them in Jello for the dessert at dinner." The Captain paused to let his words sink in. "*Mr.* Helm,"—the "mister" was used to show the Captain's utter disgust with Blatz—"you're letting your stewards get away with murder." Canned peaches, murder? "Your fitness report will reflect your unsatisfactory performance." At this, according to Blatz, a sly smile crept over the Captain's face. He added, "You get Ruhe to relieve you as mess treasurer as soon as possible." I did so in a few days.

On the 12th, the skipper inspected the personnel. Everyone was ordered to be in full dress and standing at attention on the main deck topside. Members of my C Division were not prepared to have their uniforms critically looked at. But the Captain, studying my men quizzically, never commented on the condition of their uniforms. When he looked me up and down, his jaw started working and an ominously dark look with eyes squinted seemed to indicate that he thought I was downright unclean. Again, he said nothing and moved on to the next division. Not now, but later, he would tell me off.

Shortly, the Captain initiated a physical fitness program for the entire crew. Hence, after quarters each morning, I took my C Division men out on the dock beside the *Roe* to run them through a stiff workout of calisthenics. The men sweated and grumbled, and some scarcely moved their feet when jumping around was part of the exercise. There were always some who would "dog" anything that resembled work. Theoretically, the men were being conditioned for the tough times ahead. But like all such surges of readying the crew for the demands of war—which included damage-control drills, physical fitness lectures, etc.—they were dropped by the end of the month. Almost any excuse sufficed not taking the crew out on the dock for exercise. We found it was easy to succumb to the isolationist attitudes of the U.S. public and media and worry little about the possibility of entering a war that at that time was confined to the European theater.

However, out in the field beyond the dock where the workouts were taken, steel submarine nets from World War I were laid out, with checks made to ensure that the links were still strong. The rust was scraped off the links and they were repainted, since eventually it was felt, the nets would be strung across the entrance to Hampton Roads.

On the 17th, the *Roe* went to sea to have her radio direction finder (RDF) calibrated. As arranged, the patrol chaser *PC 451* lay to in Lynhaven Roads five miles away and then continuously transmitted messages on several different frequencies. The *Roe* rolled heavily as she was swung through 360 degrees. This affected the accuracy of the transmitted signal's direction, which we took every ten degrees of rotation. The distortion of the *PC 451*'s radio signal due to the varying metal configuration of the *Roe* caused additional irregularities as the *Roe* rolled. Captain Heim, who was intensely interested in this piece of countermeasure equipment, got mad as a hornet when he looked at the plotted results of the calibration. He said that he had hoped to keep track of his flock of tin cans by getting them to transmit a message when they were over the horizon. Then, the *Roe*'s RDF receiver could give him a good bearing on the broadcasting four-piper. From that bearing, Captain Heim could send a steer-course to bring the distant destroyer close to his flagship—the *Roe*.

Captain Scruggs, of course, had to needle me with: "You can do better with your RDF equipment than this, Bill." Captain Heim was more generous in his comments about the *Roe*'s RDF equipment: "I'm pleased that your RDF receiver is so sensitive," he said. "Even though Nazi U-boats have good directional antennas for sending radio messages to their bases in Europe, we should be able to pick up the antenna-radiated side lobes when their U-boats are near our coast. It will give us warning that a U-boat is somewhere close and it will give us a direction to its position. Moreover, we'll have German submarines firing torpedoes at U.S. ships soon, despite this Neutrality Patrol business."

The results I had with the active sonar were more upbeat. During the *Roe*'s return to the Naval Operating Base, while practicing with the active sonar, I was much pleased to get clear echoes off a small island. When I pinged my initials toward this little target, they came back a readable "W.J.R."

The distance to the island was more than eight miles. The gear was finally well peaked for actual antisubmarine operations—an important activity of the Neutrality Patrol.

On the 23d, the Captain directed me to find a sample strip-ship-bill and prepare one for the *Roe*. A classmate on the cruiser *Wichita* produced a copy of her bill, which I easily adapted to determine what of *Roe*'s equipment would have to be put ashore and stored on the base. Luxury items such as couches, stuffed chairs, and commercial mattresses were high on the list to go. Dog kennels, cargo pallets, wooden ice-box flooring, blackboards—inflammable things—were also put on the list. That was the easy part. Getting each officer to agree that certain items could be stripped from his division's spaces was more difficult. Mr. Parish refereed all differences and invariably decided to "get rid of it."

On the same day, the base put out its air raid defense bill. It included measures for totally blacking out the base and its berthed ships. A black-out bill for U.S. shore facilities made little sense. However, U-boats operating off the U.S. East Coast were said to use the lights of military activities to position submarine-laid mine fields. It was a nasty development.

Near the end of October communication officers from the old four-pipers about to be transferred to the British ran in and out of the *Roe*'s radio shack. They were seeking all the information they could acquire about turnover problems. Unfortunately, I knew little about such things.

Classmates who'd just returned from Halifax after handing their old-age destroyers to British crews had only hilarious stories to tell about the "Limeys'" amazement at the impracticality of our paperwork for their bare-bones ship operations. They'd sailed for a year in a war at sea where only highly essential records were kept. One classmate, Red Welsh, told of handing his engineering logs, records, and instructions to British "black gang" crew members and their immediately throwing all of his destroyer's stuff into a trash can.

Interestingly, the British engineering gangs did few, if any, repairs at sea, believing that their equipment would remain operable until they returned to port. If something broke down, they made do with what capability was left. It was an "if-it's-broke-don't-fix-it-at-sea" philosophy. The U.S. communications officer on the destroyer *Evans*, which was being turned over to the British, said that "Sparks" (the nickname for the leading British radioman) and his "wireless" gang were simply mystified by the lockers full of radio instructions, back-files of messages, technical manuals and maintenance records. Their radio rooms had been literally denuded of all paperwork: "There's too much danger of fire, mate," a Limey commented.

The whole business of imminent war made me a sucker for a Prudential Insurance agent who came aboard. He offered a five-thousand dollar double-indemnity life insurance policy for only five dollars a month for the first year. Although I thought that I would never lose my life, war or no war, sixty bucks seemed like a good hedge against an unexpected death—such as being blown up by a mine.

Perhaps the Captain felt I wasn't busy enough twenty-four hours of the day, so he had B.D. transfer his commissary job to me. The myriad ledgers involved in running this department and keeping track of our provisions added many hours to my workload. Which I didn't need.

Throughout the month, my shore liberties were filled with tennis, bowling, parties, dancing, gang singing late into the night, and romancing quite a few of the Norfolk society girls who congregated at the country club outside of Norfolk. But I wasn't getting involved with any particular woman. Lucrece remained of first importance in my future.

During October I experienced sleep deprivation—only two hours on some nights when I'd either be up at six o'clock to make "nest inspections" or the cheap autos I borrowed from friends failed to get me back to the ship. One sixty-seven-dollar Chevy required me to hold the gearshift lever in place while in high gear. And a fifty-dollar borrowed car had a run-down and virtually unchargeable battery, which always required pushing to get it started. One time, I awoke early to find that my alarm clock had stopped during the night and that I'd overslept. (It was the most-dreaded thing when sleeping off the ship.) A dash to another borrowed car revealed a flat tire. After feverishly working to change the tire, I noted that the gas gauge showed empty and the nearest gas station was out of gas. But I did get back to the *Roe* in time for morning quarters.

In late October, my father wrote that both his probe at the State Department plus information from a Pennsylvania U.S. senator had indicated that although Miss Dolée had been contacted and offered help in getting out of Holland, she had shown little interest in leaving. She was reported to be healthy and active in helping her Dutch people bear up under the German restrictions on food and communications with each other. Lucrece, with her considerable intelligence, would help ameliorate hardships by working closely with the Germans. It was a risky business.

My father, the editor of the Allentown *Morning Call*—an influential newspaper with a large circulation—had applied at my request his proven ability to pull strings. He had done so frequently for the realization of civic projects. As president of the Pennsylvania Humane Society, he helped craft state laws to protect animals. When juvenile crime was rampant in Allentown, he founded the Boy's Clubs and worked to jack up the Boy Scout program. (His scout work was promoted with the benefit to his six sons in mind.) The establishment of the Walter E. Baum Art School was part of his vision to bring cultural talent to all children of Allentown, including his sons and two daughters. His most memorable work was directed toward building an Allentown park and recreation system unmatched by other similar communities throughout the United States. I knew this because, while a high school student, he used me as a part-time reporter on his newspaper. This job developed my note taking and news sense, which was transferred to the copious journals that I kept of my everyday experiences.

Just before leaving Norfolk for Halifax, I received another letter from Lucrece, smuggled out of Holland by the Red Cross. She told of working closely with the Reich's boss for food distribution to ensure that the Dutch weren't going to go hungry through their first winter of occupation. Her letter sounded so optimistic and devoid of tragic undertones that she seemed willing to cooperate with the Nazis. She made no dire predictions of trouble ahead. The letter explained in some detail why she saw no immediate need to leave Holland to come join me. Finally, she noted, "I haven't had a letter from you since the invasion. Don't you love me anymore?" To this, I would have answered, "More than ever. But my letters aren't reaching you." Paradoxically, absence was making my heart grow fonder.

On the Saturday before the *Roe* sailed from Norfolk, I was invited to a cocktail party at the Captain's home. No other *Roe* officers had been invited. It was evident that the Captain's wife, Louise, had included me in order to help entertain Eva, the daughter of her best friend who was in port with her yacht. My assignment was not unpleasant, and the Captain's performance as a gracious host gave me a new insight into his character. He was surprisingly polished and gentlemanly in his handling of his guests. His small talk was intelligent and affable and his *savoir faire* indicated that he was well bred and in comfortable circumstances. I guessed that his wife, Louise, a thin, angular woman somewhat taller than the Captain, had added wealth to their marriage. Taking my cue from this favorable situation, I took the cute Eva back to the *Roe* for an excellent dinner of rice and curry and then we went dancing at the Cavalier Beach Club in Virginia Beach. The evening was anything but punishment.

At noon on the following day, the Captain took me along with his family, including Eva, to the Pine Cone Inn at Virginia Beach for a lunch of baked clams. The Captain again proved a gracious and thoughtful host by insisting upon a table at a window looking out on the sunlit array of fall-colored trees. He also selected a fine wine for the meal. And little Dickie behaved beautifully—coached by his mother. Louise told Eva of my accomplishments, giving Eva clues for easy conversation. It made me realize that the Captain had told his wife a good deal about me, and not all of it was bad.

Only too soon, Eva was delivered to her mother's yacht in Norfolk harbor, because they had to depart early enough so as to still have some daylight for their next stop.

All in all, I had to change a lot of my thinking about Captain Scruggs. He had two sides. One was tyrannical, demanding perfection in his officers. The other was amiable, willing to please, and showed he actually liked his officers. Yet he never let us know that.

On Armistice Day, 11 November, the flagship *Roe* with ComDesRon 33 aboard, departed Norfolk at five o'clock that afternoon. Ten four-pipers followed her to sea. The entire squadron headed for Halifax for the historic transfer of the last of the old-age tin cans to the British. The old tin cans proceeding smartly astern down Hampton Roads was a glorious sight. Once clear of the Capes, however, the roll and pitch became so heavy that the old destroyers began to straggle badly and looked like a bunch of drunken sailors lurching behind the *Roe*. The Captain, of course, was seasick, so a great peace settled over the *Roe* as she steamed north.

Emergency drills punctured my feeling of optimism. On a damage-control drill my men failed to bring half the equipment called for by the checklist. It made me wonder why those who worked for me weren't acting serious under my leadership.

The next day, we transited the Cape Cod Canal. The scenery with a long sand spit at the lower entrance, the green "Go" light at the beginning of the canal, the shining white summer houses along the canal, the red-leafed mountains patched with green cedar trees, and the winding path of the canal made the three-hour passage memorable. When in Cape Cod Bay, our flock of ships ran into thick fog. With fog horns moaning, the *Roe*—leading the destroyers—blindly groped her way toward Provincetown. A barrier of fish weirs complicated our course. Thus, with an identifiable sea buoy seen close at hand, we dropped anchor while the other destroyers randomly let go their anchors on the *Roe*'s whistle signal. Visibility, moreover, was too low to allow the use of ship's boats for taking liberty parties ashore.

On the following morning, the destroyer squadron was led into Boston Harbor, where the destroyer tender *Denebola* awaited the arrival of the eleven destroyers that she would service during the planned six-day layover. The *Roe* was finally tied up at a pier in the Boston Navy Yard with four of the old destroyers lashed outboard of the *Roe*—constituting a "nest" of destroyers. Another nest was formed by six of the four-pipers tied up on the other side of the pier where "Old Ironsides," the War of 1812 frigate *Constitution*, was berthed. At that time Britain had been our great enemy; now we were close allies. The *Constitution*'s presence, thus, lent flavor to the historic transfer of tin cans to the British.

Nest watches were begun. They were a stupid, useless bore and necessary only in heavy weather when there might be a straining of the lines holding the nest together. Captain Heim also ordered the nest duty officer to march the first liberty party from each nest out to the main gate. Thus, as a nest duty officer, I discovered when I escorted enlisted men going on liberty to the gate that nobody else was doing it. So I got ComDesRon 33's flag lieutenant, "Dickie" Bird, to rescind the commodore's order. He did this gladly, without referring the problem back to his boss. The rest of the day proved just as irritating. The commodore's flag secretary having agitated to get all crews inoculated for diphtheria—their Schick tests had proved positive—forced an inoculation spree on the *Roe*. Ironically, he who had yelled the loudest for vaccinations, Lieutenant Commander Sperry, the flag secretary, had the worst reaction. He threw up and fainted after his shot. Dickie Bird turned a pale green and had to sit quietly for many minutes to recover his strength. At the same time, I felt no reaction from my shot, nor were the other *Roe* crew members fazed by the inoculations. A lesson in all this? Only that staff duty, perhaps, makes a man soft?

Before dinner, the Captain acted like a thunderstorm when he found a classified publication lying on a wardroom chair. It was checked out to Bill Norvell. He dressed down Bill for "being so careless."

At dinner, beef stew was served. I watched the Captain's reaction to this plebeian dish closely from the corner of my eye. Indeed, he glowered in my direction. But it was not because of the food. "Ruhe," he complained bitterly, "your boy, Ross, didn't serve me coffee in my cabin at six o'clock this morning." This unforgivable glitch by one of the stewards was evidently all my fault. The Captain was forgetting that the wardroom menu had been greatly improved since I took over the mess treasurer's "hot seat" from Blatz Helm. At supper, a warm cream soup was the first course. A lettuce or fruit salad was a side dish. Then T-bone steaks were frequently the main part of the menu. And freshly baked pies were the dessert.

Not unexpectedly, at the Captain's inspection of the *Roe* the next day, he gave me a tongue-lashing for the officers' "dirty rooms" and the "dirty boys"—the stewards. He failed to recognize that for the first time oatmeal and creamed dried beef were on the breakfast menu and that I had gotten a new thermos jug for the coffee served away from the wardroom. The old one had begun to stink and taint the coffee.

During the inspection, a fire siren in the yard screamed urgently. My fire and rescue party was rushed to the site of the fire, looking very snappy if not practical in their dress blues. Marines in fatigues, however, had the fire well in hand, with about fifty men on a roof that looked ready to collapse. It was overkill. Also, there were three hoses at the fire and someone turned on an unmanned hose, which sprayed the crew of the manned hose. Although the fire was satisfactorily extinguished, the Marines who fought the fire made their fire fighting a clown act.

Blatz, who had gone on weekend liberty, sent B.D. a kiddiegram saying, "Brush your teeth, comb your hair. Go to bed, and I'll be there." It was signed, "Master Dickie." B.D. read it aloud and then muttered, "The eternal freshman." And Charley King left the ship to go to a cruiser.

All afternoon of the 17th I worked on the Robinette court martial case to complete its paperwork. I'd prosecuted this case in which two enlisted men, Robinette and Smith, had pleaded "not guilty" to the charge of having stolen the purse of a young girl and taken her ten dollars. When I had cross-examined Smith, it became evident that Robinette was the guy who'd stolen the purse and that Smith had merely stood by watching it happen. Both had come to me later to say they would plead guilty, which made Robinette's counsel utterly disgusted and mad at me.

Before dark, I tried a quick watercolor of Old Ironsides and the three four-pipers beyond her. I felt great drama and excitement in the historical reality of having the forty-four gun frigate *Constitution*, which had defeated the English frigate *Guerrière*, next to our modern warships readying for war. But it was so cold I had to stop and finish the painting indoors.

On Monday, after three hours of deliberation, the court for my two seamen, Smith and Robinette, found both men "guilty of theft" and both were hung—i.e., given the maximum sentence for that offense. Later, Captain Heim, Mr. Sperry, and Lieutenant Bird left the *Roe* to go aboard and fly ComDesRon 33's flag on the *Denebola*. After clearing up the confusion caused by having to separate the staff's classified publications from those of the *Roe*, I went to bed for a well-deserved sleep, but was awakened at eleven-thirty that night by the yard's general alarm. A fire had broken out in the stack of a newly built destroyer. When the *Roe*'s fire and rescue party arrived at the scene of the fire, the yard's fire party was easily controlling the fire. So I took my gang back to the ship and climbed back in my bunk. But I was up at four o'clock for the nest duty watch. It was a wretched night for a tired destroyerman.

In the morning I sat on a board of investigation to look into "irregularities" in the books of the chief commissary steward of the destroyer *Sigourney*. He had evidently jacked up the general mess accounts to take care of a shortage that was getting quite large. His attempt to balance books that wouldn't balance was just stupid, so it was easy to write up my findings by noon.

Happily, at two o'clock the *Roe* departed from Boston for Halifax, along with nine of the ten old-age U.S. destroyers. The destroyer *Robinson* had momentarily been left behind to repair a blown gasket in an engine fuel-feed pump. All of the four-stackers along with the *Roe* were to meet up with the destroyer tender *Denebola*, flying ComDesRon 33's flag, early on the following morning. The *Roe* went to sea leading a column of five of the dark-gray, drab tin cans. She looked impressive with her gleaming almost-white paint, single broad stack, and far greater size and tonnage. The battered old *Bailey* led the second column of four destroyers and awaited the joining up of the *Robinson*. Compared to the *Roe*, the *Bailey* looked like a poor country cousin.

Taking charge, the *Roe* sent maneuvering instructions to the other ships by radio telephone. Ship positions however were initiated by flag hoists run up on the *Roe*. It was a glorious moment.

The Boston scenery left behind as we stood out to sea was a reminder that the British had landed in Boston and fought their first major Revolutionary War battle at Bunker Hill— which could be seen to the north of the main part of the city. The bright, late-fall sunshine illuminating this historic land-mark made it easy to recall that the British were then trying to subdue an American attempt to gain independence. Now, we were supplying the British a large number of antisubmarine warships to ensure their freedom from a fascist German foe bent on enslaving all of Europe.

At twilight, while taking some practice navigational star sights, I was dumbfounded suddenly to see a star that first blinked red, then white, then green—a red, white, and green star! When I pointed it out to Mr. Parish, he said, "Well, I'll be damned." The air was clear and cold and the darkening skies had provided a solid backdrop for a brilliant display of twinkling, white stars. This strange star was a truly unique phenomenon.

Lucrece had told me that when she was a young girl she was crewing on her uncle's collier when, amazingly, she had seen such a star. It was on a voyage from Rotterdam to Wales, where her uncle's ship took on a load of coal. I had laughed at her seriousness about seeing a star that changed color. To this, she said that her uncle had laughed at her in the same way. "But then when I showed my uncle the star, he said that he had never seen one like it in all of his thirty years of sailing the seas. Yet there it was." Her uncle had rationalized that the star had an atmosphere around it that alternately filtered different frequencies of light toward the earth. This caused different colors to blink on and off.

When I questioned her more about her experiences at sea, Lucrece said that every year she begged her uncle to take her with him on his cruises. Soon she had learned to navigate when she was ten years old. From then on, she became his navigator. "So you see, I know why you love your Navy life so much," adding that "I know I could never take your Navy life away from you."

The remembrance of this brought Lucrece front and center into my thoughts. It made me feel guilty for not working harder to bring her to my side.

At three-thirty in the morning, when I got up to go on watch, the seas had begun to toss up. When I reached the bridge, the *Denebola* had just been sighted and the *Roe* had begun to maneuver with her column of old-age destroyers to get into a screening position on *Denebola*'s starboard side. Only the running and masthead lights were visible on the warships. But with the arrival of daylight, *Denebola*'s lights could no longer be seen nor could she be spotted above the rising, choppy sea. Hence, the *Roe* was steered to a collision course that closed the *Denebola*.

By nine o'clock, the *Roe* and the other ten destroyers—the *Robinson* having caught up—had joined up with the *Denebola*. The waves continued to increase in height and force. The *Roe* thus began to roll heavily and, by noon, the roll was so heavy that we strapped chairs to tables and tied down all loose gear. Moreover, in order to take bearings on the *Denebola* it became necessary to hold on for dear life to the pelorus on the wing of the bridge—or get tossed overboard by the heavy pitching action generated by the wild seas.

The *Roe* would ride up on a wave and quiver and groan as she tilted far over to port with her bow swinging off course almost out of control. She would then slowly right herself like a drunken sailor picking himself up off the ground. The nine-knot formation speed dictated by ComDesRon 33 was too slow to adjust to the violent effects of the high seas. The *Roe*'s speed had to be changed continually to compensate for the waves' actions. In fact, all of the destroyers in the *Roe*'s column gradually straggled out of their screening positions—four thousand yards on the flank of the *Denebola*.

Sleep during the day between watches was virtually impossible. It was too battering an experience to lie in one's bunk with the guardrail raised. The snap and lurch of the *Roe*'s motion tossed me roughly from guardrail to wall and back against the heavy metal guardrail. I tried sleeping on the transom in the wardroom as a more humane solution.

By my midnight watch, the *Roe* was rolling thirty-eight degrees on a side, and seawater from the tops of the big waves momentarily poured down the stack. The engineroom gang, however, assured the OOD that they could easily pump to sea the amount of water intermittently pouring into the engineroom bilges.

The watch on the bridge was a wild affair. Men were falling away from their stations. Heavy metal doors to the wings of the bridge were torn out of a man's grasp as he attempted to get out of the enclosed pilot house to take pelorus bearings. The quartermaster's log was being tossed to the deck. Coffee cups slithered across the deck and smashed into the bulkheads with a loud, porcelain-cracking noise. Frequently, the helms-man, with an agonized cry would yell, "I can't hold her on course!" But finally he did.

Then a misty rain began falling and totally obscured the *Denebola*. Dutifully, I shouted down the voice tube leading to the Captain's stateroom: "Due to rain, Captain, I've lost sight of *Denebola*'s lights."

The Captain was in his room directly below the bridge and was prostrate in his bunk because of his incapacitating sea-sickness. As usual, when the seas were rough, he'd automati-cally turn in and communicate with the bridge through the voice tube. This time a weak mumble came floating up the voice tube. Barely audible, the Captain ordered, "Come left and close the *Denebola* until you have her in sight."

"But Captain," I shouted back down the tube, "we can't come left without taking the seas broad on our beam. They're liable to roll us right on over." (A few more degrees of roll and the water would pour continuously down the stack and cause the *Roe*'s righting-moment to be eliminated and then she'd soon capsize.)

At this point, I had the very disturbing remembrance, which ran a chill down my spine, of having read that the *Sims* class of destroyers, of which the *Roe* was one, when under construction in 1937, had been the subject of a congressional investigation into their stability in a heavy seaway. After considerable tes-timony from Navy ship designers, it had been recommended that "to play it safe," forty tons of pig-lead should be put in the keels of each destroyer. This would increase the metracentric height, or righting-arm, and supposedly eliminate the possibility of the ships rolling over in unusually adverse seas.

When I'd arrived aboard the *Roe*, I was assured that forty tons of pig-lead had actually been installed in the *Roe*'s keel and was well secured so that it couldn't shift despite excessive rolls or pitches. Hearing that had been comforting.

"Dammit, Ruhe. Dammit, Ruhe," the Captain weakly mut-tered, "Come left. Come left. Don't argue with me, Ruhe. Come left. Come left!"

Hence, I ordered the helmsman to put on ten degrees of left rudder and then waited for all hell to break loose.

As the *Roe* moved fully into the trough of the waves, a large wave with the wind blowing heavy spray off its top slammed into the *Roe*'s starboard side and rolled her sickeningly far over to port.

"But not to worry," I thought. "She'll right herself once more as she always does. . . ." But she didn't.

I was holding onto the chart desk for dear life and noted that the bubble in the bridge's inclinometer was at forty-three degrees while the *Roe* just lay there, making no attempt to roll back to an upright position.

"Do something!" the Captain screamed up the voice tube. "Dammit, Ruhe, do something." Evidently he was too weak to struggle to the bridge and was probably still tied into his bunk to prevent his falling out onto the deck. I was very much on my own and for a moment I had the thought that, "Here's an ensign who the skipper says 'doesn't know his ass from a hole in the ground' and now he's expecting me to save the *Roe* from capsizing."

Consequently, I ordered the helmsman, who was tightly clutching the steering wheel with both hands for support: "Put on hard right rudder." And I ordered the man at the engine annunciator to "ring up two-thirds speed on both engines," giving the *Roe* about fifteen knots of speed. But nothing happened. So I stopped the starboard screw, which I realized had been turning over completely out of water and churning the air and had "standard speed" rung up for the port screw.

Many minutes of just lying there seemed to tick on by. Yet the *Roe* wasn't rolling any further over to port. She was stuck there—wallowing in the trough of each succeeding wave that rolled past the stricken ship.

Shouts and curses and disjointed orders from the Captain kept being shrieked up the voice tube. They didn't make any sense as to what the Captain wanted done. And no one, not even Mr. Parish, pulled his way to the bridge to help save the ship. Moreover, I was unable to look back at the smokestack to see how much water was pouring into the *Roe*. All reports from the engine room had stopped. I wondered if anyone was there to answer my commands for a change in speed.

Then there was a slow roll back to starboard of about twenty degrees—enough to get the starboard screw under water. At this, I ordered, "Starboard engine back two thirds, port ahead two thirds." That made things start to happen. The *Roe*'s bow slowly swung to starboard, into the side of an oncoming wave, and she was rolled back to only forty degrees. The *Roe* kept turning into the following waves until her rolls were reduced to no more than fifteen degrees. But the *Roe*'s pitching had gotten so heavy that I had to slow the port screw and stop the starboard one. This cut down the extent of the pitches and made the *Roe* ride the waves in a tolerable fashion.

A quick glance at the clock showed that only about four minutes had elapsed since the *Roe* had rolled to forty-three degrees and gotten locked into the trough as the waves swept past her. During this period, I'd looked longingly at the radio telephone hanging on the after bulkhead. But I couldn't figure out how to travel across the intervening few feet so I could notify nearby ships that the *Roe* was in deep trouble and that her people might shortly have to be saved from the raging sea. I then had tried to spot a life preserver that I might carry through an upside-down open door and out into the sea below a capsized *Roe*. I also had wondered if I could hold my breath long enough to get to the surface from fifty feet down, while being buoyed upward by my life jacket. Evidently, I didn't have time to let fear seep through my body.

Now that the *Roe* once more was in a fairly stable condition, I could decipher the screams and yells coming up the voice tube: "What are you trying to do? Kill all of us? You idiot, when are you going to learn how to maneuver this ship? Get somebody else up there to take over! Anybody else! Where's Mr. Parish?" The Captain had the clarity of thought to suggest, "You'd better be looking around for the other ships so we don't ram one of them."

It was a good suggestion. I went out on the starboard wing of the bridge and studied the sea around the *Roe* through my binoculars. The rain had stopped and the lights of the ships were now clearly visible. They showed the *Roe* to be well clear of all of the ships.

The Captain staggered to the bridge. His face was haggard, ashen, and tinged with a touch of sickly green. He growled, "I'm taking the deck. And get the hell out of here," as he entered the pilothouse. I'd been driven ignominiously from the bridge.

At this, I felt relief rather than misery. The Old Man was back to normal. He was punishing me by banishing me from his sight. It was a moment to be happy about.

But more than that, it was actually Thanksgiving Day, as so decreed by Franklin D. Roosevelt. It was a week earlier than usual and our cooks were furious to have to change their menus. But I felt that we had a lot to be thankful for, even if the Captain didn't agree. And I also had the thought that "the North Atlantic is a wild beast that can do in those who sail across her surface if they aren't skillful enough to handle her violent moods."

5

Wartime Halifax

THE *ROE*'S SQUADRON OF DESTROYERS entered Halifax Harbor at six o'clock on the morning of 21 November. We entered between two lightships, a red and a green one. They marked the position of the submarine nets that were pulled apart to let the destroyers and the *Denebola* through. The *Roe* then tied up alongside the *Denebola* while the other ten old destroyers were tied up on the far side of the pier.

The air was crispy and crystal clear. It was a beautiful day. In the afternoon I hiked into the main part of the drab, old but clean town and up to the Citadel, the ancient fort guarding the harbor. There, I found much military activity. Men were camouflaged with strands of dry grass on their helmets and shoulders and were practice-crawling through the brown, long grass of the old parade ground. On my tour I met Captain Scruggs, who greeted me warmly. He suggested we walk together to see the lovely park at the edge of the town. We did, and the conversation was pleasant. When back at the *Roe*, I met Bird and Mr. Sperry, who had commandeered the commodore's gig. The three of us then went to the Royal Yacht Club for a beer in the staid British atmosphere.

By evening it was raining hard and was very cold. The town no longer sparkled in bright sunlight, but had become gray and dreary. Soldiers and sailors were everywhere, and many pairs of plain, unattractive girls walked up and down the streets looking for a pickup. Blatz and I, however, found a rather cute waitress whom we took to see a movie. Air raid precautions were tacked to many trees and poles. It was certainly a laugh to think that the people were worried about being bombed. Also, the Duke of Windsor's picture was pasted

on many walls. The people, I was surprised to note, talked like
Americans instead of like the British. And the exchange rate
was $1.10 Canadian for a U.S. dollar. Merchant ships packed
the harbor. They were poised to sortie to sea as part of a huge
convoy bound for England. And almost a hundred more ships
were anchored upstream. It would take at least eight hours for
all of the ships to clear the harbor.

At skipper's inspection of the *Roe* the next day, the Captain
criticized my men's compartments for being dirty and said he
wanted their bedclothing stenciled immediately. I guessed that
the Captain on yesterday's walk had assessed my attitude as
being too free and easy, so he wanted to get me back into a
more serious mood. It also seemed that he deliberately created his storms to keep me sharpened up. When all sheets,
blankets, and mattresses were labeled "C Division" in black
ink, I dashed ashore to paint two watercolors of the bleak,
wintry, rock-lined inlets with their dark, somber fir trees along
the shores under cold gray skies. It was Nova Scotia as I'd
expected to see it in the winter. My paintings were done in
such a hurry because of the bitter cold that they were only half
finished when I gave up on them. I would finally complete
them when I was forced to stay aboard.

On Sunday I slept late deliberately, in order to miss early
church. It gave me a bad conscience to give up religion for the
aesthetics of a beautiful scene on a bright, cloudless day. The
scene would have been ideal for an oil painting. Yet I couldn't
risk having a smudge of oil paint accidentally rubbed on the
Roe's sides. If the Captain spotted a smudge, his reaction
would resemble a lion sending forth a dangerous roar while
meditating on an animal just killed. Consequently, I used
watercolors and carried them in an attaché case—a container
that was unlikely to arouse the suspicions of the Captain when
I went ashore. In fact, on one occasion when he saw me carrying the briefcase as I left the ship, he asked me about my destination. I told him that I was on my way to the Boston Public
Library to research naval battles of the Revolutionary War. He
liked that. Actually I was on my way to paint one of the nests
of old four-pipers.

Thus, before noon I headed on foot to paint the scene of
Herring Cove featured on a Pan American Airline ad. It
showed fishing huts at an inlet about four miles from Halifax.
Unfortunately, no signposts were in evidence to guide my
search for this lovely Nova Scotia scene. All signs had been
removed for wartime security so that German agents put
ashore from U-boats would have to grope their way toward

the defenses that ringed the important military seaport of Halifax. A macadam road winding to the west seemed the correct path to get to my objective. A mile beyond the city of Halifax, however, I approached a guard house beside the road. It was empty. There was no sentry to stop me. So I kept walking in the direction of Herring Cove. After two more miles of plodding away, and just after I'd gotten a glimpse of weathered roofs on fishing huts, another dirty-gray guard house appeared ahead. But again, the post was empty and no Canadian soldier barred me from proceeding on. Thus, I took it for granted that what was once a tight security area was no longer of military importance.

Feeling no constraints, I trudged on to the locale of the fishing huts and finally chose a scene showing four of them. They were shuttered and seemingly abandoned. No fishing boats were in sight. The ice-green water surrounding the huts was unruffled and the tall red-brown grasses growing along the shoreline showed no signs of being trampled on by soldiers or fishermen.

Herring Cove had all the charm of the northern woods. Dark evergreen trees hemmed the inlet. A few wild ducks placidly floated on the still water, which provided shimmering reflections of the huts. The day was gemlike and close to freezing in temperature. But the sun was brilliantly friendly and kept my hands warm enough so that I could sketch and apply color rapidly to my scene. I experienced a great feeling of well-being as I worked on my painting for more than an hour without interruption. And being far from the *Roe* was delightful.

Suddenly, a delegation of four enlisted army personnel, followed by an officer wearing a black beret, jumped out of a large army truck that had arrived at the end of the dock on which I was sitting. The group loudly clomped their way toward me in precise rhythm, their thick-soled heavy shoes beating an ominous tattoo on the boards of the walkway as they closed in on me. The officer held a swagger stick under his arm and chanted "Hup, hup, hup." That kept the men marching in a threatening military fashion. I didn't turn my head to find out why they were approaching and continued to paint my picture.

"Sir," the officer imperiously snapped, "You are under arrest."

Without looking up from my work, I merely grunted an "Oh?" showing no recognition of his official action.

"Come with me," the officer barked. "You've violated the security of this area."

But I continued to ignore him, indicating that I wasn't about to obey his orders. I did mutter, "That's nonsense. There's nothing here. You can see that as well as I can." It was a difficult situation that I'd walked into. So I felt that I would have to stay on the offensive to solve this problem. I painted frantically on to get as much down on the paper as possible before I'd be forced to stop. I could then finish the painting back on the ship.

The arresting detail stood silently behind me as the officer quietly pondered how to handle this troubling situation.

"You'll just have to stop your painting, sir," the officer demandingly said, "or we'll have to use force on you—you know." A begging tone had crept into his voice, which made me certain that I had the upper hand in this business. It was the only comforting thought, however, as I began to sweat profusely and felt a bit queasy.

Reluctantly and with tantalizing slowness, I put all my brushes and paints back into the briefcase and, looking up, said, "Okay, I'll stop. Now what do you want me to do next?" It occurred to me that the Canadians had exhibited a certain laxness in not having security checkpoints manned. This could be my ace in the hole to get out of this jam.

When I stood up, briefcase in one hand and the painting in the other, the officer pleaded, "Please move along with my men. We've got to take you to the duty officer at headquarters to explain how you got to where we found you." I noticed that the arresting officer was only a lieutenant and wanted to pass the buck along to someone more senior.

At first, I marched toward the truck in the middle of the enlisted men, like Edmund Dantes being led off to prison in *The Count of Monte Cristo* movie. However, I felt that acting independently would be a better idea. It would indicate that I was doing the lieutenant a favor by letting him take me to his headquarters. So I lagged behind the detail and gestured with my hand to show that I wanted them to get ahead of me. Then I ambled along after the group—out of step—and finally got into the front of the truck after the officer had climbed in. By squashing him against the driver of the truck, I made clear my stubborn nature.

At headquarters, I was introduced to an army man wearing neatly pressed brown woolen pants, brightly shined heavy black shoes, and army captain's bars on his collar. He was the duty officer.

"We found this man painting a picture of the huts at Herring Cove," the lieutenant explained. "How he got there, the Lord only knows. He probably jumped over the outer fence." This was muttered so unintelligibly that the captain had difficulty actually understanding why I had been arrested.

"Let me see the picture," the captain demanded. He reached for it to pull it out of my hand.

I moved away and cooly protested, "I didn't climb over any fence and none of your security people were along the road to Herring Cove. If this is a security area, perhaps you've not properly done your job here and something should be done about it."

The air around me got chilly. The captain stiffened perceptibly. And the lieutenant began edging toward the door. I could see that the army captain was puzzled as to how to end this situation. Finally he suggested, "If you just surrender that picture to me, we can forget the whole business and you can go on your way." Beads of sweat had appeared on his forehead. Obviously, I held the upper hand.

Obstinately, I asked, "What's so all-important about those fishing huts?"

For a few moments the captain declined to answer. Then grudgingly he admitted, "they house some fast patrol boats that we can employ against an enemy warship that comes close inshore to threaten shipping."

Perhaps. More logically ammunition was stored inside those weather-beaten shacks. But even if PT boats were tied up inside the huts, there was no need to surrender my painting. It showed absolutely no details that would indicate a military use of the fishing huts.

"I'm not handing over this painting," I stoutly declared. "Take me to your area commander. We've got to talk about this violating of security business." I made this sound like an order. Then I showed him my identification card to show that I was a member of the U.S. Navy and that I was just as interested in security as he was supposed to be.

Reluctantly the captain said, "Come along, sir, and we'll go see the colonel."

A short walk took us to a large stone house, where we were ushered into the colonel's study by his enlisted "batman." A blazing wood fire was raging in the massive stone fireplace before the colonel's armchair, in which he was sitting. The heat generated by the fire had a welcome warmness. I'd been getting colder and colder with concern as each step brought me closer to the top Canadian army commander for the Herring Cove area.

The colonel smiled pleasantly and addressed me respectfully. To him, I was a fellow officer in arms who had only a minor difference to be resolved. He gazed steadily at the Herring Cove scene in my hand. Apologetically, and with good Oxford diction, he began, "Oh, you're the ensign in the American Navy whom I was telephoned about a few minutes ago. My duty officer seems to think you violated our area security. But I don't believe you have anything to worry about. It seems that some mistakes have been made which I believe are easily resolved if you just hand me that painting in your hand and let me burn it up in my fireplace."

It was the same refrain I'd heard twice before. And I still saw no need to accede to this request. I'd lose my painting that way. "Sir," I emphasized, "Nothing in that painting reveals what the huts might be used for." My answer was uncompromising.

"Throw it in the fire," the colonel snapped, his patience worn thin.

"Why?"

"Throw it in the fire. I want to see that thing burned up— destroyed. Now!"

"But you can't accuse me of getting to Herring Cove illegally," I slyly countered.

"Throw it in the fire!"

I stood there silently, certain now that I could force some other solution that would involve my retaining the picture.

"What's the name of your ship, young man?"

"The *Roe*, sir. It's a destroyer."

"And the name of your commanding officer?"

"Commander Richard Scruggs, Sir."

At this, the colonel told the captain, who was standing in the shadows of the firelit room: "Get Commander Scruggs of the U.S. destroyer *Roe* on the phone. And tell him we're holding one of his officers for a security violation and that I'd like to talk to him."

The phone beside the colonel's desk rang shortly. It was Commander Scruggs on the phone demanding to know the name of his officer involved in a breach of Canadian security.

"It's Ensign Ruhe, commander," the colonel explained, in chipped nasal tones. "He was painting a picture in our security area out here and we've had to put him under arrest for it."

"How do I get him back to my ship?" Captain Scruggs loudly asked.

"All he has to do is to destroy his painting and we'll forget about the whole matter. I've suggested that he throw it in my fire, but he's been adamant about that."

"Get Ruhe on the phone," Captain Scruggs demanded.

When I was handed the phone with the advice to "go ahead and talk to your captain," I respectfully said, "This is Ruhe, Sir."

"Dammit, Ruhe," the Captain shouted, "Throw that damn fool painting of yours on the fire and come right back to the ship . . . and that's an order!"

There was no further possible way to save my painting, so I reluctantly tossed it into the fire and watched it burn up. The colonel's low chuckle could not easily be forgiven—even if he was a Canadian. Then I turned to the colonel and said that I would just walk back by myself to my ship, on the same road I used coming out to his place. And that I wasn't worried about any of his soldiers stopping me because—as I smugly added— "there don't seem to be any on duty."

Both officers in the room muttered a few low-toned curses as I went out the door and headed back for the *Roe*.

It was the end of my problem. Or was it? I'd still have to cope with some form of punishment the Captain would devise to "teach me a lesson."

When I walked aboard the *Roe*, Mr. Parish met me at the top of the gangway and sadly told me that I was being confined to my room for the next two days and taken off all duties as punishment for something. "You'll have to ask the Captain why you're being disciplined. He didn't tell me what it's all about, but I'm also supposed to enter your punishment in the Ship's Log. And that means that you're being put in hack." Mr. Parish's voice held much fatherly concern as he delivered the bad news.

I was certain why I was being punished. I'd embarrassed the Canadians. In the eyes of Captain Scruggs I had created an international incident at a delicate moment in history when the United States was using Halifax as the port of transfer for U.S. destroyers to the British Navy.

But that wasn't the actual reason why the Captain was putting me in hack, as he explained when I went to his cabin to hear the charges he was preferring against me. "Ruhe," he said coldly, "I'm punishing you for your neglect in not properly preparing your radio room for inspection."

For inspection? When I left the *Roe* to go painting, nothing had been said about there being an imminent inspection of the communication spaces.

"I held a surprise inspection this afternoon, Ruhe, and found that the new 'Warning' tag on your high-voltage radio transmitter was bolted down with only three bolts. The fourth bolt had no nut on it and was useless. That's a helluva way to

treat a critical warning sign!" Then, to emphasize the gross-
ness of my offense, he added, "Your indifference to safety on
this ship will be noted in your next fitness report and you're
being put in hack for the next two days to think things over.
You'll surrender your sword to Mr. Parish."

Surrender my sword for a nut missing from a bolted warning tag? What nonsense! This archaic punitive action was
meant for heinous crimes. Even if I had inspected the radio
room just prior to the Captain's inspection I might easily
have missed that deficiency. But I felt the Captain's demand
that I be always thorough and painstaking in carrying out
my duties was somewhat justified. He was trying to make me
a top-notch officer—the hard way. Yet, I had the disturbing
thought that only when he'd heard about my painting incident had he sprung into action and called for a surprise inspection. Then, he had headed straight to the radio room to find
a discrepancy.

As with my experience in the past, naval officers in general
have an ingrained prejudice against those officers who dabble
in the arts—music, painting, writing, acting, etc. And an officer poet? He'd be shunned as an outsider.

My crime of the moment was in having my interlude of painting discovered by the Old Man. It was a mistake, moreover, to
begin thinking that the Captain was a pretty okay person. I'd
even started liking him and wondered why all the officers on
the *Roe*, including Mr. Parish, seemed to disapprove of him so
much. But then the ax had fallen. I didn't know whether to
laugh or cry. Since I was not the crying sort, I decided to laugh
and try to forget about this nasty business. In fact, I decided to
be like the three monkeys, the don't-see-speak-hear little guys.
But I would add a fourth with a tourniquet around his head so
he couldn't even think about things . . . not even about the
Captain. I'd be happier that way and do my work better.

While I was in hack, the British crews went aboard the
four-pipers to learn from the U.S. crews how to operate those
old crocks. The Limeys even brought their noonday ration of
rum with them. Then at ten-thirty on Tuesday the 26th, a
turnover ceremony was held on each destroyer. The American
crews had left their ships at ten-fifteen and the U.S. flags then
were hauled down. At the same time, the British and Canadian relieving crews came aboard to take over the old four-
pipers and raised their own flags.

Evidently, some of the planned British crews had been lost
to U-boats on their way across the Atlantic. Canadian crews
were thus substituted on some of the Lend-Lease destroyers.

Twenty U.S. engineering ratings from the turned-over tin cans stayed on the *Roe* in order to help the British and Canadian crews on their trial runs during the next few days. Meanwhile, the Captain entertained some of the British skippers of the transferred destroyers at dinner on the *Roe*. One said that on the first big enemy air raid on London, some fourteen Axis pilots had dropped their bombs in the Channel and then glided to the nearest English airfield to be interned there for the rest of the war. Another guest, a newly arrived Mrs. Burton from London, was overheard telling the Captain how she had walked through Knightsbridge in London and found a sign on a fashionable dress store that had been gutted by a bomb, which read: "Don't think this is anything. You ought to see what the RAF [Royal Air Force] did to our dress shop in Germany." The forced gaiety in her voice showed a tenseness and anxiety about the war that was missing from the talk of women back in the States.

The day after I got out of hack it snowed heavily. In fact, so much snow fell that the awnings that stretched over the quarterdeck had to be dumped periodically to prevent the canvas from tearing. The clean, beautiful whiteness of the ground beyond the ship made me eager to get ashore and paint some watercolors. Unfortunately, I had to teach five new seamen how to conduct an efficient lookout watch. Then I joined the other *Roe* officers in preparing Condition II and Condition III details for the ship's battle bill. Condition II meant doors were on the latch and condition III meant everything was buttoned up so that a shell hit or a mine blast wouldn't finish off the *Roe*. A torpedo might. We were hard at this job when the Captain at two o'clock remembered that it was Wednesday and that the crew should have a rope-yarn Sunday, with the afternoon off. This didn't, however, stop the officers from continuing with their work for the rest of the day. There was little rest for the weary on the *Roe*.

During the afternoon several big British merchantmen arrived in the harbor in badly damaged condition. One had an eight-foot jagged hole in her side and the ship was listed to keep the hole out of water. Another ship had taken two direct five-hundred-pound bomb hits, ripping her up badly, but not a person was reported as having been badly injured. A third ship had been hit by a torpedo that had torn her bow off. Then at two in the morning, the *Roe* was rolling so heavily that all hands had to get up to move her forward along the dock about fifteen feet to prevent her from slamming into the bridge of the destroyer alongside.

On Saturday, 30 November, Navy beat Army 14–0. It was a
good reason for considerable drinking at the three-hundred-
dollar reception thrown by ComDesRon 33 for the people of
Halifax. The three hundred dollars was all that was allotted for
the party—but Scotch was a dollar a quart and gin half that. I
was assigned the job of barman. Me? An authority on mixed
drinks? After sampling a couple of my own mixed drinks, I successfully passed off a gin-and-scotch mixture. Then, in going to
the head, I accidentally bumped into a reeling, sloppy-drunk
Canadian—tumbling him down the stairs. It looked like I had
shoved him and so there were some angry growls from our
civilian guests. At this, I furtively looked around to see if the
Captain had observed my blunder. He hadn't, because he was
nowhere in sight.

As the party wound down, I canvassed every eligible girl for
a date but struck out on all of them. Despite that, I went to the
Lord Nelson for some dancing and did the Cokey Okey and
Bumps-a-Daisy with some wallflowers. Blatz, who followed
me there and who was an expansive, happy drunk, proceeded
to give away five-dollar bills to every "lovely lady" he saw until
he declared himself "broke." When I caught up with this silly
charade and determined that Blatz had started the evening
with eight five-dollar bills, I asked for the bills back from some
of the girls who were flashing their "American money" at their
friends as though they'd made some sort of conquest without
being prostitutes. Blatz, watching this, stammered, "Ruhe,
you've embarrassed me. Never again shall I call you friend."
Out of money, he tried to give his gold class ring to a girl. I put
a stop to that, with more protests from Blatz. Big tears welled
up in his eyes. It was difficult getting him into a taxi. And
when we got to the pier, he opened the door on his side and
fell out onto the ice-covered dock. He lay there with a cherub-
like sweetness to his face and then promptly fell asleep. Passed
out. I paid the taxi driver with a retrieved five-dollar bill.

On Sunday, Bill, B.D., and I went to St. Paul's Episcopal
Church for the vespers service. Built in 1740, it was Canada's
oldest church and had many interesting tablets that told about
King George V of England and other high-ranking people who
had worshiped there in the past. After a drink at the Nova
Scotian Hotel, I joined a group of young Canadians who were
rehearsing for a show. At a pause in their acting, I played the
on-stage piano and sang "A Tisket a Tasket." They all sang
along, knowing all the words. So the singing continued until
they had to go home. And it was late. And cold—twelve
degrees Fahrenheit.

The day before leaving Halifax, I calculated the wardroom mess bill for each officer for the month of November to be twenty-nine dollars. That would produce some sort of tirade from the Captain. More importantly, Mr. Sperry spent several hours figuring out how to help get the *Roe* an "E" in engineering for the competitive year. He made some weird calculations, based on the *Roe*'s doing twenty-one knots after departure. Then it would be claimed that the *Roe* was doing only fifteen knots, when she was actually transiting at twenty-one knots with a "month out of harbor" factor, "cold water factor," etc., etc. These were doubtful parameters. He felt the *Roe*'s resulting score could win the engineering "E." This game was played by most destroyer skippers, who saw "Es" as a path to promotion to a higher rank.

After going out into town to pay the commissary bills for fresh produce and returning back aboard, I received a letter from Lucrece. I'd finally gotten a letter through to her. It was a recent one in which I asked her for her third-finger-left-hand ring size. She didn't supply that information. But she noted that my letter "was most welcome" and that "nothing has changed." Did that mean that we were still devoted to each other, or were we "just friends"? The rest of the letter I would rather not have read. It told of her attending parties in Germany with Nazi bigwigs—Bormann, Clovius, Funk, etc. Was she now a collaborator? It was a hateful thought, which I immediately banished from my mind. Finally, at eleven that night, Blatz and I went into town to spend our remaining Canadian money on "souvenirs of Halifax." Nothing practical.

6

Phony War

ON THURSDAY, 3 DECEMBER, the *Roe* got under way at twelve-thirty, but not before a lavish lunch of lobsters, dipped in browned, melted butter, had been served—more than enough for all of us. Everyone in the wardroom gorged themselves on the low-cost, but very delicious, creatures. They were our undoing. The heavy wind blowing outside should have forewarned us of trouble when once at sea.

On the way to sea, as the *Roe* passed one of the old-age destroyers just turned over to the British, a shrill bos'n's whistle floated across the water toward us. It was calling all hands to that ship's main deck for a special event. From the doors in the sides of the four-piper's superstructure at least half the ship's crew issued forth and crowded the rails. Then, from the bridge came a shout, "Hip, Hip." The men on deck raised their blue caps and answered with a loud, "Hooray!" This was repeated three times. The cheers of appreciation from the Limeys produced a lump in my throat and a warm spot in my heart for the men of England, who were close to being defeated by the German U-boat campaign in the Atlantic.

What great guys we had handed our destroyers to—our Allies with whom we were already fighting a restrained war called the Neutrality Patrol, as ordained by our president, F.D.R. To most East Coast American destroyers, this meant escorting Allied convoys half way across the North Atlantic. It was not a pleasant business, particularly during the winter months with their raging seas and blinding blizzards. The usual subzero weather helped make tin-can operations thoroughly miserable.

Fortunately, however, according to dispatches that I'd picked up on the *Denebola* prior to sailing, the *Roe* was headed for

San Juan, Puerto Rico, to play a different Neutrality Patrol role—in the balmy calm seas of the Caribbean. What a break!

When well beyond the submarine nets, the *Roe* steamed into a violent sea that rolled and pitched her mercilessly. All officers became debilitatingly seasick from the too-rich luncheon. Only B.D. and I were strong enough to stand a watch on the bridge. This watch was almost pleasant because not a single squawk or whisper came up the voice-tube from the Captain's sea-cabin. We could only imagine (and enjoy a little) his suspected discomfort.

For the eight o'clock to midnight watch on the bridge, I wore heavy, cold-weather clothing including wool-lined mittens. Although the pilot house was heated, the windshield wipers on its front window cleared only a small arc of visibility ahead, so I had to go out onto the wings of the bridge to look for ships that might be closing on the beam or coming up from the stern. The large rolls of the *Roe* made the heavy iron doors a hazard to pass through; it was only a matter of time before, in my weakened condition, one of the doors caught me off guard.

I had grasped the sharp-edged doorjamb to steady myself before stepping back into the pilothouse when a lurch in the snap roll of the ship suddenly banged the door shut—crushing my hand. When the heavy iron door slammed down on my glove, I was certain that my hand had been either badly mangled or cut in half. The force of the blow caused my stomach to churn and waves of nausea to sweep over me. I pulled the door clear and stepped into the pilot house and found that my legs were so weak that I had to ease myself into the Captain's chair in order to continue the watch. I was braving the Captain's wrath by sitting in "his" chair. The few minutes out on the bridge's wing had frozen my hand numb, so I could only guess at the extent of damage sustained. It was terribly depressing to think that the injury might end my piano playing. With my hand dangling at my side, I contemplated the need for a speedy relief and help from "Mac," a hospital corpsman and the *Roe*'s doctor. After putting in a call for B.D., who was the only qualified watch officer able to respond to my appeal for help, the word was passed over the public announcing system: "Doctor to the bridge." I waited.

As my hand warmed, it started to throb painfully. It also felt soggy, which indicated a good deal of blood was inside my glove. I hesitated to test the extent of the bleeding, but finally put my hand into the air to let the blood dump out of the glove. I was encouraged to see no more than a half cupful of the red stuff. Still, I didn't have the heart to pull off the glove. I'd wait for the doctor to reveal the bad news.

Mac was the first to the bridge. When he carefully removed the glove from my injured hand, a deep cut across the top of the hand and a badly crushed thumb were revealed. Nothing more. He patched the cut with adhesive tape and wound a tight bandage around the hand. My thumb, which Mac ignored, caused the dominating pain as pulsing blood built up pressure under the thumbnail. Hence, after B.D. had relieved me of the bridge watch, I asked Mac to bore a hole through the top of the thumbnail to release the blood underneath it. He'd forgotten to bring a scalpel with him, but he did have a pocket knife. When Mac's penknife opened up a hole through the nail, blood spurted into the air to a height of more than an inch. The relief was glorious. Consequently, when I turned into my bunk, I was actually able to go to sleep. My last thoughts were about how tough was the life one led on a destroyer. Might a Purple Heart be awarded for an injury sustained in this phony war? I wondered.

By morning, the seas had calmed enough that all of the officers were up and around—except for the Captain. The ocean's swells, however, were still rolling the Roe heavily. At first light, two yard patrol craft (YPs) were seen wallowing out of control in the troughs of the sea. The YPs were about the same displacement as the three tiny vessels of Columbus's fleet. Both small craft were stopped and were crazily bouncing around on the seas. They appeared to have been abandoned to the raging waves. Yet, the Captain steered the Roe close to one of the vessels to hail anyone who might be aboard the YP. For a minute or so there was no answer. Then a feeble, barely audible voice shakily called back: "We're all so seasick that every man is helpless and is tied down at his station. . . . My engines are stopped. . . . Could you send some men over to help get us underway. . . . and back to port?"

The Captain, after estimating that it was not too dangerous to transfer men to the YPs by means of the motor whale boat, told Mr. Parish to round up two quartermasters and two men knowledgeable in the operation of diesel engines and send them over to the stricken craft. The relief crews of two men each were then instructed to get the YPs under way and to follow the Roe to the safety of Cape Cod Bay, where our men would be brought back aboard the Roe. It was taken for granted that, with the quartermasters steering the two tiny vessels, in due time the seasick men would recover enough to regain control of their craft.

This episode emphasized the hardiness of fifteenth-century seamen who took small vessels such as the *Nina* and *Pinta* across the Atlantic. It was also easy to realize why Vikings in their longboats made their transocean cruises only in the summertime.

By the early afternoon, after the *Roe* entered Cape Cod Bay and recovered her four men, we headed down the Cape Cod Canal. A big merchant ship was aground at the entrance, and we had to maneuver carefully to avoid it. A developing blizzard reduced the visibility to a hundred yards as the *Roe* transited the canal. Foghorns were heard ahead and behind as the *Roe* groped her way down the winding, two-hundred-yard-wide cut, which followed an old riverbed. The houses of Cape Cod were deserted but looked very American and friendly. Many Cape Cod–style cottages were in evidence along the east bank of the canal. Their popularity as a "cozy" home had caused them to be built everywhere around the United States, as I had observed as a teenager when I went to the '32 Olympics in Los Angeles.

After clearing Hens and Chickens Shoals and Block Island, the *Roe* headed for Norfolk, which was to be our home port for the time being. It was pleasant to contemplate being back in Norfolk, for although it was not an exciting place, the people were exceptionally hospitable and the girls were classy and lively and fond of naval officers.

Finally, we tied up alongside the destroyer *Borie* on Thursday, 5 December, B.D.'s birthday. We received word that the *Roe* would leave for San Juan on Saturday. After doing a Neutrality Patrol job off Martinique, we'd head for the Pacific. Later in the day, we received a confidential message directing that all ships begin "stripping ship" to be ready for combat. However, since no other destroyers were taking immediate action in response to the directive, the Captain granted regular liberty.

The day before departure, I had to pay mess bills and draw a full bag of publications, whose covers were so heavily weighted that when thrown overboard they would sink to the bottom of the ocean and be irretrievable. If forced to abandon ship, all classified publications would be "deep-sixed." Burning was too slow. Heaving the pubs over the side and into deep water was now the accepted way to prevent important matter from falling into enemy hands.

When a well-tanked-up Blatz came back aboard, he routed me out of my bunk and drunkenly insisted that together we celebrate B.D.'s birthday. So while B.D. was ashore, we filled his bunk with coat hangers and dirty brooms. As Blatz put it, "B.D. needs our caring attention. . . .We've got to do something to show that we remembered his birthday. Right?" Right!

First, over the doorway to B.D.'s stateroom I rigged a contraption that would dump water over him when he entered to go to bed. It worked fine. Doused and about as angry as I'd ever seen the placid B.D. get, he snarled at Blatz and me, "You guys are adolescents who'll never grow up!" And with considerable venom he growled, "You're both forces for evil on this ship."

When it came to getting into bed after unloading all the coat hangers and brooms, he did it, however, quietly and sadly. He complained no further about the tricks played on him to celebrate his birthday. But B.D. was morose all of the next day. This made Blatz and me repentant and ashamed, feeling that B.D. was suffering too much from our pranks and the Captain's incessant needling. Perhaps we had provided the last straw. And B.D. was too nice a guy for that to happen.

On Saturday the *Roe* was under way before noon and followed the division flagship, the *Morris*, to sea heading south.

There was a touch of the flu in my system, so getting up at dawn on Sunday, along with the entire crew, to conduct an early morning battle problem was torture. A battle problem on Sunday? But that was par for our division commander's programs. He never got seasick!

The *Morris* had raced out of range at high speed during the night and, with the start of the exercise at dawn, began closing for an attack on the *Roe*. I was on the RDF's plot and got amazingly good tracking results from the radio bearings of the *Morris*'s radio transmissions that Chief Radioman Feath intercepted. When we finally sighted the *Morris* barreling in toward the *Roe*, she was at the range predicted by my plot. Quickly setting up the torpedo director for curved fire ahead, I called to the bridge to "come to course 248 degrees for firing torpedoes." Nothing happened. So I climbed down to the pilot house to discover that Commander Swenson had thrown a monkey wrench into the battle problem by declaring that all people in the *Roe*'s pilothouse had been killed by a shell hit. This included our Captain. The problem thus was thrown totally in my lap. So I called the waist torpedo tubes to "stand by to fire torpedoes." At the last minute, with confusion having taken over and with the supposedly dead Captain jumping up and down yelling, "Get them off, get them off," I changed the ship's course and shifted to straight fire of the midships torpedo tubes. Fortunately, I got the simulated launch of the *Roe*'s torpedoes off okay.

At the end of this frantic battle problem, there was a heavi-
ness in my feet and I felt terrible. But that could have been
mainly from the flu I was suffering through.

The remainder of the day held more drills because the eager-
beaver division commander thought up more and more ways
"to get his ships ready for war." In the midst of an evening
drill, a darkened ship was sighted. That was real excitement for
Captain Scruggs, who called for twenty-five knots speed "to
close the enemy." He was certain that it was a German raider
hunting Allied shipping. His impulsiveness sent a chill down
my back—as if someone had brushed it with a chunk of ice.
The Captain ignored the possibility that if the big ship actually
was a German raider it might open fire on the *Roe*, pouring
large-caliber shells at her. Moreover, the *Roe* wasn't buttoned
up in condition III, the fully ready condition for minimizing
battle damage. And the unknown ship was not answering the
beamed signal light challenge that the *Roe* was sending.
Luckily, the blacked-out ship finally identified herself, using a
green-light searchlight. She was a British merchantman en
route to England. I breathed easier after that identification.

All day Monday we held more drills. They were conducted
three hundred yards astern of the *Morris* while running in Dog
formation. In this formation, which resembled a bunch of sled
dogs slightly offset from each other, the odd-numbered ships
were slightly to starboard of the even-numbered ships. Hence,
when any ship had a breakdown, the odd-numbered tin cans
would turn to starboard while the even ones would turn to
port—preventing collisions. There were simulated tactical
drills, signal drills, radio communication drills, and finally
another battle problem, which began at five-thirty with the
Morris out on the ocean somewhere and about to attack.

The *Roe*'s radio direction finder rapidly located the distant
ship. However, when she closed to visible range, she illuminated the *Roe* before I ordered "Shine a light on the enemy."
There was no "Dammit, Ruhe!" from the Captain for this failure. Then, when I ordered the simulated launching of torpedoes, only to discover that the *Morris* had turned away and all
torpedoes would have been wasted, there was still no violent
reaction from the Captain. His blow-torch rhetoric was missing.

At the end of the drill, Mac, our enlisted medical man,
reported a bad case of measles on the *Roe* and said that he
had isolated the man in the shell-handling room of the forward five-inch gun. A little later Mac returned to the bridge to
report that he'd just discovered an acute appendicitis case.
The Captain, with this opportunity to break free from the divi-

sion commander's mania for more and more drills, received permission to dash to San Juan in order to get expert hospital care for the two sick men.

The next morning, after dropping the hook in San Juan's inner harbor, the appendix patient was hospitalized. He proved to be far gone with tuberculosis and, even after removal of his appendix, would be a long time convalescing before he could return to the *Roe* and resume his shipboard duties.

At midday, the uniform for all hands was shifted to "whites"—short-sleeved white shirts, white pants, and white shoes. The *Roe* had moved into the tropics. From her decks I could see emerald green hills framed by distant gray-blue mountains, while close at hand, the brilliantly sunlit buildings of San Juan dazzled my eyes. Old forts, brightly dressed people, and pastel colors on stores and houses created scenes that I was excited to paint. Although the sun beat down mercilessly, a cool breeze was always blowing in from the ocean.

By the afternoon, the heavy harbor traffic close to the *Roe* so disturbed the Captain that he ordered us to shift berths before he granted shore liberty. I was in the first liberty boat with my painting attaché case. At first I hurried around the main part of town, looking for a good scene. Then I headed for the abandoned El Morro fort at the western end of San Juan. Close by the fort, I found the most wretched living conditions that I had ever seen. Garbage was piled up in the front yards of shacks that had rusty tin roofs and were built on stilts. Pigs rooted under the packing-case-constructed houses where women, wearing only shifts to stay cool, sat on rickety porches—picking lice out of each other's hair. Goats gobbled up refuse in the streets and emaciated dogs that looked like overgrown rats followed kids as they dumped slop jars, their primitive plumbing, into the streets. Radios loudly blared rumba and "La Cucaracha" music. The radio announcers could be heard several miles away. The din of noise was deafening. The scenery, but not the racket, needed to be recorded. When I started painting this scene, I was immediately surrounded by a horde of ragged, dirty children who showed a great interest in "the American painting pictures." Later, when I unwrapped some sandwiches prepared by Ross for my lunch, the kids were so agitated at the sight of thick-meat sandwiches, that I decided to surrender them to the mob around me. That started a near riot. Hands from everywhere tore the sandwiches apart and the children wrestled with each other—like a pack of hungry dogs—to get a fragment of my lunch. This was San Juan, our commonwealth possession?

On the way back to the ship I ran into a '39 classmate who was on the destroyer *Sims* that had just completed two weeks of patrolling off Fort-de-France, Martinique. She'd been conducting the Neutrality Patrol job that the *Roe* would shortly do—i.e., keeping an eye on the Vichy French warships inside the harbor there. The United States felt that these warships would constitute a threat to the Allies if they were allowed to return to France. Hence, our job was to follow close behind a warship that sortied from port and seemed to be headed east across the Atlantic. We would report the situation to Washington and await further orders. To sink the French ship? And what about a Vichy warship firing without warning on a shadowing tin can? My classmate said while his destroyer was doing the blockade job, he had continually felt nervous about the situation.

Although terms of the French surrender to the Germans on 22 June 1940 called for an immobilizing of French warships in French ports, the warships holed up in Fort-de-France were evidently being kept fully operational and might attempt to join the German Navy at any time. Off Oran, Algeria, on 3 July 1940, the British Navy had attacked French warships at sea and caused great loss of French lives—probably generating another lasting keen dislike of the British by the French. So I hoped that the *Roe* wouldn't be ordered to fire on Vichy French warships.

After suggesting that we keep a close lookout for Nazi subs that might sink U.S. destroyers, my classmate, John Muhlenberg, advised that we could trade tin boxes for lobsters at Port Castries, where we'd go on our days off. He also described the best patrol areas for keeping an eye on the French warships inside the harbor.

The *Roe* was to do her patrol job over Christmas and then return to San Juan for a New Year's Eve celebration.

On the following day, the *Roe* went in to a pier to take on fuel oil. The land alongside the *Roe* choked off the sea breezes, and those of us on board began to drip with sweat. Nearby, all kinds of small, broad-beamed sailboats were tied up and were being hand-loaded with burlap bags of foodstuffs. The cargoes resembled those carried into darkest Africa. In fact, the pier looked like an outpost of civilization. Moreover, it was the rainy season and deluges of water dumped on the dock workers—but for only about five minutes at a time. The Captain sent me to the *Morris* for operation orders. She was commanded by my nemesis at the Naval Academy, Lieutenant Commander "Beanie" Jarrett. He had almost had me kicked out of the Academy for amassing too many demerits. Each successive time he caught me playing my guitar during study hour, I received an escalating number of demerits. Beanie Jarrett, as a duty officer, had loved to fry repeat offenders, who he felt were a vicious sort of criminal. Fortunately, I managed to avoid meeting him on the *Morris*.

All morning of Friday the 13th I supervised the cleanup of my division's spaces. I was certain that the Captain would be out to get me at the afternoon ship's inspection. During the morning his eyes held a threatening sullenness that indicated that he was spoiling to teach me greater respect for him. However, the Captain precipitously left the ship after lunch and Mr. Parish took over the inspection. He only glanced at things and noted no discrepancies.

Saturday morning the Captain held a long-winded conference on the operation orders for the *Roe*'s deployment to Martinique. At one point, he noted a need to see CSP 963, a confidential publication that "I need on Monday." So I went to the Naval Station that afternoon to draw it, but the issuing activity was closed until eight-thirty on Monday morning. I related this to the Captain, who then said, "I want you to go over to the Station on Monday and draw that publication. Leave at seven-thirty to make sure you get it at the earliest time."

Stupidly, on Monday morning I'd taken the eight o'clock boat over to the beach and returned with CSP 963 at ten o'clock. On my return, the Captain was at the gangway and snarled, "You didn't leave this ship at seven-thirty as ordered on Saturday. You're late in getting me my instruction, so I'm suspending you from all duties and confining you to your room for two days. You've got to learn to obey my commands *to the letter*. Nothing else will do!" Then he delivered his broken-record old saw: "Life is real and life is earnest. . . ." Curtly, he snapped, "Get to your room, Ruhe. You've had it."

"Am I in hack again, Captain?" I ventured.

"Not this time. You're getting off easy!"

Again, Mr. Parish, with sad eyes and a doleful tone to his voice, advised me that I was not getting an official punishment, but it meant that I'd get an unsatisfactory fitness report. Oddly, I thought I was working harder to do everything one hundred percent right. Yet I was sure looking inept. Perhaps the Captain was getting the results with me that he was seeking. But this time, I felt he was just showing poor judgment. It was evident that I was engaged in a phony war conducted by the Captain against me. At the same time, he was also in the midst of a phony war in support of F.D.R.'s friendly neutral actions.

As I sat alone in my bunkroom for the next two days, I angrily thought about the need to have the Captain respect *me*. I had to find some way to frighten him—without his being certain of my role in his denouement. He had to be made so fearful of what I might do in retaliation that he would no longer risk restricting me for my blunders. Complicated? Yes. Possible? Yes. But it would take time and patience. Draconian treatment of me demanded draconian responses. But what to do? Above all the Captain wanted to score well in the *Roe*'s drills so that he'd get an outstanding fitness report from the division commander. "Aha!" I thought, "This might be his Achilles' heel." But his fanatical regard for security seemed a better route to explore. There must be some sort of opportunity that would pop up that I could capitalize on. It was only a matter of time and of continued survival.

On the bright side, I recognized that the Captain was using me more and more in key roles aboard the *Roe*. He seemed to regard me as his best officer OOD, even though I was relatively new to the job. The *Roe*'s communications were somewhat better than the other ships of the division. And he'd made me the key man in the *Roe*'s torpedo exercises. However, everyone was getting a good laugh out of my getting confined to my room. They failed to recognize that my being disciplined was an example for all officers to be more serious about their work.

In the afternoon, the *Roe* steamed to St. Croix and dropped the hook off Frederiksted. During the night a fisherman in a power boat came close to the *Roe*, supposedly to fish. He wouldn't leave, despite shouts from the deck watch to "pull clear of the *Roe*." So the OOD, using his forty-five-caliber revolver, shot into the water off the bow of the boat. That chased the fisherman away. At this point in this phony war, the danger of sabotage in a foreign port seemed quite likely.

On Wednesday, the *Roe* got under way for St. Thomas. My restriction was over. Yet I felt on edge, certain that the Captain would try to get me for some other offense—no matter how small. Perhaps he was achieving his goal of making me respect him by demonstrating that he could kick me in the teeth any time he pleased.

At St. Thomas there was a French freighter that was being restrained from leaving port by a U.S. Coast Guard cutter. There was also an Estonian ship whose skipper I was told had been ordered by Stalin to return to the Soviet Union or to face the prospect of losing his wife, who was back in Estonia.

When I asked a large, fat Negro what was made in St. Thomas, he said, "Bay rummmm." Laughingly, he claimed, "If you knew how good ours is, you'd use it on your hair every day." The air of St. Thomas was sweet with a rum odor. The streets were clean, the houses were freshly whitewashed, and the inhabitants loading small boats along the waterfront wore colorful, untorn clothing. Most were barefoot. By my estimate, there were fifteen blacks for every white person on the streets of Charlotte Amalie.

Later in the day, we learned that the *Roe* would get under way early on 20 December in order to relieve the destroyer *O'Brien* on patrol station off Martinique. Since a great deal of wardroom laundry was ashore, I had to get to the town laundry establishment at six o'clock the following morning and roust the lady owner out of bed to recover the still-wet wash. Fortunately, I found a townsman on the nearly vacant streets who guided me to the laundry owner's home. Inexplicably, the laundry's owner was actually home at six in the morning— normally she was out at that time, playing an organ in her church. In the darkness of the early morning it was frustrating to sort out the wardroom's laundry.

Back on board, I directed the sullen stewardsmate, Ross, to iron the wet wash. Only when I threatened to cancel his shore liberty for a week did he do it.

As the *Roe* left for Martinique, I had a moment to reflect on the fact that the Captain, when I had met him ashore the previous day, hadn't spoken to me in a civil way. Normally when off the ship his manner was friendly and he would suggest we walk together and eat together. But now he was evidently feuding with me.

The scenery, as the *Roe* headed down through the Virgin Islands, was so pleasant that my problems with the Captain seemed trivial. The small islands to port were lusciously green, very steep, and had few people in sight. But lots of cattle were grazing everywhere and most islands were topped by extinct volcanoes. At Saba I saw a Dutch village with bright red chimneys that was built inside a crater.

Most of the Leeward Virgin Islands—St. Kitts, Nevis, St. John, Montserrat, Guadeloupe, Dominica—might easily, with their broad sandy beaches, become choice vacation spots when lower prices for air travel were available. The gentle movement of green-blue waves onto the gleaming beaches had an allure that made me want to request the Captain to drop the hook off one of the islands and order "swim call."

7

Martinique Blockade

THE *ROE* ARRIVED OFF the mouth of Fort-de-France, Martinique, early on the morning of 21 December. As she closed the U.S. destroyer *O'Brien*, which was monitoring the ship traffic in and out of the French port, I was routed out of my bunk to accompany the Captain to the *O'Brien*. Once there, I took notes on questions Captain Scruggs asked, along with the answers they elicited. He asked how the other ship's skipper handled the sorties of merchant ships and warships from Fort-de-France. What should be done at night if they refused to blink back their identity? Had ships been shadowed for some distance back toward Europe? If so, what instructions had Washington sent when the White House was made aware of the ship's probable intention to escape back to Vichy France? What French warships were inside the harbor? And what difficulties had the *O'Brien* experienced with communications?

The answers were worthless. Nothing of note had happened in the *O'Brien*'s two weeks of Neutrality Patrol operations. Her skipper said he was bored by it all and was eager to get back to San Juan for some upkeep work and a little fun. Still, Captain Scruggs asked question after question, and each one became more piddling than the previous one. As usual, the Captain showed his great thoroughness. Evidently, this long-winded demonstration of leaving no stone unturned was as much for my benefit as for his own understanding of how the *Roe* could best carry out her patrol duties. I was being taught another lesson!

One useful suggestion by the *O'Brien*'s skipper was that on dark nights we should closely watch the lights along the shore. The only indication of a darkened ship steaming close to the beach would be a blanking out of those lights. Ashore, no

lights had been doused because of the European war, but at
sea all ships ran in a blacked-out condition. The threat of U-
boats off Martinique seemed small, however, since the best
torpedo targets, the oil tankers out of Aruba or Curaçao, transited north to the United States far to the west. Vichy French
ships, moreover, were not believed to be U-boat targets.

Shortly after return to the *Roe*, the Captain sent a message
to confirm that the *Roe* had assumed her patrol duties. The
O'Brien was thus free to head north to recover from her two
weeks of blockade operations. Then, while the *Roe* was holding the bag and keeping a sharp lookout for emerging ships,
the Captain passively watched the French cruiser *Bonfleur*
enter the harbor and join the aircraft carrier *Jeanne d'Arc* and
three other warships whose topworks could be seen from the
Roe's patrol position. Suddenly, the Captain snapped to and
shouted at me, "Ruhe, you've got to report this to Washington!" At this, I smugly said, "I've already had that message
sent in accordance with our patrol instructions, Captain." This
made him twist around and glower at me as though I was
being a wise guy.

Later, when there was no further activity as the *Roe* ran up
and down a ten-mile line four miles off the harbor's entrance,
the Captain called me into his stateroom. "Ruhe," he began,
and paused. With squinted eyes and a tight jaw, he looked up
from the paper he was scanning on his desk. A frown deepened in a menacing way. He didn't like what he saw. Me. I was
respectfully standing at attention and not quivering nervously.
It seemed that he wanted to frighten me before he continued
talking. Eventually, he snapped, "I'm concerned with how you
handle the classified publications on this ship. And I don't
want to have a 'lost document investigation' because of your
sloppiness."

I sensed that he had heard about my last inventory of all the
classified documents for which, as communications officer, I
was the custodian. My checkoff of items had shown that one
was missing. It was the one that Hop Nolan had drawn and
had, he assured me, promptly returned. Unfortunately, I had
no record of it having been burned along with other superseded publications. Perhaps I had failed to scratch it off when
it had been actually burned. My problem was that my workload was so heavy that, to stay caught up, I was working too
swiftly for my own good. There was just too much correcting
of publications, decoding of messages, and doing inconsequential things for the skipper that he always claimed were of
first priority. For a week, I'd sweated out what to do about the

document's loss. But then I'd found a piece of paper upon which a scribbled notation indicated that it had been burned separately in accordance with a special note in the publication saying: "Immediately destroy after reading." I'd just plain forgotten about this unusual procedure.

"What I'm going to insist on, Ruhe," the Captain continued with much gravity, "is that from now on the person who is issued a classified thing signs a log you maintain, acknowledging receipt of the item along with the date on which it was drawn. You keep that log in your safe until that classified thing is returned. Then you break out the log and scratch the item off your list and initial your action in view of the person who has just returned it. That should be a foolproof way, Ruhe, for keeping track of your Secret documents." The Captain appeared much pleased with his cleverness. Feeling that the Captain was protecting me from blowing my future career in the Navy, I enthusiastically initiated his classified-document-control system within the next hour.

After dark, we spotted a freighter without lights leaving port. This caused the Captain to run back and forth around the bridge while calling for a signalman to challenge by blinker light the unidentified merchantman. When no response was forthcoming, the Captain shouted to the OOD, "Head toward her and put on some speed." And to the quartermaster, "Shine a searchlight on her bow and see if we can read her name." To me he appealingly said, "What are we supposed to do, Ruhe?" I was now the authority on how to conduct this Neutrality Patrol?

When the ship blinked back her name and Estonian nationality and where she was headed, things quieted down.

It was hard to imagine two weeks of a rat race like this.

The next morning the *Roe* was relieved of her patrol duties at seven o'clock by the *Morris* for the next twenty-four hours. She'd left San Juan a day after the *Roe* and was going to share the surveillance job for the next two weeks.

Down the *Roe* went to Gros Islet, twenty-six miles to the south. She was headed there "for recreation and rest." The crew's idea of recreation, however, hardly squared with doing any resting.

I went ashore just before church bells started ringing. The people who thronged the hard-earth, clean streets were dressed in their Sunday finery. All were Negroes of very dark complexion —though I was told that two white derelicts were asleep somewhere in the many small, one-story shacks that stood on stilts and nestled in a grove of breadfruit trees.

Everyone was cheerful and greeted me with a "Hello, Joe"—
the only English most of them knew. They talked a French
patois. Even little children barely able to walk grinned up at
me and would pipe, "Hello, Joe." The women wore huge straw
hats, colorful neckerchiefs, and gaudy bandannas on their
heads. Large brass earrings and necklaces jangled as the
women swayed their full, baggy skirts on their way to church.
The men wore any sort of bedraggled suit and most wore
faded green felt hats. Few had shoes. All appeared joyful and
eager to attend the church service. A quick look inside the
church as the service began showed about three hundred
orderly and attentive blacks. They responded to the preacher's
harangue with, "Ay-men," "Praise the Lord," or "Hallelu-yah."

The days at sea in the open-air environment had made it
intolerable to be confined in a church and sit through a two-
hour service. Thus, I chose to swim in the flat sea in front of
the village. Men from the *Roe* were everywhere, playing softball, hiking into the jungle back of the beach, or just "looking
for action." A group of cute little black fellows followed me
everywhere begging for articles of my clothing. At one point,
an old wrinkled hag propositioned me for my swimming
trunks. "You give me them for some love, Sah . . . okay?" Not
okay. But I did trade her one of the several tin boxes I'd
brought ashore with me for a bunch of bananas she had in her
boat. Moreover, I discovered that it was far easier to trade
things than to try to use American money, which they didn't
seem to understand. British money was barely usable, but
French money was very "okay."

At four o'clock, after I'd acquired a red tan from lying on
the beach, the *Roe* departed for her patrol station. On the way,
the division commander on the *Morris* detailed over the tactical radio a battle problem involving a torpedo attack by the
Roe against the patrolling *Morris*. The Captain ordered me to
the bridge to "handle the torpedo attack." Luckily, everything
went well. All settings for the simulated torpedo firing
appeared to be perfect. Throughout the exercise the Captain
sat quietly in his bridge chair, never changing his instructions
or producing nasty comments about my procedures. Perhaps
that's why it all went so well.

We spent another day going up and down the patrol line off
Fort-de-France. Then next day the *Roe* went to Port Castries,
St. Lucia, the next island south of Martinique. It was a
bustling port of wooden schooners being loaded by sweat-
stained men wearing only shorts. Glistening white buildings

flanked by palm trees were in the background. There were a few cars and many bicycles and donkeys. Dugout log canoes floated all over the harbor. There was a long delay getting clearance to land because the *Roe* had two cases of measles on board. When clearance was granted, we tied up to a wooden pier, and I immediately left the ship to look around. The place was somewhat more civilized than Gros Islet. A little black fellow proved this when in answer to my question, "Does everyone here say, 'Hello, Joe'?" he said, "Never. We greet you men with, 'Hi-ya, mate, how's she going?' and stuff like that."

More civilized or not, I saw a water tree that squirted water when a branch was broken off, oysters clinging to the roots of trees, and a marketplace selling dead tropical fish of varieties I'd only seen in New York's Aquarium. Also, there were some black and white eels that I believed were poisonous. Most mystifying, however, was the black-meat pudding encased in intestine-covering that everyone was buying and eating by the slice. Then there was the nine-year-old, Gildeth, who lived in a packing case on the dock and who stayed close beside me as I went painting. He sang songs from recent movies in their entirety with the correct words and tunes. When he sang "Murder on Tenth Avenue," I asked how long it had taken him to learn that one. He said, "I just heard it in a movie yesterday." And he knew it by heart! The kid was a genius and didn't know it. In Port Castries! A perfect auditory memory—like Winston Churchill's photographic memory; his biographers claimed he could read a page of a book and recite it verbatim flawlessly a few days later. He was also like the Eskimo who, according to Sir Richard Grenfell, the Arctic explorer, had devised his own form of recording Eskimo words—in a world where no written language existed.

Buying supplies for the wardroom required much time-consuming haggling to bring prices down to a reasonable level. Being cheated by the merchants was against my principles. So I stridently argued against every exorbitant initially quoted price. By late afternoon, when the *Roe* left port to resume her patrol job, I was worn out.

It was Christmas Eve. We hoped that the Captain would let up on the officers for at least the next twenty-four hours. But after an early morning watch on Christmas Day, my attempts to get more sleep were frustrated. I was awakened three times in succession to do "high-priority" but actually insignificant jobs for the Captain. That made me lose all feeling of "good will toward men." Then mail came aboard. A few Christmas cards with warm greetings and best wishes promptly put me back into the Christmas spirit. The holiday dinner of roast turkey, stuffing, cranberry sauce, and pumpkin pie raised the wardroom spirits. At the head of the table the Captain looked glumly at his food, but refrained from making caustic remarks about the meal. His silence was deafening. Luckily, it was interrupted by a report from Mac, the corpsman, that he had discovered another acute appendicitis case. So Doc Brown, the division doctor, was boated over to the *Roe* from the *Morris* to take charge of the patient. At his recommendation, the *Roe* was rushed down to Port Castries to get the sick man into the small but decent hospital there. A boat was waiting at the harbor's mouth on our arrival and the sailor was put on a stretcher and taken into the port. Doc Brown accompanied him to ensure the best of care for the man. Immediately after transfer of the patient, the *Roe* returned to her patrol area. This allowed the *Morris* to shove off for San Juan under special orders and leave the *Roe* to conduct the surveillance-blockade job, alone.

Shortly, the Captain went into a near panic. "Ruhe," he yelled, "do you know what's going to happen now? Do you have any instructions for this patrol that I haven't seen and don't know anything about? Dammit, Ruhe, you've failed me again! How can I operate this ship without knowing what I'm supposed to be doing? I ought to kick you out of the Navy and do everyone a big favor."

I kept wishing that he'd just shut up.

The Captain continued to rant the rest of the day about not knowing "what's going on." Then, the destroyer *Howard* hove into sight, coming from the north. Soon, her skipper and several other officers were ferried over to the *Roe*. They wanted instructions on how to conduct the patrol off Martinique in place of the *Morris*. As senior skipper, Captain Scruggs verbosely told the junior *Howard* skipper exactly how he expected the surveillance patrol to be conducted. But then an SOS distress signal from an unknown ship was intercepted by the radioman on watch. The appeal for help, which we heard on the wardroom's speaker, interrupted our Captain's harangue. A jumble of English words with some German words mixed in was all that we could distinguish. Eventually the name *Marie Louise* of Belgian registry was vaguely heard. Evidently, she was in distress and her broadcast for help was being jammed by a German voice using spurious words to prevent the stricken vessel's message from being understood. Everyone in the wardroom looked helpless. Fortunately, the radioman said that a patrolling U.S. aircraft had picked up the SOS and was heading down the bearing of the ship's broadcast. So it was up to the U.S. pilot to help the ship in distress. We never learned the outcome.

When the Howard's officers left the Roe, it was evident that they had paid little attention to our Captain's arrogantly demanding instructions. As might have been expected, patrolling with the Howard became less than pleasant. Each time she'd pass the Roe along the patrol line, she'd be steered so close to the Roe that a ramming appeared possible. It seemed that the Howard's skipper was showing his disdain for his senior patrolling partner. We were amused by our Captain's chagrin.

On the day of the 27th, the Roe returned to the Gros Islet area. Like the previous visit, many small black boys were hanging around to cadge my clothing. At lunchtime all of them cracked coconuts, drank the colorless coconut milk, and then munched on the snow-white meat inside the hairy husks. Like a plutocrat, however, I drank water from a canteen and ate my lettuce sandwiches—which the little fellows looked at with disgust. After a long swim, I read a newspaper I'd brought with me. As I discarded sections of the newspaper, the children snapped them up as though they were treasures— even though they couldn't read a word. Kids were everywhere, interfering with the softball games, and they were begging money while trying to line up their sisters "for some loving." The Roe's shore patrol detail wandered the beach and sidled through the groves of trees behind the beach, to keep order. Eventually, most of the Roe's men were herded back to the ship by the shore patrolmen at the end of their liberty. The villagers had peddled much beer and the women had grown more aggressive and "friendly" than on the previous visit.

On 28 December the Roe chased ships. It was a day of many ship departures from Fort-de-France. Unfortunately, my signal gang had much trouble getting the cargo ships to identify themselves. So I caught hell from the Captain. But when he held his usual Saturday personnel inspection, and I was called off watch to accompany him and record all the discrepancies, he found little to criticize about my wardroom boys. That was most unusual. And then the bad news: A message indicated that the Roe would remain on station until New Year's Day and then return to San Juan—with a further two-week patrol in the offing.

The next day, the Roe went to Port Castries to tie up for the usual recreation. With the in-port duty, I had a lot of trouble keeping the young islanders from trying to force their way aboard. At one point, we broke out a fire hose and used it to force a horde of pushing and shoving children off the gangway.

Then a Negro came running down to the dock to say, "The Captain wants Mr. Ruhe to pull the *Roe* aft about a hundred feet." With all duty hands hauling on the ship's mooring lines, the *Roe* was slowly dragged along the dock to a new location. It was amazing how easily the job was done. We only had to overcome a small amount of ship friction with the water. The weight of the ship was inconsequential.

As usual, I had a good deal of trouble converting dollars to British pounds for Ross to buy supplies in the town. I had to use Ross to buy wardroom mess provisions because he was the only steward who'd drive a hard bargain and keep the cost of our food down. The pound was still pegged at $4.50, which was a rotten rate of exchange. Finally, at three-thirty with all hands back aboard, the *Roe* returned to her patrol station.

The next morning I had the early watch on the bridge; I tardily remembered at six-thirty that the routine six o'clock, plain-language "on station" report had not been sent to Washington. Feeling sleepy and exhausted on the watch, I finally realized that I hadn't initialed the release of the required message. The discrepancy had slipped by me. But not by the Captain. At quarter to seven he came storming to the bridge. Smoke was coming out of his ears. He yelled about the message going out late. "Ruhe," he growled, "You're not fit to be an officer and take the responsibilities demanded. The fitness report you'll get for this should get you right out of the Navy. And the letter I'll write to go along with the fitness report will detail your incompetency!"

The Captain was truly dangerous at this point. More than ever, I'd have to do something soon to cool him down. But then again, perhaps I'd be better off leaving the *Roe* and the naval service. Going to Submarine School might be even a better solution. But I'd have to wait until the Captain turned friendly again before I submitted a request for Sub School.

Mr. Parish was quite disgusted with me for letting this slip up happen. He had that you've-just-got-to-do-better look on his face. Defensively, I said that I'd completed all my correspondence courses and had a $19.40 wardroom mess bill for the month of December—a new record. "And all my publications are corrected up to date." Understandably, Mr. Parish looked doubtful and amazed. Yet there was a good chance that he'd continue to be my best ally on the *Roe*.

The last day of December was also the *Roe*'s final day on patrol station. On New Year's Day, the destroyer *Buck* was scheduled to arrive and take over the *Roe*'s job. Things should change in the New Year! But with one day left of 1940, the Captain, true to form, insisted that sixty thousand gallons of fuel oil be transferred to the *Howard* before the *Roe*'s departure "in case she has to stay here longer than expected," he explained, "and has to chase a couple of French ships halfway across the Atlantic." The Captain was always thinking ahead and trying to impress everyone with his sound reasoning and foresight.

The *Howard*'s skipper, being junior to Captain Scruggs, obviously had to graciously accept this kind offer.

Thus at four o'clock, after telling Mr. Parish to have all available *Roe* officers on the bridge "to observe how it is done," he directed Mr. Parish to "impress on them the great value of each officer making his own silent judgments about how the seamanship used by the Captain is successfully getting the job done." Then he added, "They can check their guesses with how I actually do it and thus learn good destroyer seamanship."

The Captain certainly wasn't bashful about his ability to handle a destroyer. He liked to show it off at every opportunity. Normally I couldn't fault his handling of the *Roe*. But this refueling-at-sea evolution was new to me and I didn't know what to expect. So I stayed close to Mr. Parish to compare the orders I would give versus the exec's sound views on handling a destroyer. That way I could make conclusions as to how correct and effective the Captain's orders were.

The Captain, having relieved B.D. as OOD, called to his side Chief Yeoman Sheehy, an intense, efficient little man whom the Captain rarely growled at. Sheehy held a steno notebook in his hand at the ready. Sheehy was instructed: "I want to address a letter about this to all destroyer skippers and those who will shortly get destroyer commands so that they can profit from my handling of this novel seamanship evolution."

"Yes, Sir."

"We'll title the letter, 'A fueling operation between destroyers at sea.'"

"Aye, aye, Sir."

The Captain, after much testing of windspeed and direction by holding up a wetted finger just outside the open windscreen in front of the helmsman, said: "I've got only a slight breeze blowing from the northwest. Record that."

This was noted by Sheehy.

The Captain then ordered the destroyer *Howard* to "take a course of 332 degrees true directly into the wind. And make three knots." A glance at the sea showed only a calm smoothness that should make the fueling operation uncomplicated. So far so good. "It will take only about two hours to transfer the fuel and we won't get very far away from the harbor entrance." That was extraneous information, so the Captain advised, "You don't have to note that, Sheehy."

Sheehy scratched out the last sentence.

My thought was, "What happens if the *Jeanne d'Arc* comes charging out of port just about now after we've hooked up the fuel hose?" I looked at Mr. Parish to see his reaction to the Captain's refueling strategy. His face was a blank.

"I'll bring the *Roe* alongside the *Howard*'s starboard side," the Captain dictated, "and we'll pass a hawser over to the *Howard*'s bow. Then we'll tie our bows together leaving a lot of slack so that both of us are sailing on the same course with the water flowing aft between the bows of the two ships. This will provide a cushion of water between the two of us. . . . Sheehy, make this a second paragraph."

There was furious scribbling by Sheehy.

I whispered to Mr. Parish, "Won't the water flowing between the destroyers pull them together in accordance with Bernoulli's theorem?" (This theorem postulated that water flowing between two bodies would produce a force that sucked them together.)

"Probably not," Mr. Parish whispered. "I think we're going too slow to produce sufficient force to bring us together." I trusted Mr. Parish's judgment on that. Then I carefully listened to Captain Scruggs's cautious commands as he eased the *Roe* close to the *Howard*. When the *Roe* was steadied on the same course as the *Howard*, the Captain observed that the ships were being kept apart by the water flowing between them toward the stern. And that was true.

The refueling hose from the *Roe* was passed over to the *Howard* from a station aft of the *Roe*'s single stack. We then began to pump fuel from one destroyer to the other.

The Captain's commands, as well as all the reports received over the intercom from the fueling station, were feverishly recorded by Sheehy. "Captain, do you want all of these reports included in your letter?" Sheehy frustratedly asked.

"Make the reports a separate paragraph, Sheehy," the Captain directed. "I want everything written down and we'll decide later what should be included in my letter."

With the transfer of fuel progressing nicely, the Captain turned the deck back to B.D. and went below "to attend to some paperwork."

Sheehy had been instructed to "stand easy on the bridge until my return. Then we'll do a paragraph on how I plan to break free from this hookup." B.D., moreover, was ordered to call the Captain ten minutes before the refueling would be completed. Consequently, the officers, except for B.D., drifted off the bridge to check their people involved in the refueling operation.

Just before six-thirty, the word was passed throughout the *Roe*: "All hands, stand by to complete fueling and break clear of the *Howard*."

Back on the bridge, I estimated the situation. The wind had freshened considerably and was now blowing from fifteen degrees on the starboard bow, pushing the bows together; the seas were now sufficiently ruffled to cause both destroyers to pitch slightly.

The Captain, on returning to the bridge, put a wetted finger into the air, smiled smugly—really pleased with his seamanship. He glanced only momentarily at the seas and the way the destroyers were riding them. His face showed no realization that the situation had changed.

"As soon as the fueling hose is brought back to the *Roe*, I'll have the *Howard* let go the bow line," the Captain dictated to Sheehy. "But she'll continue on the same course and at the same speed. Make this paragraph four," the Captain noted. "Then, I'll back the *Roe* one third and we'll pull clear of the *Howard* and go on our merry way." This description of a happy ending to "a difficult evolution" showed the Captain's great satisfaction with his handling of this refueling.

At this, I glanced at Mr. Parish to see his reaction to the Captain's plan of action. Mr. Parish's jaw was tight and his eyes stared at the deck.

"He doesn't seem to know that the wind has gotten stronger and is blowing from a different direction," I whispered to Mr. Parish. "Shouldn't we warn him what might happen?"

At this, Mr. Parish looked steadily and sadly at me. "It won't do any good," he muttered. "The Old Man won't like any suggestion that he isn't doing this thing exactly right. He won't pay attention anyhow to what we might think. He'll just get angry with us. So we'll have to hope that he doesn't damage the *Howard* too badly when he backs the *Roe*."

When the Captain saw Sheehy complete his notetaking for paragraph four, he ordered over the TBS tactical radio: "On the *Howard*, maintain course and speed while the *Roe* pulls clear." Then in a firm, confident voice he ordered: "Both engines back one third." The *Roe* picked up speed going astern; the backing wash of water pushed the *Roe*'s stern away from the *Howard* and forced the *Roe*'s bow to swing into the *Howard*'s bow. At this, the increased wind helped to push the *Roe*'s bow tight against the *Howard*, while the *Roe* increased her speed astern.

It was a disaster! The *Roe*'s bow was pinned against the *Howard*'s starboard side. As the *Roe* moved aft, I heard the loud screeching and clanging of damaged metal as the *Roe*'s bow swept away the *Howard*'s stanchions, lifelines, davits, cleats, chocks, and other gear fastened along the *Howard*'s side.

Confused by the cacophony of noise and the mess being created, the Captain sputtered, cursed, and muttered incoherently. In a panic, he ordered, "All back two thirds"—hoping to stop the damage. But it only made things worse.

Fortunately, the *Roe*'s bow broke clear of the *Howard*'s side before reaching the depth charge racks on her stern. More importantly, the *Roe*'s bow just missed the *Howard*'s starboard propeller.

Finally, with the *Roe* well astern of the *Howard*, the Captain ordered "All stop." Then he surveyed the havoc he'd created. Soon, over the TBS, he apologized profusely "for messing things up." The *Howard*'s skipper, who was much junior to Scruggs, had no response. Promotion in the Navy would be very tenuous if a destroyer skipper acted displeased with the performance of a senior skipper.

Sheehy, with a downcast look, folded up his notebook and pocketed his pencil. He looked at the Captain with shadowed eyes as the Captain said, "We'll have to write our paragraph five later on when things cool down." But I was certain, after glancing at Mr. Parish's tight little smile, that the Captain's letter to the destroyer skippers on how to refuel another destroyer at sea was due for the wastebasket—before the fifth paragraph was ever written.

"Parish," the Captain snapped irritably, "take over the deck and bring us back to our patrol line. I'm going below." He was too agitated to pause and give an excuse for what had gone wrong.

The *Roe*'s sharp and protruding bow was rumpled and crumpled. But it could easily be repaired. The *Howard*'s damage was something else. It wasn't bad enough to cause the *Howard* to leave station; yet extensive repairs taking many days would be required when she was back in port.

At dawn on New Year's Day, the *Roe* left station and headed for San Juan. Shortly, she passed the *Buck* coming south to work with the *Howard*. The *Buck* made no effort to raise the *Roe* by radio or flashing light. Evidently her skipper didn't want a ration of good advice from Captain Scruggs.

It was a new year and my only resolution was to be more thorough in my assignments.

The following morning San Juan glistened like a jewel in the bright, clean sunlight. The port was such a friendly one that I felt like I was returning home. With the *Morris* tied up nearby, all hands on the *Roe* were paid by the division's paymaster. A letter from Lucrece, addressed in her cursive, script-like writing, stood out of the mass of mail I received. My heart thumped noticeably and my hands trembled as I tore her letter open. First she wished me a "Happy New Year," Dutch customs being similar to ours. Then she described how nicely she was being treated by the German occupation people, who she said were trying to alleviate the hunger of the Dutch people because the war had destroyed their crops and food stores. Some, she noted, were even useful in helping her carry out her Red Cross duties. "A few of the Germans are sympathetic to the suffering they have caused our people." Nazis, sympathetic? Again, I wondered if she was getting too friendly with the enemy.

Then she spent a paragraph wondering why I preferred her to the many glamorous American girls that I met "every day." The fact that Lucrece in her letter pictured herself as a plain woman who was dressed in unexciting clothing and whose hair was rarely styled in a beauty parlor was actually very charming to me. The emphasis by American girls on glamor turned me off. Lively good looks, combined with intelligent, humorous conversation were what I found attractive.

Lucrece did not mention anything about her ring size, nor its implication that I wanted to be engaged to her despite our separation. Perhaps she hadn't received that particular letter of mine. But I suspected she had, with her mention that "maybe we should cool our relationship until things look more promising." That wasn't what I wanted to read, since I felt that marrying this unique, beautiful woman was the wise thing to do. My passion for her perhaps was diminished because of our long days apart. But my good judgment, I felt, should still be relied on.

The *Roe* remained in San Juan for the next two weeks, at the conclusion of which she was ordered to resume for a week her surveillance patrol off Martinique. After this she'd head for the Pacific with Destroyer Division 17.

During the time in San Juan, the wardroom mess treasurer job was handed back to me. Evidently, the Captain was more satisfied with my stewardship of the wardroom mess than might be inferred from his daily harangues about my sloppy mess boys, poor planning of menus, and messy conditions around the wardroom area.

We wasted great amounts of time trying to decode an avalanche of classified messages of only general interest to the *Roe*. But the Captain wanted to know about "everything that's going on in the Atlantic." The encoded messages were frequently so faulty—wrong code, wrong heading, wrong procedures—that I thought, "We'll lose our first major naval engagement in a war, if the encoding of messages is not done better." Already, communication staffs were being expanded with inexperienced, recently commissioned officers.

On Monday the 12th, the Captain raised so much hell with everyone on the ship that when he exploded on Bill Norvell about discrepancies in the forward five-inch gun turret, Bill yelled back at the Captain (within hearing of many of the crew): "You're so inhuman and so inconsiderate of all the officers that you've reduced their efficiency one hundred percent." Bill, with a flushed face, was madder than I'd ever seen him before. Bill's reaction made the Old Man's shoulders slump. Looking downcast, he retreated to his stateroom.

Before lunch he called all officers to the wardroom "for a conference." At great length he explained that he was unreasonable at times because he was dedicated to making the *Roe* excel over all other destroyers. "And we've got the talent right here in this wardroom to make it so."

After this things quieted down. The Captain seemed willing to undo the harm he'd done to all of us. He suggested that he would not send to the Bureau of Personnel any of the bad fitness reports that he'd threatened to use as a club to achieve better results. And he promised not to dress us down before our men. He also praised the improved performance of all the divisions on the *Roe*.

The Captain sounded sincere and repentant. So in response to an all Navy (ALNAV) message requesting additional volunteers for the April Submarine School for officers, I decided to risk submitting my request the next day. Thus, in the afternoon I dashed over to the Naval Station clinic and took a submarine physical exam. The results were discouraging, but the doctor there said that I had "passed." Evidently, he'd had instructions to go easy on submarine-duty volunteers because there was a great need for more officers to man the expanding submarine force.

On the 14th of December the *Roe* left San Juan, stopped at St. Thomas for two hours to take on twenty thousand gallons of fuel oil, and then headed south. Off Rollo's Head, Guadeloupe, the *Roe* passed the *Buck* on an opposite course. As before, there was no exchange of messages. The *Buck* was now painted a startling dark slate gray color as an experiment for decreasing the visibility of destroyers at night.

The next day, the *Roe* joined the *Morris* and the ships patrolled up and down the ten-mile line, five miles off Fort-de-France. It was monotonous. Every other day one of the destroyers went to Port Castries for "recreation." The radio guard was also split with the *Morris*. That produced fireworks when the *Morris* delivered the "press news" in a fancy format. Not to be outdone, our Captain ordered me, when it was *Roe*'s turn to copy the news, to produce an even fancier layout of the press news to send to the *Morris*. Nothing that I produced, however, satisfied the Old Man, who kept snarling, "Ruhe, you can do better than that." He wanted some of my artwork combined with the press news to make it more attractive. His irritability made me decide to delay the submitting of my request for Sub School.

Blatz, however, was floating on air because he had received his orders to the school's April 1941 class. This meant that sometime earlier the Captain had given Blatz's request a favorable endorsement. Perhaps he'd do the same for mine, if it arrived on his desk at a propitious moment. I decided to wait a few more days to risk submitting my request.

On Monday the 20th, the Captain announced plans for a big ship's picnic when on the following day the *Roe* went to Port Castries. Clearly he hoped to improve his standing with the crew, whom, according to Bill, he'd thoroughly alienated. Thinking that the Captain was in a repentant mood, I mentioned to him my intention to volunteer for submarine duty. To my surprise, he said that he hated to think of my leaving because I had become necessary to the ship and that he greatly valued my contribution to his command. After all that had gone on between us, I felt like laughing—not "ha, ha" funny, but more like "yeah, yeah" bitterly.

When we arrived at Port Castries the next day, all the officers hurried ashore to play golf while the crew had their picnic with two bottles of beer for each man. They drank the beer
so fast that I organized foot races "for extra beer." Everyone
wanted to compete, so there were lots of races and lots of
extra beers dished out. The races got crazier and crazier: men
tripped each other and fell on one another in heaps. At the
same time, at least four softball games were in progress along
the beach. All in all, the men decided that the *Roe* was "a really good ship." Nothing was said about the Captain.

Emboldened by the success of the picnic, I completed my
request for Sub School. Shortly after I had laid it on the
Captain's desk, he called me to his room. He appeared displeased by my action and tried to dissuade me from trying to
get off the *Roe*, saying, "Ruhe, you've showed much promise
of late. You've become a good officer. And I hate to see you
quitting your job here before you've achieved the excellence
that your potential has promised." Words words words. Under
my breath I muttered an "Oh, yeah?" I knew one little bust on
my part would cause him to climb all over me and he'd reject
my Sub School request outright. He did, moreover, shove it at
my face as though giving me a chance to take it back. But I
didn't grab for it. I'd decided that I'd have to see his forwarding endorsement before I'd make up my mind either to stay or
to go. But going more than ever seemed imperative.

On the 23rd, the *Roe*'s neutrality patrol was ended and she
was headed for San Juan for several days of refit before sailing with the other destroyers of Destroyer Division 17 to
Guantanamo Bay, Cuba. From there, all four ships would go
to the Pacific. Evidently, the Japanese threat was developing
ominously.

8

Transfer to the Pacific

THE NEXT MORNING THE *ROE* met the *Morris* off the east end of Puerto Rico. As expected, Commander Swenson had made arrangements for exercises. This time they involved antiair gunnery firings. The commander had arranged for a plane towing a red sleeve, and the *Morris* had the first firing runs. I was a member of the observing party on the *Morris* when the sleeve was towed up her beam about two hundred yards off. Her guns managed to knock down the sleeve with five hits, the last severing the tow wire. She had pumped out about twenty shells when the sleeve came floating down.

After returning to the *Roe*, I was turret officer of five-inch gun number three when the *Roe's* antiair gunnery was tested. Captain Scruggs initially requested a practice run with simulated firing and at my gun everything went smoothly. Lynch, the gun captain, expertly simulated pumping out five shots without a hitch. On the first firing run, however, Lynch forgot to close the breech of the gun after a five-inch shell had been loaded into the barrel. I had to yell at him to "close the breech." Then, the rammer jammed and on the first shot the main antenna was nicked and the plane flew directly over the *Roe*. My gun had to be loaded in an almost vertical position before the gun hit the safety stops and failed to fire. Hence, gun number three registered only four hits in the sleeve. This was not decent shooting. None of the other guns did any better, so it was not a good day for Bill Norvell and his gunnery department.

When the division commander was boated over to the *Roe*, he looked as though he was going to raise hell with Captain Scruggs about our shooting. But he merely indicated that he wanted to ride the *Roe* to San Juan—and browse around the ship. He explained to the Captain: "I just want to get some feel for how well you are prepared for war."

The Captain's hands quivered on hearing this. He probably was thinking about the black mark on his fitness report he might get from Commander Swenson as a result of our gun shoot—and how it would affect his chances for promotion. But by the time the *Roe* arrived in San Juan, the commodore had said nothing about the *Roe*'s readiness for using her guns.

After lunch, my attempt to draw publications for the *Roe*'s imminent deployment to the Pacific resulted in the usual closed-on-Saturday-afternoon treatment. The Naval Station duty officer paid no attention to my plea to have the issuing activity opened. On returning to the ship I reported my failure to get the latest classified information. The Captain's wife, Louise, was on board for dinner. She had flown to San Juan to be with her husband—as usual. (Perhaps she didn't trust him out of her sight.) In her usual nosy fashion, she asked question after question about why I couldn't get the duty officer to help me. "And why didn't the station's paymaster pay our crew when my husband's ship arrived in San Juan?" Etc. Finally, she observed with a sorrowful smile, "You'd think the Navy people here really dislike the *Roe*." Perhaps she was right, since the Captain did a lot of throwing his weight around when dealing with the Naval Station officers.

On Sunday morning I went to church, though there was no service in progress. I just wanted to find a little peace of mind by saying a few simple prayers. Then I went to a beach on the northern side of San Juan with my watercolors and painted a large seascape. This was a form of recreational therapy where I could blot out all bad thoughts about the happenings on the *Roe*. The intense, unbroken concentration on a painting not only gave me considerable aesthetic pleasure from depicting the lovely scene, but also renewed my tolerance for enduring my tin-can experience. The act of painting was a catharsis.

When back on board the *Roe*, I had a chance to read some bizarre Sunday supplement articles from Hearst newspapers that were scattered around the wardroom. They had been included in a packet sent over from the *Morris* to alert the *Roe* officers to a mission that Destroyer Division 17 was being asked to carry out while en route to San Diego. The division's four destroyers were expected to explore several deserted islands off the west coast of Central America to see if they were as described in the tabloids' stories. These articles depicted the islands as bases for smuggling activity or for the likely staging of Japanese attacks against the Panama Canal and U.S. activities in Baja California. The stories quoted yachtsmen and merchant marine people who had landed on these islands and found proof that piers and foundations for buildings were being prepared for smugglers to use and that flat areas were being bulldozed to prepare airfields for making bombing raids against mainland objectives. The sensational, hair-raising stories made it seem that what we'd find on the islands would confirm the worst fears of U.S. citizens as to the Japanese efforts to prepare for a war in the Pacific. The smuggling business, on the other hand, was hard to get worried about. Using high-speed motorboats to land drugs and other illicit cargoes clandestinely in Baja California was certainly a lesser threat to the American public.

Much later in the evening, I was called to the telephone on the dock to answer a call from Hop Nolan, our engineering officer. He sounded frantic. "I'm down sixty bucks in a poker game here, Bill, and they won't accept my I.O.U. I'm dead tired and can't play a decent game anymore . . . and I've got to get back to the ship for some rest before we leave tomorrow . . . and there's lots of work to be done in the morning to get ready for our long trip to Panama." After pausing for a deep breath, he added: "So what I'd like you to do, Bill, is to bring sixty bucks over to me as soon as possible." Then he gave the location of the gambling club where he was being detained.

I had only ten dollars available and B.D. had only ten. So I hit Mr. Parish for the other forty, which he grudgingly produced with much head shaking and the comment that "Hop's got to be cured of this bad habit or we're liable to have a dead naval officer on our hands." Then Mr. Parish ordered me to "escort Hop back to the ship, Bill, and report to me when he's back on board. We've got to get under way at noon tomorrow."

On the way out to where Hop was playing poker with a bunch of sharpies, I thought about how I had first met Lieutenant Rathel "Hop" Nolan on my second night on the *Roe*. He had come back to the ship for dinner, bringing with him a sleazy, gangster-type friend. He had first showed his "friend" around the destroyer and then they joined Blatz and me for the meal in the wardroom. The nice meal, politely served by two white-jacketed mess stewards, made a great impression on Hop's thuglike friend. His battered nose and thick Brooklyn accent made me wonder at the company that Hop kept. At the end of the meal Hop's friend declared, "I really like dis ship of yours and the hansom fellas here. So I'd like to give youse a horse to bet on—next Tuesday at Hialeah.

He's a sure ting in the fifth race." At this, he named the horse and urged the three of us to bet heavy and make a killing because "He can't lose."

When Hop left the ship with his guest, Blatz and I discussed the proposition. Blatz thought it was a gimmick to get suckers like us to invest in a horse that was bound to lose but in so doing would increase the odds on another horse the gangsters were actually laying their money on. I didn't see how it was possible to fix a race to the degree promised. But perhaps the horse might have a chance to win if the gangsters had threatened violence against the jockeys on the good horses to ensure that they were held back in the race. And Hop's friend certainly looked as though he could be a party to a betting coup of that sort. So when Hop returned to the *Roe* I cautiously asked him to place a five-dollar bet on "the horse" for me along with the bet that he, Hop, would make. Hop agreed to this and then looked at Blatz to see if he also wanted to risk a little of his money. But Blatz wasn't risking anything.

On the following Wednesday, Hop's friend was back to find out how much we'd won on his sure thing—which had actually won the race going away. He was much distressed to learn that Hop had only bet twenty-five follars at eight to one and that I'd only bet five dollars. He stared incredulously at Blatz, who looked sheepish for not risking a cent. Then Hop's friend said, "I got anudder sure ting for tomorrow's seventh at Hialeah. Play it heavy because dis might not happen again."

We thanked him, and when he left Blatz decided to risk four dollars while I, not believing that it was possible to fix two sure things in a row this close together, decided to bet only four dollars as well.

The horse in the seventh won, as before.

Again, Hop's friend was back to enjoy our profound appreciation for his money-making tip. But again we disappointed him. Hop, however, had by now won almost six hundred dollars. As before, Hop's friend was much disgusted with our chickenness. "I'm really sorry you nice fellas won't take me seriously. Now listen to dis real hard. I got a sure ting in the second on Tuesday. Dis will be your last chance to make a bundle. So go down wid everyting you have on my horse." Then he looked sadly back at the three of us as he proceeded down the *Roe*'s gangway. He was evidently convinced that we wouldn't take the risk to make a fortune on his betting tip.

And we didn't, because it didn't seem possible to repeat this gambling coup a third time. We again bet cautiously—satisfied with the small amount of money that we had won on the first two horses.

When the horse in the second race won handily, gloom descended on the three of us. How could we be that dumb? Although Hop had won more than a thousand dollars, Blatz and I cleared less than a hundred dollars each. But then naval officers are a mighty conservative, cautious bunch.

When the telephone call came from Hop's friend the next day, Hop was almost too embarrassed to tell him how little money we'd actually risked. "Dis was duh last one," the friend said. "Dere aren't no more." He cautioned, "Don't tell nobody about any of dis business or all of us are likely to be dead men." So we never retold "dis business" as long as we were close to New York. And I never recorded it in my journal.

How had the gangsters managed to fix the three races? It was something I often thought about without even hazarding a guess as to how it could have been done. And I was still thinking about it as I handed Hop the sixty dollars in front of five tough-looking poker players who were enveloped in cigarette smoke. After Hop handed over the money to the banker of the poker game, he arose unsteadily from his seat. Then he walked out of the room with squared shoulders and at a slow, even pace—never looking back. I followed close behind him as we returned to the ship.

On 27 January 1941, Commander Swenson, the commodore of our division, came back aboard the *Roe* to ride her to Panama. His "browsing around" had induced him to watch the *Roe*'s crew in action. His presence on board made the Captain a mass of jitters. And the signal bridge resembled Grand Central Station, with its high level of noise and confused activity of apprehensive people rushing around in all directions. The commodore's subsequent orders to his four ships for all sorts of exercises and drills caused an even greater pandemonium.

At Guantánamo Bay, Cuba, on the next afternoon, Division 17 joined the submarine *Sailfish*, which would accompany our tin cans to provide a submarine target en route to Panama. The *Sailfish* was the old *Squalus*, which had sunk in 1939 when its main air-induction valve failed to close on diving. Twenty-three men lost their lives in that tragedy. After being raised from the bottom she had been refurbished and renamed the *Sailfish*. A big fleet boat, she should prove a valuable asset in a sea war.

Guantánamo Bay was full of odd-looking transports, fleet oilers, tenders, aircraft carriers, and lots of other warships.

Evidently, this anchorage had become the main basing area of the Atlantic Fleet. After only two hours of layover, with undue haste Destroyer Division 17 shoved off, headed for the Pacific.

An hour later, Mr. Parish, with great gravity, showed me my request for submarine school with the Captain's forwarding endorsement appended to it. The ALNAV I'd responded to had said: "Applicants for Submarine School should be able to pass a submarine physical examination, be recommended by their commanding officer for submarine duty, and be qualified to stand an underway officer of the deck watch on a surface warship." I had "passed" the physical exam in a marginal way and I was definitely a qualified OOD for underway operations. The Captain even fully relied on me to stand the low-visibility watches on the bridge because of my excellent night vision. Lastly, the Captain had unequivocally said a few days earlier, "You've become a good naval officer, Ruhe."

Thus I was aghast when I saw what the Captain had written about me in his endorsement to my request: "This officer has advanced very slowly in his professional development since he arrived on this destroyer. His communications department shows considerable need for him to be more thorough and diligent in the oversight of his men and equipment. Some of his officer qualities need honing."

Honing? What did that mean?

"It has been difficult to make him serious about his naval duties," the endorsement continued (the old "life-is-real, life-is-earnest" crap) "and hence, his reliability as an officer seems questionable. He is therefore not recommended at this time for submarine duty." As I read the Captain's words my hands became clammy and it felt like a heavy rock had settled in the pit of my stomach. I couldn't believe my Captain had written such vicious, discouraging words about me.

Mr. Parish watched my reaction. With considerable pity he consolingly said, "He did that so you'd withdraw your request for Sub School. He doesn't believe all that he wrote. In fact, he's said that he's pleased with your performance and that your communication department has improved greatly in the past couple of months. What he's trying to do is keep you aboard because he feels he needs you."

What a way to keep me on the *Roe*! To help the Captain make commander?

Sick at heart, I stood there helplessly. I was so deflated that the impish smile that spread across Mr. Parish's face didn't register with me until he said, "Why don't you go ahead and have it forwarded just as it is? Some of the people who'll see that request will know how tough a skipper Scruggs is to serve under. And anyhow, with a war coming pretty soon, the Bureau of Naval Personnel might need volunteers for submarine duty so badly that they won't pay any attention to what Scruggs has written. Your high class standing at the Naval Academy should also be of some help. Give it a try." So I dropped my request for submarine school in the ship's mailbox.

Dear, sweet Mr. Parish. A real friend! He thought that I had a chance to be accepted. *Despite* the Captain. I wouldn't hear from the Bureau for a month or so. Suppose I was accepted— how would the Captain react to that? Only time would tell!

Mr. Parish's smile looked like the much later Alfred E. Neumann, "What, me worry?" smile. It warmed me like a fireplace blaze on a cold, wintry night.

On the following morning, sonar drills were held, employing the *Sailfish* as the submarine target. Using an Aylwin plot, the ranging by the sonarman was well controlled—the sonarman, Fletcher, looked particularly good on his instrument as he held constant contact on the sub at two thousand yards' range. On one occasion Fletcher called out, "I hold a submarine at two hundred yards on our starboard beam." But as the *Roe* was turned away to evade this close contact, it was evident that Fletcher was pinging on a knuckle in the *Roe*'s previous wake as she had zigzagged in accordance with the antisubmarine doctrine for destroyers.

After a conference about the deserted islands that the *Roe* had been tabbed to investigate on her way to San Diego, I did a virtual Easter-egg hunt on the ship for applicable confidential charts and letters that might be on board and that the Captain was unrelentingly demanding, despite their actual scarcity as shown by my records. Of course, he questioned my records incessantly. He was certain they were, "as usual," faulty. More black marks on my next fitness report? I had to believe that I was being singled out as an on-board example of inefficiency, except that B.D. got the same mistreatment for his performance. And, Mr. Parish, whom the Captain snidely called "a passed-over lieutenant" took the worst beating of all of us. He got unsat fitness reports regularly.

On Thursday morning we again held sonar-tracking drills. At lunch, the commodore proposed that before we arrived in Panama he'd have the *Roe* protect the patrolling submerged submarine *Sailfish* near the entrance to the canal while the *Morris* was designated to attack and simulate her destruction.

A wild flurry of signal bridge activity started. The commodore wanted all directions to the *Morris* sent by flag hoists

and messages sent to the *Sailfish* by flashing light. The
Captain spun almost out of control as he dashed about the signal bridge creating confusion with everyone.

"What does Hypo, Queen, Roger, and then the designator
Sail mean?" he yelled at Chason, the first-class signalman, as
he saw the four-flag hoist two-blocked on the *Roe*'s yardarm.

"That's 'Conduct antisubmarine operations with the *Sailfish*,' Sir," Chason answered. There was a second flag hoist of
numbers that was also two-blocked and meant "at 1500." The
Captain questioned where Chason had gotten that information. "From the commodore, *Sir*," was the answer given—
Chason emphasizing the "sir" without looking back at
Commander Swenson, who stood close by for verification.
Chason, a burly, short-necked, cocky eighteen-year Navy man
with spit-polished shoes, wore his white hat on the back of his
head and hadn't made chief because of a spotty record—that
showed such offenses as "resisting a shore patrolman." He
took the Captain's tongue lashings with a small smile.

"Dammit, Ruhe," the Captain softly snarled, "you've got to
keep me informed on what's going on here." And so it went.
He checked every signal but was never quite certain that the
signal gang was using the right procedures or even the correct flags. The commodore's presence proved very unsettling
to Captain Scruggs. The sooner the *Roe* got to Panama, the
better.

Somehow the *Roe*—without further flails—arrived at Coco
Solo, the Panama submarine base on the Atlantic side, and we
tied up there. The moment the gangway was secured, I was off
the ship and heading to Colón nearby to get wardroom mess
supplies. Ross went with me to help, but at some point he
drifted off and I lost him. I had also directed the stewards
Valdez and Gentry to deliver all wardroom linens, including
the officers' dirty stuff, to the base laundry with instructions
for the clean wash to be shipped on the Panama Railroad to
Balboa on the Pacific side. There, it would be picked up
Saturday night after the *Roe* had transited the canal.
Unfortunately, the rest of my time ashore until supper time
was consumed in finding applicable charts for the Pacific
islands. Then I had Frank Lynch for supper. From the Naval
Academy's class of '38, he was Navy's largest football player
at six feet four and 230 pounds and our best lineman—a
tackle. After the meal, he showed me around his old crock of a
boat, the submarine *R-1*. And we had a good talk as I told him
that I expected to get into submarines despite all my troubles
on the *Roe*.

On the following afternoon the Captain held a party on board the *Roe* for his many friends in the area. Although it was the dry season, six flash downpours had confused the preparations for the wardroom party. That was expected, since during the wet season the Panama people, it was said, went to the movies in dugout canoes. Then I almost had heart failure when the stewards Ross and Jameson, who were designated to serve at the Captain's party, came back to the ship too drunk to do anything except sleep. Luckily, Gentry was available with clean whites and saved my skin.

In the evening Frank Lynch and his wife, Emily, invited me to dinner at their quarters, after which we went to the Atlantic Night Club in Colón to see the notorious, raunchy floor show—a must for all visitors to Panama, I was told. Blatz was there alone, sitting with a "hostess" who ordered Blue Moon after Blue Moon at a dollar a glass. It was an innocuous drink with little or no alcohol. Blatz on the other hand was drinking double whiskeys while the "hostess" got 40 percent of the money Blatz shelled out for his and her drinks. The hostesses were far from pretty. They were chaperoned and were miserable dancers. And they could scarcely provide an intelligent conversation. Interestingly, if they put their Blue Moons on the edge of the table it meant that their table partner was making headway. Their dresses were low-cut and slashed to the hip provocatively to make them look sexy. Yet their job was supposedly to provide only companionship for lonely servicemen—without going any further. When a serviceman got too drunk, he was helped to a taxi and dispatched to his place of duty.

Before the main attraction of the floor show was staged, Blatz had disappeared—carted off to the *Roe*, no doubt.

Until the moment when the advertised "Beauty and the Beast" act began, the floor show seemed to have a premium on ugly-looking women. But "Beauty" proved to be a lovely, middle-aged woman with excellent breasts and soft, slim thighs. She was dressed in a nightgown of what looked like see-through mosquito netting and she reclined on a couch while smoking a cigarette with languid, graceful gestures of her snow-white arms. She was truly a delicious dish and just waiting for something nasty to happen. The stage set beyond her had a large spot-lighted window through which one expected the "Beast" to arrive. The tension grew, as the band's music increased in tempo. Then, a large gorilla appeared at the window and ogled the reclining Beauty. There was lots of amorous growling before the Beast pushed his way into the room and grabbed the frightened, beautiful woman. Slowly, and with much lustful tenderness, the gorilla stroked his victim's body while he tore the mosquito netting off her. (I now understand the economics of using cheap mosquito netting for a costume.) What a climax when she, totally naked, was clasped tightly to the gorilla's hairy chest. The lights went out. I heard loud scraping and banging as the set was removed. And then the lights were turned on. The stage was empty. Wild cheering and clapping followed.

Shortly afterwards, Frank, with a devilish look, pulled out his calling card and wrote on it, "Ensigns Ruhe and Lynch would be honored and delighted if you'd have a drink with them. Your act and your elegance deserve much praise." Frank liked the little-used word "elegance" and thought it would get results. It did. After Frank's calling card had been delivered to Beauty's dressing room by a waiter, she appeared on the dance floor and had the waiter point out our table. Then she graciously joined us and Frank made the introductions. She virtually ignored Emily's "How do you do?" with an incoherent, uncivilized mumble. But the bemused and admiring smile she beamed at Frank Lynch and her cultivated speech were quite unexpected. More and more, she seemed a true enigma. Eventually, and rather casually, I asked her how it happened that she had come to Panama to do this night club act. Very tolerantly, and with a "dear boy" smile, she said that she'd been on the stage in New York doing some small parts and earning only a little money when she was approached by a vacationing Panamanian night club owner who saw her on stage and who thought she was just what he needed for his club in Colon. "He offered me a lot of money to do this thing I'm doing now. And since I was having trouble scraping up enough money to keep my son at Harvard, I agreed to his offer. And it's quite a pleasure meeting handsome young men like you two." I wondered at her "son at Harvard" explanation. Harvard? How about CCNY (the City College of New York)?

On Saturday, 1 February, I was up at dawn for transit of the canal and still musing about the "Beauty and the Beast" act of last night. I was perplexed by a radio broadcast item that Chief Feath had typed up for routing. In essence it said that President Roosevelt had taken action to divide the U.S. Fleet into an *offensive* Atlantic Fleet and a *defensive* Pacific Fleet—at least until the "two-ocean Navy" that the president had decreed in July 1940 would be realized in late 1942. Destroyers escorting Atlantic convoys were offensive? And destroyers supporting the Pacific battle fleet was defensive? How could a young ensign understand such a policy?

The *Roe* went through the Gatun locks in an hour and a quarter, while being raised eighty-two feet above the sea level of the Atlantic Ocean. No pumps were necessary. Gravity caused water from Gatun Lake to flow into the locks. The *Roe* and the *Morris* went through together. All handling in the locks was done by means of heavy manila lines hooked to electric locomotives that ran along the top of each lock. The locks were equipped with emergency gates to make them more secure against sabotage or bombing. However, I saw little sign of any canal defenses. No antiair guns. No army encampments nearby. But I did see debris nets at the bottom of each lock to catch anything dropped overboard from a transiting ship. "One German ship," I was told, "dropped a flat iron into a net—holding up the passage of the German ship for an hour until the iron was recovered and closely examined." There was two-way traffic all the way across Gatun Lake and through the passes leading to the Pedro Miguel locks on the Pacific side of the Canal. Gatun Lake was exciting. I saw alligators slithering into the water as the wash of the *Roe* scared them off the mud banks at the edge of the lake, and I frequently heard the loud cries of large flocks of birds that rose en masse from the nearby luxuriant dense jungle.

By one-thirty, the *Roe* had gone downhill through the Pedro Miguel locks and by two-thirty was clear of the Miraflores locks. She was almost a hundred feet lower than the waters of Gatun Lake and was at the water level of the Pacific. Each successive lock was pumped out almost noiselessly and very rapidly. The U.S. Panama Canal Zone Authority handled the world's trans-Isthmus ship traffic with great efficiency. The canal was lighted for night transits. And seventy-three pilots with salaries of about four hundred dollars a month guided the ships through—each piloted a ship no more than two or three times a week. Soft duty! A few of the pilots should try a month aboard the *Roe* and they'd stop griping about their tough job and low pay. An ensign, it might be noted, received only $125 base pay plus $18.75 ration allowance per month as a bachelor, if married $40 more for a housing allowance.

By three o'clock the *Roe* was tied up at a fuel dock in Balboa. Then after fueling she was shifted to pier fifteen and was nested with the other ships of Destroyer Division 17. It had been sweltering hot all day, yet I took off for a few hours to paint a quick picture of the barrio in the middle of Panama City. As I painted a watercolor of the densely populated, poverty-stricken, inner-city housing area, many Panamanians crowded around to watch me and to comment in broken English about their lives and living conditions. There was no running water, electricity, or sewage-disposal means within the barrio. The people were well paid by the Canal Zone Authority. But on Friday—their payday—they quickly spent most of the money on lottery tickets, gambling, and wild drinking parties. Many of the kids looked starved, probably because little money was left to buy food for the rest of the week. The place was a rat's nest; rodents darted and ambled around the tin-roofed shacks as though they were pets. I felt that if at some time this ghetto was destroyed by fire or dynamite, the inhabitants would have been done a great favor. Then the benevolent "Uncle Sam" would have the whole place rebuilt with concrete houses, electric lights, sewer pipes, and running water in each dwelling. According to the people who watched me paint, most Panamanians were dependent on Canal Zone jobs and the medical services that they badly needed.

We were scheduled to leave at midnight, and as in-port duty officer I had to listen to a lot of returning drunken enlisted men ranting about how monotonous it was for men having duty in Panama and how basically evil the whole place was with its emphasis on drugs, drinking, lewdness, and making money. The *Roe*'s crew was not surprised that all a serviceman could do on liberty was to get stinking drunk. Two men tried to jump ship after returning aboard, but were caught leaving the ship. However, Martin the radioman never did come back to the *Roe* after he'd gone ashore without authority earlier in the day.

Destroyer Division 17 broke up their nest just after midnight of the third of February 1941 and followed the *Morris*, with a canal pilot aboard, to sea. The pilot guided the four destroyers in column through mine fields off the Pacific entrance and then was transferred to a boat to return to Panama. Destroyer Division 17 headed for "the deserted islands" of the Pacific Ocean.

9

Sinister Islands

DESTROYER DIVISION 17 STEAMED toward Clipperton Island, about due west of Panama and sixteen hundred miles away. Exploring deserted lands was not a new mission for naval officers. Robert Peary, a captain in the Navy's Civil Engineering Corps, had spearheaded the exploration of the Arctic in the early twentieth century. Other naval officers had gone ashore in the Antarctic and recorded their findings. Naval Lieutenant Edward Beale in the mid-1850s had explored the southwest United States. Now the *Roe*'s officers were about to land on a few deserted islands to determine the status of supposed clandestine preparations for their smuggling or bombing use.

All day on 3 February the division commander continually maneuvered the four destroyers. He was now riding the *Morris*. All directions were sent by flag hoists. These flags created such a flail on our signal bridge that Roger, one of my best signalmen, vowed that he would "get off the *Roe* when she got to San Diego." Roger was a slim, quiet, conscientious second-class signalman who took Captain Scrugg's criticisms too seriously.

When the commodore formed a scouting line, the Captain nixed my recommendation to go to a position five miles on the starboard side of the *Morris*. The Captain insisted that the *Roe* belonged five miles on the port side of the *Morris* and headed her that way. When the *Roe* arrived at the Captain's directed position, the *Morris* raised a flag hoist questioning the *Roe*'s position. At this, I matter-of-factly said to the Captain, "We're in the wrong place and had better get over to the starboard position in a hurry, sir." Without hesitation the Captain had

flank speed rung up and raced the *Roe* over to her correct station. He had actually believed me for a change. Then, with the
Roe in her proper position, the flag hoists ceased for the time
being.

The next day when I had the morning watch on the bridge,
Barber, a gunner's mate, fell overboard while he was washing
down the after five-inch gun. The Captain did everything correctly, turning to port from our formation dog. But I was first
on the whistle, tooting it and warning the other ships in column of "man overboard." I kept Barber's head in my binoculars and coached the Captain as to how to maneuver the *Roe*
for a pickup. The man was back on board in three and a half
minutes. "That's a record," the Captain gloated. Then he casually said, "Well done, Ruhe."

When the division commander ordered, "Hold flag hoist
drill at 0900," the Captain snidely said to me, "See, the commodore thinks your signalmen need more practice."

Later at general quarters, the *Morris* and the *Roe* as a sec-
tion attacked the *Buck* and the *Wainwright*, simulating the firing of torpedoes when the range was down to four thousand
yards. "That's too close for this type of engagement," the
Captain snapped. But then, when a "Well done 418" (the *Roe*'s
hull number) was run up by the *Morris*, I let only a tiny smile
curve my lips.

The Captain kept simmering and growling while flags were
being raised and lowered. Finally, I told him à la Bill Norvell
that "No seaman aboard this ship has volunteered to strike for
signalman, even though I've pressured quite a few to go for
this rating . . . You've just made it too hot to work on the signal bridge." The Captain took this to heart and he calmed
down noticeably.

When the *Morris* signaled the *Roe* to "close me for transfer
of mail," the Captain allowed me to conn the *Roe* to a position
forty feet off the starboard beam of the *Morris*. When there, we
shot a heaving line over to the *Morris* and hauled back a
packet of mail plus a small heavy box. As the *Roe* backed clear
of the *Morris*, the Captain pleasantly said, "That was *really*
well done, Ruhe." The mail was then sent below to Sheehy for
routing, while the box was opened to show a gallon container
filled with chocolate ice cream. Appended to the container
was a note signed by Commander Swenson that said, "We
make great ice cream on this ship with real cream and
Hershey's chocolate syrup. I know how much you like chocolate ice cream. So here's a little gift for one of my finest skip-

pers. Keep up the good work." The Captain glowed with the compliment he'd been paid. But then, with eyebrows lowered and not to be outdone, he critically asked, "Why isn't there an ice cream–making machine on this ship, Ruhe?" Defensively I mumbled that it was on requisition but not delivered as yet. My excuse deepened the Captain's frown. He then muttered: "I don't like being bettered by that *Morris* crowd."

I guessed that the Captain would start eating the ice cream then and there. However, flipping the public announcing system's switch, he said, "Ross to the bridge," and in an aside to me, "There's so much ice cream here, we'll have it for dinner in the wardroom tonight. Have Ross keep it frozen in the pantry refrigerator until we can get to it." My "Aye, aye, Sir" was enthusiastic, since I also loved chocolate ice cream. But I should have known better than to let Ross get involved.

When Ross took the box of ice cream, the Captain, with his usual thoroughness, told Ross to put it in the pantry refrigerator's freeze compartment personally and "report back to me that you've done just that." In several minutes Ross was back, saying with a backhand salute, "Mission accomplished." The "sir" was missing and that spelled trouble.

When the officers sat down for dinner, the Captain, with a big, pleased smile, reminded them to "save a little space for that chocolate ice cream that we got from the commodore today." Then at the end of the main course, the Captain in a lordly fashion directed Valdez, the steward, to "serve the chocolate ice cream for dessert." Valdez looked as though he'd been struck by lightning. He nervously went to the pantry window and incoherently mumbled something to the steward inside the pantry. After this he returned to the Captain to report with a frightened stutter, "Gen . . . Gen . . . Gentry, s . . . s . . . sir, . . . says there ain't no ice cream in the refrigerator."

At this, the captain roared with disbelief. "It can't be. That can't happen on my ship!" Then with a little more rationality he decided, "It's been stolen. Get Gentry in here right away."

As mess treasurer, I rushed to the pantry window to see if a whole gallon of ice cream could actually be missing—and to tell Gentry that the Captain wanted to talk with him. Both Gentry and Ross, who was also there, looked sheepish. Guilty? I couldn't be sure, but Ross looked like the more likely culprit to dispose of the ice cream. When I looked back at the officers gathered around the wardroom table, my wide-eyed, raised-eyebrows look of amazement told the whole story. But what was worse, B.D., Blatz, Mr. Parish, and the Captain were staring at me suspiciously. Me? Well, why not? They all knew I loved chocolate ice cream and easily downed a pint or more of the good stuff whenever it was available.

But then the Captain zeroed in on a better possibility. "Where's Ross?" he yelled. "Get Ross in here right away and look for chocolate stains on his whites." Then he had another questionably brilliant suggestion. "Find the empty container. It will be hidden somewhere on this ship—perhaps in a trash can—and when it's found we'll be able to zero in on the person who stole *my* ice cream." This last instruction was directed at B.D. who was quivering and sweating because he'd assumed that the Old Man would blame him for this crime— the way he did for other things for which B.D. was not responsible.

For my part, I watched Mr. Parish closely, recognizing that he had the body volume to consume much of a full gallon of ice cream and that he always ordered chocolate ice cream at the end of a drinking session ashore. But Ross was still the best candidate for the purloining of the Captain's ice cream. Had he eaten some and then dropped the rest overboard? Did he first share it with his pals and then throw the container overboard? Hell! Of course he was the best bet to grill.

When Ross reported to the wardroom, all eyes studied his whites for a tell-tale brown spot. There was none. But Ross was so cocky and acting so blameless that his brazen "You gonna blame me for stealing the ice cream? You got the wrong man, Captain" convinced me that he was the right man to investigate. His not saying "sir" was pure affrontery.

Then the Captain had another striking thought. "It would take two people to eat all that ice cream, Ruhe, so you figure out who the other guy was." Then he added, "But first check the crew's ice box. You might find *my* ice cream hidden there."

I wasn't certain that Ross had stolen the ice cream and now I was supposed to find the other man who benefited from the theft. The Captain seemed to think that he was a modern-day Sherlock Holmes—carefully picking the perfect incriminating question to ask. I might have suggested that the Captain get Blatz to examine the passageway outside the wardroom for a trail of brown drippings. An excellent clue. But to suggest something the Captain hadn't thought of would only get him mad. As though reading my mind, however, the Captain said, "We'll call this 'The Case of the Purloined Chocolate Ice Cream.'" Then he tittered at his great cleverness.

Turning to Bill Norvell, he said, "Get on the public announcing system and tell the crew about this theft. Add that if anyone withholds important information about this loss it will be a mast offense. And the Captain will not go easy on any offender." Norvell, pleased to get away from the wardroom, headed for the bridge to put out the word over the 1 MC system. The Captain followed him, tossing over his shoulder, "I'm going to the bridge to coordinate the hunt for the culprit who stole *my* ice cream." He sure had a groove in his brain that played "*my* ice cream" over and over like a broken record.

Throughout this ordeal, Mr. Parish with knit brows would intermittently study my face quizzically, looking for some sign of guilt. He knew that I didn't scare easily, and that I wouldn't show any sign of nerves. I guessed that he wasn't trying to discover some sign of proof that I'd eaten the stuff but, more likely, that I'd thrown the carton of ice cream overboard before dinner. As mess treasurer, I could move in and out of the pantry without arousing any suspicion and could have removed the box of ice cream without being seen. B.D., however, confronted me when we were alone together and said, "You adolescent, this kind of trick is carrying things too far." B.D. accusing me? Evidently, my hazing of him on his birthday still rankled. Later, Norvell accused me of dropping the ice cream overboard. But Hop Nolan guessed that "it was Ross. He must have dropped it overboard." By now, nobody seemed to think anyone had eaten it.

In due time, every person with a sleuthing assignment reported negative results to the Captain. Hence, at the limit of his patience he frustratedly appealed to Mr. Parish. "You tell me who ate *my* ice cream." Giving credit to Mr. Parish for being able to think straight was not like our Captain. The whole business was pretty dumb. So I threw in the suggestion that we dangle another gallon of chocolate ice cream before the nose of the thief—in the wardroom pantry's refrigerator. "I can get the *Morris*'s commissary officer to give me a gallon of ice cream, disguised in a bag so nobody will know what has arrived aboard. Then we'll keep a watch on the pantry and when the lover of chocolate ice cream lets his hunger for the stuff get the better of him, we can swoop down on the thief and spring the trap." The Captain liked the idea and thought that whoever stole his chocolate ice cream was stupid enough to fall into "our trap." Real pleased with himself, he gloated: "That will work."

Yet the bag of ice cream shortly received produced no results. It stayed untouched in the refrigerator for the next three days. Finally Mr. Parish said he was convinced that the original gallon of ice cream had been deep-sixed. At the same time, his disapproving look every time his eyes alighted on me suggested that he *knew* who'd stolen the Captain's ice cream. The Captain, on the other hand, was dissatisfied with the situation and stayed in a bad mood for a couple of days. The rest of us silently cheered the "no solution" result.

Wednesday was a true day of celebration. An ALNAV listed Lieutenant Herman Olaf Parish as having been selected to be a lieutenant commander and was "best fitted." There was much good feeling throughout the *Roe* because Mr. Parish was such a fine fellow and so deserving of this promotion. There'd be no stopping him now. He'd get his own destroyer to command and there'd soon be a war in which he would prove himself. For me, the day was also a banner one because the Captain said I could pass along my mess treasurer job to B.D. Blatz had wormed out of the assignment by claiming that his orders might come through at any moment for him to go to Sub School.

By the end of the day, the *Roe* was well ahead of the other destroyers in a competitive flag-hoist drill monitored by the commodore. However, it looked very much as though Roger the signalman would crack from the strain of trying to overachieve while the Captain was watching him in action.

After the midwatch I was awakened to decode a confidential message from the commodore and to acknowledge it as quickly as possible. So I got Blatz out of his bunk and the two of us had the decoded message in the hands of the Captain and acknowledged back to the commodore a half hour before the other ships were able to do so. This pleased Captain Scruggs so much that he said, "I'll recommend you for submarine duty when we get to San Diego, Ruhe. And remind me to do that . . . then."

More drills, drills, drills.

The night-steaming in column formation with three hundred yards between each destroyer proved an irritating last straw. When the darkened *Morris* suddenly turned to starboard because of engine trouble, I missed ramming her stern by only about twenty-five feet. The Captain dashed to the bridge to see what was happening—but didn't curse me for being slow in responding to the emergency created. I wasn't getting enough sleep, what with being woken frequently to decode messages, respond to calls from the Captain to issue a publication to him immediately, or catch hell for some glitch made by my communication gang.

Then on the midwatch, I had the wrong number of turns rung up because I thought the *Roe* was closing the darkened

Morris, only to discover that the *Roe* had been slowed too much and fallen back on the *Wainwright*, which almost climbed up the *Roe*'s stern before I realized my mistake. At this, the Captain blew up and ranted that one more bust on my part and I'd be "taken off the watch list." It made me realize that perhaps my "busts" weren't a matter of bad luck but might be inherent to a flawed character. Perhaps it would be wise for me to get out of the Navy before I did some serious damage to a ship or caused real harm to the *Roe*'s crew. But that was a defeatist attitude and wouldn't be of any help for the next couple of months—until I got off the *Roe* to go to Sub School. By then, however, the Captain might have wrecked all my chances for making the Navy a career. I'd have to fight back. Soon I'd have to do something that would be so threatening to the Captain's chances for promotion that he'd stop needling me rather than see his naval future go up in smoke. I had to stop his seesawing between "You're doing fine, Bill," to "This should finish you off, Ruhe." Evidently a more imaginative solution to this problem was necessary.

Saturday morning of 8 February 1941 was when *Roe* personnel would explore Clipperton Island. I knew that I'd go ashore with the *Roe*'s landing party, since there was a heavy surf to get through and I was probably the strongest swimmer aboard. I'd thought a lot about what clues to look for in order to identify Japanese preparations for mounting an attack against the Panama Canal. As an avid reader of mystery stories, I recognized that I could apply the investigating techniques of Agatha Christie's detective, Hercule Poirot, to this intriguing investigation of a circular coral atoll, which was about two miles in diameter and had no land wider than about two hundred yards that enclosed a shallow lagoon. What sort of cigarettes did the Japanese smoke? Cigarette butts strewn around, if identified as the type smoked by the Japanese would reveal their presence on the island while the freshness of the butts would place in time when they were smoked. How about the hand tools used for clandestinely leveling the atoll to develop an airfield? But was there enough area on the narrow rim of coral to provide a takeoff strip for a bomber? How about empty Coke bottles or cans? Also, was the enclosed lagoon wide enough for seaplanes to get airborne for a sixteen-hundred-mile flight to the Canal—while carrying a few small bombs? And could one discern Japanese plans for a pier built out into the ocean for logistically supporting a seaplane base? Were the Sunday supplement articles at best only unsubstantiated guesses?

On schedule, the *Roe* and *Morris* lay to three miles off the French-owned Clipperton Island—the *Roe* to land an exploring party while the *Morris* took the day off and observed the *Roe*'s efforts. Half of the *Roe*'s officers, including the Captain, were embarked in the motor whaleboat that headed for the beach. The French government had granted permission to visit the island for one day only. And no warships were to violate the international three-mile limit. At the same time, the *Wainwright* and the *Buck* were released to proceed to Clarion Island some seven hundred miles to the north to look for smuggling activity on that island.

When the *Roe*'s motor whaleboat moved close to where the surf was breaking heavily, we dropped two anchors to keep the boat just outside the dangerous surf. We then streamed a buoy on the end of a heavy manila line toward the beach. Officers used it to ease hand over hand along the line through the crashing waves. One after the other, however, lost their grips on the line and were tossed and tumbled into the shallows at the water's edge. B.D. had his Naval Academy class ring stripped from his finger—never to be found again. All emerged from the water with their summer white uniforms covered with sand and their hands lacerated by the sharp coral at the shoreline. Fortunately, the sharks that cruised offshore were of no bother.

Only a single palm tree rose starkly above the white, barren, low-lying rim of land. A rock about thirty feet high lay at the southeast side of the atoll. It was there that the Captain found, alongside the remains of an old stone lighthouse, a weathered wooden sign saying, "Los Angeles City Limit." This was stretching the popular joke about the exaggerated area that was claimed to be part of L.A. We found no cigarette butts on the glistening coral. Nor were there any signs of pounded coral indicating airfield construction. Also, we saw no empty bottles. Moreover, there were no indications that the lagoon had been dredged to provide a safe takeoff area for sea planes. There were, however, a few twisted, rusty iron beams and fragments of a wharf on the western side of the atoll. These were clearly part of a pier that had been used long ago to take potash out of the island—a French industry described in one of the Sunday supplement articles.

Our exploration of the island was not, however, a total washout. The lack of human habitation for many years had created an island that would have delighted Charles Darwin. The sheltered lagoon was full of brightly colored tropical fish, and Hop Nolan reported seeing a half dozen scrawny pigs that could swim and were leaping into the lagoon to catch fish. Evidently, the pigs subsisted on the fish. They were not the only animal life we saw on Clipperton. Crabs, lizards, and sea birds in great abundance were on the atoll and were so tame that it felt eerie to wander amongst them; a flock of birds standing around on the beach merely shuffled aside to let a tourist pass.

Before dark, the *Roe* and the *Morris* headed for the Mexican owned Socorro Island, eight hundred miles north of Clipperton. Two days later and just before first light, the *Roe* lay to off Socorro and readied a landing party for another day of exploration. This time, two enlisted gunners mates carrying rifles were included in the *Roe*'s investigating team. Visiting yachtsmen reportedly had seen dangerous wild animals on Socorro—according to a Sunday supplement article. Unhappily, I was excluded from the exploration team and was assigned the deck watch while the *Roe* lay at anchor in Braitherwaite Bay. The Captain was punishing me for something. But then, there was no need for a strong swimmer in the landing party, since the *Roe*'s motor whaleboat could move close to the shore in the quiet bay and ground itself, so that the officers only had to get their shoes wet as they stepped out of the boat and slogged ashore.

During the day, Hop Nolan and Chick Sayles, a new ensign on board the *Roe*, used the Captain's gig to take soundings in the bay—using a weighted, fathom-marked line that they dropped over the side of the boat.

Socorro proved just as barren as Clipperton, but it had steep hills and a mountain that rose thirty-seven hundred feet into the air. The *Roe*'s explorers reported on their return that there was much volcanic ash to tramp through and that they had observed steam issuing forth from fissures in the mountain's sides. We were disappointed to find no area of the island that might be leveled to make an adequate airfield. And there were no cigarette butts dropped by smugglers nor any debris that could be connected with smuggling activity. Yet, according to the Sunday supplements, Socorro was a dope-runners' sure thing—only three hundred miles from Guadalajara, which was a good Mexican market for drugs shipped from South America. Covertly carrying drugs to the mainland of Mexico in high-speed motorboats at night, the smugglers would supposedly operate much like the rumrunners of prohibition days off the East Coast of the United States.

We saw many mountain rams and ordinary sheep and a gunners mate of the landing party shot one. It was then skinned. He proudly brought its long-haired hide and heavy, wide-spread horns back to the ship. I felt it was all wrong to kill such a fine animal.

The real excitement of the day, however, occurred on the anchored *Roe*'s stern. A dozen members of the crew fished from the fantail, and Johnson, the bos'n caught a twenty-one-pound blackfish. This created some scattered cheering. But then Walsh, the electrician, reeled in a huge tarpon. This caused a large number of the crew to flock to the stern who "oohed" and "ahed" at the marvelous catch. Walsh immediately became the ship's hero, and this status lasted at least through the next day. There was much discussion as to how to skin the fish so it could be stuffed and permanently displayed on a board in the crew's mess. By unanimous demand, the fish's meat, in large chunks, was served in the crew's mess on the following day. When the meat proved delicate and delicious, Walsh, the expert fisherman, decided that what he'd caught couldn't be a tarpon but must be some sort of huge tuna. "Tarpon meat," he said, "is coarse and bad tasting."

The *Buck* and *Wainwright* officers also failed to find any signs of smuggling activity on Clarion Island, far to the west of Socorro. It seemed apparent that the reporters who wrote the Sunday supplement stories about smuggling were smoking opium and hallucinating as they described fictional happenings.

Shortly, all four destroyers of Division 17 joined up and headed for San Diego. The *Roe*, however, on the 13th peeled off from the other destroyers for a few hours to visit the Mexican-owned island of Guadalupe. This island, only two hundred miles from San Diego and its naval installations, was a far better bet for finding Japanese activity. Here the Japanese might conceivably build an air base—that is, if they were intending to go to war with the United States. The prospect of actually finding some incriminating evidence was exciting. So when the Captain said that I'd be part of the exploration team, I did my homework—rereading the Sunday supplement article on Guadalupe and looking up all available data on the island.

Guadalupe was a former penal colony but was now uninhabited. In the past it had a cannery for seal and goat meat. It had a peak that rose forty-six hundred feet from the sea, and compared to Socorro was hillier and far larger. I thus suspected that I'd been substituted for Bill Norvell, who went ashore at Socorro, because I was expected to do a lot of tough climbing around the hills and up the mountain. The Captain particularly wanted me to explore several plateaus that became visible as the *Roe* closed the island. Mountain goats were said to abound there. The island was also the wintering spot for the rare sea elephants of the eastern Pacific.

When the whaleboat left the *Roe* it proceeded clockwise around the island. At first it skirted a three-hundred-foot-high vertical cliff of granitelike gray rock, unbroken by any fissures or projections. At the very top of the sheer cliff, several motionless, white mountain goats were visible. They peered down at the passing boat with a seemingly quizzical interest. Shortly, a narrow beach came into view and it was there I was deposited—in the midst of a herd of sleeping sea elephants— after being instructed by the Captain "to reconnoiter the area and go as high as you can. But be back here in five hours to be picked up." At that, the whaleboat chugged off to land the other officers at other beaches.

The many harmless-looking, massive, dark-brown sea elephants quietly slept in the bright sunshine. They paid no attention to me as I threaded my way past their motionless bodies. Many were big enough to weigh close to a ton. Their half-trunks and huge shiny shapes were no more menacing than the big boulders scattered around the shore. Thus when I saw a large, fat mother with a small—about thirty-pound—orange-haired baby sea elephant sleeping alongside her, the temptation to kidnap the cute little animal was overpowering. I'd take it back to the ship to show the crew. So I picked it up and cradled it in my arms.

At this, the mother and the entire herd of sea elephants awoke with a loud racket of snorting and shrill barking. All of the beasts started thumping and bumping across the rocky beach toward me. This thunderous charge of enraged, pop-eyed animals caused the ground to quake. I realized that if they caught me I'd be crushed by their heavy bodies and torn apart by their pointed tusks. But rather than drop the baby, I fled with it up the slope. I felt that I could get away from the trumpeting beasts—knowing that such huge creatures would have a tough time following me upward. But when I started to slip on loose stones and the baby felt heavier and heavier, and I heard the mother's heavy breathing very close behind me, I gently placed the baby on the ground and scrambled faster up the hillside.

That halted the charge of the furious sea elephants. The gnashing of their tusks stopped. And a quick glance backward showed the mother nuzzling her child and probing for injuries. The rest of the herd looked as though they'd gone back to sleep.

For my part, I kept climbing up the steep hill until I reached a plateau. There I found some scratchings on the hard-rock surface that were apparently made by a pickax. Perhaps it had been wielded by a Japanese worker trying to determine the difficulty of leveling the ground. Or perhaps random geologists were looking for indications of mineable minerals. I was amused to find on a plateau a cairn of rocks and in it a tin can of English cigarettes. A note stuffed in with the Player cigarettes said, "Help yourself, pal." The note was dated 1926. It seemed possible that the writer of the note was the last person to explore the island. Thus, to respond to this gracious offer I scribbled on the back of the note, "Thanks, but I don't smoke," and signed it, "Ensign W. J. Ruhe, USN, February 1941."

I discovered nothing else to indicate a Japanese presence— as I threaded my way around the hills and finally followed a path down to another shore. There I found the remains of what had been a seal and goat cannery. About fifty weathered skulls of these animals and a few broken rams' horns were all that remained of that long-ago enterprise.

Shortly, the *Roe*'s whaleboat came around a bend in the coast and picked me up. On the way back to the ship, our boat skirted the same sheer cliff we'd passed on arrival off Guadalupe. This time, a single mountain goat, a ram with a wide span of horns, was perched sentrylike at the top of the cliff framed by the sky and contemplatively staring down at us. For a minute I was distracted from watching the goat. Three wide seams of coal that showed on the cliff face had attracted my attention. Yet nothing had been mentioned about Guadalupe being a good source of coal. Then, when I looked for the mountain goat he was gone from the top. Quickly I spotted him perched on something forty feet below where he'd been. Amazingly, I saw no sign of any irregularity in the cliff that might provide a narrow ledge for him to stand on. Nor was there any sign of a path down the cliff for the goat to descend to the spot where he was flattened against the vertical wall of rock—with his head slightly turned and staring at the *Roe*'s boat. His seemingly thoughtful way of regarding us indicated that we represented a once-in-a-year intrusion of his domain. Only another mountain goat could explain how he could have gotten to his precarious perch.

The other officers, including the Captain, who had investigated Guadalupe as well as the two other islands, found nothing of any significance that might confirm the facts of the many scare stories published by the Hearst newspapers. It was a good lesson not to believe everything one might read in the newspapers.

Before dark, the *Roe* rejoined the other three destroyers of Destroyer Division 17 at the north side of Guadalupe and proceeded on to San Diego. We arrived off the entrance channel the following morning.

10

West Coast Precautions

DESTROYER DIVISION 17 in column stood up the long channel into San Diego at seven o'clock on the morning of 14 February, Valentine's Day. The morning was overcast with a gathering of dark rain clouds that briefly dumped heavy rain onto the *Roe*. It was a disappointing welcome to "sunny California." The *Roe* eased along a well-buoyed path that resembled the curved blade of a sickle to the inner harbor. On her starboard side as she headed for her anchorage spot was the newly constructed North Island airfield built on an extensive landfill. At a long pier at the foot of North Island the aircraft carrier *Enterprise* was tied up. On the *Roe*'s port side we had passed many cool-colored, single-story stuccoed houses; much low, sandy expanse with a few sand jetties at which small U.S. war vessels were secured; and finally the city of San Diego itself with many high buildings—as high as seventeen stories. It was an unexpected metropolis. My visit to Long Beach for the 1932 Olympic Games had led me to believe that southern California cities were greatly restricted in building size because of the threat of earthquake and the uncertainty of foundations built on a sandy base. Apparently, this was not so.

After dropping anchor to the south of the ferry crossing from San Diego to Coronado, the Captain called an "immediate" conference to plan for the *Roe*'s docking on Monday for bottom-cleaning of the hull. Then there was a parade of destroyer-tender people through my communication spaces who discussed upkeep work to be done during the next week. And finally, a breathing space allowed me time to sift through a mass of personal mail that had been deposited on my bunk

by the *Roe*'s mailman. I was electrified to discover a letter
addressed in Lucrece's stylish handwriting. It was a letter of
the greatest importance. My heart beat faster as I tore it open:

My Dearest Bill,
I've had many lovely letters from you but this is my first letter
to you in several weeks. I want to write only happy things to
you, the one I love. Yet little happens in our occupied country
that could be called pleasant. For me it's been a dreadful time.
It's terribly cold, everyone is very depressed and always there
is not enough food. It breaks my heart to see my dear mother
nibbling on scraps of bread and acting as though she is starv-
ing. She badly needs a few fresh vegetables to bring back her
radiant color.

The Germans are not much in evidence. But there's a lonely, quiet German man—the Reich's Commissioner for food distribution—who has been friendly and nice to me and whom I
can't hate like the others. He makes me feel human and kind
when I know that I have lost all sympathy for my own Dutch
people. They've been suspicious of each other and resentful of
anyone who has made a friend of a German. They've been so
mean to me that I have had to isolate myself from them.

The war has destroyed much of the goodness I was able to
express through my Red Cross work.

I know that this is too short a letter to write to my dearest
one. But I can't find the words I want to say. My heart is heavy
because of our separation. . . .

Your Lucrece

This was not the kind of letter I'd eagerly anticipated for the
past several weeks. Was Lucrece trying to say—actually not
say—that she was losing interest in our future together?
Again, she had not mentioned her third-finger-left-hand ring
size. And again, she seemed to have more than a passing interest in the enemy; this time a German involved with food.
Perhaps she was doing this for her mother's sake—a very risky
business in a country where such actions could brand her a
"collaborator." My poor Lucrece. She seemed at serious odds
with her own Dutch people. My troubles aboard the *Roe* were
minuscule compared to what she was suffering through. The
dearth of better clues as to her actual situation was the most
disturbing thing about her letter. My attempt to guess its actual meaning suggested only pessimistic answers. This might
even be her final letter to me. I felt sick as I realized this. The

letter certainly wasn't a sentimental Valentine's Day expression of love.

Depressed, I felt overworked and unappreciated. Then the Captain decided to hold a personnel inspection after lunch—a demoralizing thing for me and for all those in the crew who were trying to clear up their workload so that they could enjoy a free weekend with girls in San Diego, horse races in Agua Caliente, or bull fights in Tijuana. We had much to look forward to.

As usual, I caught much hell for men in my division who were wearing frayed whites and scarcely polished black shoes and who had dirty fingernails and sloppy postures as they stood at attention. The Captain too frequently said: "Put that man on report, Ruhe. He doesn't meet muster." Which, when translated, meant that the Captain thought a man wasn't up to *Roe* standards of personal appearance. Didn't the Old Man realize what torture it was for my men to be delayed in getting ashore for liberty?

At the end of the inspection I was unable to break free from an avalanche of classified paperwork that I had to file—and determine which papers needed immediate routing to someone. By late afternoon, however, I was able to take an hour off to go ashore furtively and see San Diego. All the men on the streets were wearing short-sleeved shirts. They optimistically believed, like true Californians, that the sixty-three-degree temperature was not very cold. Many attractive girls, I was surprised to see, wore *long trousers*, mannish coats, and erotically painted sandals. This kind of dress for women was new to me. The movie palaces I passed on my way into the center of the city charged only fifteen cents for a double feature and the buses and trolleys cost only five cents a ride. There were many sailor "joints" of shabby dance halls, hash houses, cheap clothing stores, souvenir shops, and tattoo parlors. And there was much open space within the town, which was void of littering debris. All in all, San Diego seemed like a decent place to make a liberty.

On Saturday afternoon, Chick Sayles and I went out to the municipal tennis courts for what turned out to be a poorly played game. However, drinking a large, frosted, chocolate milk shake after the sweaty play made the afternoon worthwhile. We stayed in town for supper and saw a W. C. Fields slapstick comedy at which we guffawed loudly. Although Chick provided some sort of companionship on liberty, he preferred to have a few beers in a bar and then return to the ship.

It made me realize the difficulty of finding another officer with the same desire for the many things I wanted to do when I went on liberty—seeing art museums, going to college lectures, browsing around the old quarters of a town to understand its history, painting a scene typical of the locale, or dancing with classy girls to a top-notch band. Going places alone was a bleak business, but it was liberating. It allowed me to rapidly appreciate a region and its people. It was true adventure.

On Sunday morning I was up early to go to church, only to find several messages that needed decoding. I thus missed the church service but caught the twelve o'clock bus to Agua Caliente, just south of the Mexican border. The horse races were exciting, but I wasted all of my two-dollar bets on losers. The young girls at the track wore bright-colored, flimsy, low-cut blouses, and open-toe sandals, and they painted their faces garishly. Overdressed old women, similar to those one would see at Monte Carlo, were in abundance. Three who emerged from the race track's bar were giddy drunk; one said, "*Now we've grown too old to dream.*" That summed it up nicely.

At the end of the races I moved on to Tijuana but was too late to witness a bullfight. The place was filthy, loud, free-wheeling, and like Las Vegas, only less civilized. It catered almost entirely to tourists, with its sleazy dance halls and long dirty bars crowded with chocolate-colored hostesses who provided "companionship." In one of the bars I met the skipper of a destroyer that was anchored close to the *Roe* in San Diego harbor. He was well lit and looked ashen, as though he'd drunk too much tequila on top of hot-spiced Mexican food. Suddenly, he broke off his talk with me and bolted out of the place.

An instant later I heard a crowd gathering outside the bar and heard excited Spanish chatter. I ambled out of the bar to see the cause of the disturbance and found the destroyer skipper passed out in the gutter with a bad gash on his head that was bleeding profusely. He'd evidently collapsed and hit his forehead on the curb. The Mexican crowd was bunched around the injured man and was doing a lot of hand wringing and cursing "the gringo" for messing up "our" town. But they were doing nothing to help him. For a moment I thought it wise to let the local people take care of the drunk man. But then I gently sopped up his blood with my handkerchief and tied a bandanna offered by a sympathetic woman around his head. I called a taxi. I would have thought twice about being a good Samaritan had I remembered that the injured skipper was a classmate of Scruggs.

The taxi driver helped me haul the skipper into his taxi and took us to "el medico."

After getting the skipper cleaned up, stitched, and winding a bandage tightly around his head, the Mexican doctor asked for eight dollars for his work. I went through the unconscious man's pockets looking for some money, but his pockets were empty. I had only seven dollars left after paying the doctor. However, for that amount the taxi driver agreed to take us to the destroyer boat-pier in San Diego. So an hour later, I helped the skipper into his own gig and sent him back to his ship in the charge of the boat's coxs'n.

The next day after the *Roe* had started cleaning her bottom in the *ARD-1* floating dry dock, I borrowed the *Roe*'s motor whaleboat and went over to the injured skipper's destroyer to get back the money he owed me for the doctor and the taxi. When I arrived at the top of the gangway and requested the OOD's permission to see "the captain," a messenger was sent for him and he quickly appeared on the quarterdeck with a mass of bandages on his head. He looked like he was wearing a white turban above his pale-gray face.

"Sir," I tentatively ventured, "I'm the person who got your head sewed up by a doctor in Tijuana and brought you back here by taxi. . . ." I paused to see his reaction to my Boy Scout help. His icy stare and clenched jaw, however, were not promising.

I hesitated. Actually asking a destroyer captain for money, when he might not have remembered what had happened, was a bit difficult. Moreover, the skipper continued to look at me with squinted eyes as though to say, "So what?"

But it seemed necessary to risk Captain Scruggs's wrath by perhaps belittling one of his classmates. So apologetically, I said, "The Mexican doctor cost me eight dollars and the taxi cost me seven dollars and I'd . . ."

At this, he interrupted me and grumbled something like, "I didn't ask you to help me," and with that, turned away and returned to his stateroom.

Flabbergasted by the skipper's response, I stood there mute, helpless, and resentful. I thought of telling the deck watch what had happened. That way the word would get all around the ship and the crew would know the sort of skipper they had. But then I realized that the skipper was embarrassed by the whole business and therefore was dangerous. I had to be careful about arousing the retribution of a senior officer. He could easily wreck my career—unfairly, of course. But was

Scruggs any different? Such treatment seemed to go with seniority.

In a really bad mood, I met my classmate Bill Fargo at the boat landing and suggested we have dinner together at the Hotel Grant. Fargo, an enthusiastic conversationalist and good listener, was a whirlwind sort of guy. As a lightweight boxer at the Naval Academy, he would run at his opponent with arms flailing so fast that he made it almost impossible for the other fellow to get in a solid punch. He still moved fast, talked fast, and had dates for the two of us within minutes after we got to the Grant. Together, we had some great dancing in the basement to a Victrola gadget in which you dropped a nickel into a slot and a voice said, "What number, please?" Then you made your choice from a large number of tunes displayed in lights on the top of the music player. Dancing to great American music in the American way with neat American girls was a refreshing treat. Bill's girl, Lucia Morgan, was a real cutie and the lively, smartly-dressed date Lucia got for me followed my tricky dance steps easily as she glued herself to my body. The day had turned into a success despite my failure to get my money back after having done "a good deed."

On Tuesday, all hands worked hard stripping ship, crating the things removed, and then tagging the crates and invoicing the contents. It wasn't being done well, yet it was a start toward answering the war fears. I turned in my classified publications at Com 11 and then drew the latest classified publications for operations with the Pacific Fleet. Wearing a pistol and carrying the publications in a chain-locked suitcase were requirements. The fear of them being compromised was almost paranoid among the officers involved. Talk was rife that the many Japanese in San Diego posed a security threat. Still, there was no sign that we might soon take action to respond to such fears.

On 19 February the *Roe* was out of dry dock and an oil barge came alongside to fill her up with fuel oil. The winds had picked up and were beginning to blow strong, and the oil barge and the lighter-barge that was loaded with strip ship items, began to pound heavily against the *Roe*'s sides. This forced me, as OOD, to get a tug to haul the lighter-barge away and have it tied up at the aircraft carrier's pier. Then Kirk, the coxs'n of the Captain's gig, let its tiller be yanked out. This put the gig out of commission at a time when the Captain was about to hold a dinner in the wardroom for some of his San Diego friends. He'd hosted all of his guests to a cocktail party at the Officers' Club before bringing them aboard for dinner. Luckily, he was feeling in fine fettle as he returned to the ship in the gig I borrowed from the *Morris*. His dinner conversation was full of humor and he didn't talk any "shop" to his charming guests. In fact they showed little interest in the Navy's readiness to go to war against the Japanese. Again, the Captain amazed me with his smoothness and *savoir faire*. When I sent all the guests ashore in the borrowed *Buck*'s gig, he made no comment—either nasty or favorable.

Juggling division boats around to meet commitments required some mighty shifty maneuvers. The next day, everyone wanted to go somewhere "at once," and the boat situation got out of control. The lid was off when the Captain yelled for a boat "right away" and none was available. He ranted at me for being incompetent and "a disgrace to the Navy." At that point, I decided to cancel my invitation to Bill Fargo to come to dinner in the wardroom that evening. I was afraid that he'd hear the Captain pinging on me and gain the impression that my performance as a destroyer ensign left much to be desired. I never reached Bill, however, and he arrived in the destroyer *Manley*'s whaleboat only a few minutes before we sat down to eat.

All the officers stared at their plates as the meal began. All were waiting for the Captain to break the silence. Then he berated B.D. for all the strip ship items that B.D. forgot to box and get off in the lighter. (B.D., as first lieutenant, actually bore the brunt of the whole strip-ship operation.) Then there was more glum silence. Finally the Captain asked Bill Fargo what sort of a wardroom mess did he have on the *Manley*? To this, Bill could only mumble, "The food's good." Then more silence and more staring into our plates as the dinner was consumed.

Afterwards I asked Bill, "How bad is it on your ship?" and Bill replied: "My Old Man seems just as rough a guy as yours, but we don't seem as afraid of our Captain as you do of yours."

"Does he give you unsat fitness reports?" I asked.

Bill slowly and reflectively guessed that he probably didn't. "But we never see our fitness reports before they're sent to the Bureau. Our captain says, 'If you're interested, look them up in the Bureau of Naval Personnel when you're back in Washington.'"

At midnight the *Roe* was under way and groping its way out of the harbor through rain and fog. This put the Captain in a nervous jitter, running from wing to wing on the bridge looking for buoys, sailboats, obstructions, or whatever. He had me on the bridge watch, even though it wasn't my turn, "because you can see things others can't in low visibility." True.

By eight o'clock, the 21st of February, the *Roe* was tied up at San Pedro, a short distance north of the Long Beach Naval Shipyard. What a strange, unattractive view! I saw green hills of artificial lush-green color, billboards everywhere, and many oil derricks instead of trees. By early afternoon, after taking on eight reworked torpedoes, Blatz and I were free to bus up to Los Angeles. I wanted to talk to the Dutch consul there about the situation in Holland. When I finally got in to see him, he had bad and good news: Shipping an expensive gold ring to Lucrece was simply impractical, but mail was coming out of Holland with little delay. When I asked about rumors of Dutch collaboration with the Germans, he said that he'd heard of a few instances but no names were mentioned along with such stories. The trip in no way put my mind at rest.

Before going back to San Pedro, Blatz and I went to the Seven Seas for an early evening drink. Blatz seemed to want to spend money, and had three palm readers study the lines in his hand. None told of his shortly taking a long trip (across the continent to Sub School) nor did any see submarine duty in his future. Nor was there any mention of being in a war shortly. So much for palm readers.

The division departed for Honolulu late Sunday night; the *Roe* carried five officer passengers to Pearl Harbor for assignment to ships there. The other three destroyers of the division, on the other hand, carried only one passenger each.

One of the *Roe*'s passengers was a Lieutenant Commander Shultz, whose home was Emmaus, Pennsylvania, only three miles from my home. He was a friend of Captain Scruggs and hence ignored me, despite the fact that he identified me as a hometown associate. Another passenger was a naval reserve officer, Lieutenant Harris. He had a mandolin with him and we promptly started playing duets together—me on my guitar. Then there was Lieutenant Hind, U.S. Naval Reserves, who was a former tuna boat owner. He said that his boat operated out of San Diego as far south as the Galápagos Islands on fifty- to seventy-day voyages. During these trips with three-pole fishing for catching 150-pound tunas, they caught about forty-thousand dollars' worth of fish per trip. The profit per year for his boat he estimated to be fifty thousand dollars. He was using Portuguese fishermen to keep the labor costs down. The fourth passenger was a former bond salesman, a Lieutenant Crouch, an ex-Academy man. This was his first

Navy assignment and he called it "a real vacation for me." All four of these reservists thought they were merely going to a picnic. We'd see. Lieutenant (junior grade) Kenny West from the China Station said he had enjoyed his first tour out there so much that he had extended his tour for two years and hoped to get back, particularly to Tsingtao.

The best thing about the five passengers was that they brought pleasurable table talk to each meal, and they more or less ignored the Captain. For his part, he seemed content to listen to their stories and to act as the genial host. For the time being, no one stared at his plate. Also there were few drills or exercises en route to Hawaii, since the division commander was confined to his bunk with a bad case of the flu.

At night, we carried out visibility tests of the light-gray painted *Morris* versus the *Buck*'s dark-gray paint job. But it was no contest. The light-gray *Morris* proved much harder to see at all ranges than the almost black *Buck*. Hence we expected that on arrival at Pearl, the *Buck* would be repainted with the customary gray color. Sonar drills conducted by the *Roe* were futile. At only five hundred yards from a target ship, the sound echoes were lost in the ocean's static. Still, the Captain kept yelling, "Give me a range and bearing. Give me a range and bearing. Give me . . ."

The sea was getting violent and crashing over the *Roe*'s bow and a cold forty-knot wind was straining the halyards. But at this time, the Captain, from his sea cabin, ordered us to conduct a flag hoist drill. Weakly, he mumbled up the voice tube, "You fellows up there need the practice." Fortunately the seas grew even heavier and the Captain became hopelessly seasick. And silent. A great peace settled over the ship. But what a pity that with quiet reigning it was almost too difficult to do any work such as correcting publications, getting caught up on correspondence courses, or even decoding messages. Each heavy lurching roll of the *Roe*, would cause the decoding slips to shoot out of their slots in the aluminum strip-board. The ship was rolling up to forty degrees but righting herself nicely, since her course was many degrees off the troughs of the waves.

Chick Sayles, the new ensign, proved to be a congenital seasick victim. That meant that he'd be absent from the deck-watch rotation every time there was rough weather. Consequently, only three officers were standing top watches in the pilothouse. Captain Scruggs arbitrarily ordered that four of the passengers who were qualified OODs from their service on other ships were not allowed to stand such watches on the Roe.

By Friday, 28 February, the seas had calmed enough for the Captain to be up and about. Thus ended all the peace and quiet.

B.D. at the evening meal announced that the wardroom mess bill for February would be eighteen dollars, a new low. Everyone cheered under his breath. Then on the midwatch I sighted Molokai Light fifty-five miles away. At this I felt a momentary electrifying current running through my body as I realized that we'd arrived at the Hawaiian Islands—where grass-skirted native girls swayed to Hawaiian music and interpreted the songs with gestures of their "lovely hula hands." As a boy I'd seen and heard Hawaiian troupes performing in vaudeville shows and lately I'd been hearing *Hawaii Speaks*, the music program broadcast daily from the Moana Hotel on Waikiki beach. So it was exciting to contemplate the days ahead.

By six-thirty on 1 March, the *Roe* was standing up the channel to Pearl Harbor. The rising sun's rays breaking through low-hanging clouds dazzled the lushgreen hills and purple mountains beyond the harbor. The island of Oahu had much the same scenic quality as the island of Madeira off the west coast of Africa, where I'd avidly painted many good scenes when I was with the cruiser *Trenton*.

When we entered the main part of the harbor, the *Roe* was directed to tie up at a fuel dock. And it was there that Hop Nolan's sister Frances, with her friend Pat Taylor, came aboard carrying armfuls of leis that they draped around the necks of the officers topside and greeted us with a singsong "A-lo-ha." Pat Taylor placed two tuberose leis around my neck and even though I was a complete stranger, kissed me warmly and said another "Aloha," that sounded more like an expression of love than a "Hello." After inhaling the fragrance of the leis, I risked saying that I thought "their perfume is as lovely as you are." It seemed the right thing to say, as she beamed her approval. Draping leis on a person's neck on arrival in Hawaii was the friendliest gesture of welcome I'd ever encountered. It sold me on the islands.

After a hectic morning of transferring men, getting paid, cleaning the sides, doing touch-up painting, and getting the boats operating, Hop Nolan, Mr. Parish, and I went to the Moana Hotel to hear an eleven o'clock broadcast "to the States" of *Hawaii Speaks*, a radio show that Hop's sister produced. The Hawaiian music was super, yet my attention gravitated to the beach boys riding the heavily breaking surf far out beyond the Moana Hotel, which fronted on the beach at Waikiki. A person standing on a board all the way in to the shore on a single wave was a thrilling thing to watch. It seemed to be a better sport than skiing and probably as hard to master. And it was something I wanted to do expertly, right away.

So next day I went back and rented a surfboard at the Outrigger Canoe Club next door to the Moana. The board was solid, dark mahogany; broad, about twelve feet long; and more than a hundred pounds in weight. Yet, it wasn't too tough to get it into the water and to paddle it out to the Queen's surf a half mile at sea. But catching waves defied me at first. Then when I did catch one, I couldn't stand up on the board without losing my balance. After two frustrating hours of trying to master surfboard riding, I went all the way back in to the beach on a single wave by lying on the board the entire distance. I was exhausted from trying to control this beast of a board—and too tired to carry it back to the Canoe Club, so I had to get one of the beach boys to help me pull it out of the water. I knew that the next day the *Roe* would join the fleet in exercises off Oahu. I hoped there would be plenty of time in the next couple of months to learn how to ride the waves—Hawaiian style.

When I returned to the *Roe*, I found orders for me to report to Submarine School. They read:

> When detached, proceed to the Submarine School, New London, Connecticut, to attend the Officer's Class convening on 3 April, 1941. You may employ any means of transportation available and will be reimbursed for travel and related expenses. Ensign Kenneth Steen has been ordered to the *Roe* to relieve you.

How could I show these orders to the Captain? He'd be furious that I had my request approved by the Bureau without his knowledge.

Hesitantly I took them to his stateroom and awaited his explosive reaction. There wasn't any. In a very businesslike manner, he said, "I can't detach you right away, Ruhe. There won't be time for you to properly hand over your communication and torpedo duties to your relief when he arrives. So I'll notify the Bureau of Naval Personnel that you won't be available for the April class but will be available to attend the July class. You've still got a lot to do if we're going to win the fleet communications competition. You know I'm expecting the *Roe* to have a big, white 'C' painted on her sides." Then the Captain matter-of-factly declared, "Let's just shoot for the July class and let it go at that." For him, the matter was settled. Or was it?

11

Frustrated Searches

ON MONDAY MORNING at four-forty-five, the *Roe*, along with several other destroyers, slipped her buoy and, with all lights doused, left Pearl Harbor. Like a furtive gray wolf, she crept to the sea area near the harbor's entrance. There she scoured the waters through which the fleet had to steam en route to where war games would be played. With her active sonar pinging away, the *Roe* searched the restricted area to the west of the green-lighted entrance buoy for snooping Japanese submarines. Over the past six months, occasional contacts had been made on possible unfriendly submarines, but no sub had been forced to the surface for positive identification. According to scuttlebutt information, when the British had found a submerged unidentified submarine outside Portsmouth Harbor, England, in early 1939, they had used depth charges to force a German U-boat to the surface. After signaling "So sorry" to the British, the U-boat lit off her diesels and on the surface departed for Germany. On the other hand, U.S. destroyers lacked peacetime authorization to use weapons against an unfriendly submerged sub.

By daylight, when many fleet warships began to sortie to sea, we had made no sonar contacts on any spying submarines. But close to where the *Roe* was patrolling, a sampan drifted and a man on its main deck was taking pictures of the ships departing Pearl Harbor. The Captain was much annoyed by the intruder and conned the *Roe* within a few yards of the sampan. Then, through a megaphone, he shouted at the oriental-looking "fisherman" who had the camera held to his face: "Clear out of this restricted area at once!" The man ignored the Captain and continued snapping photographs of the passing warships. This

caused the Captain to raise a head of steam that would gener-
ate a lot of hell-raising on the *Roe*'s bridge. Fortunately, a
Coast Guard cutter hove into sight and raced over to the sampan. Several Coast Guard sailors then boarded the illicit vessel and secured a tow line from the sampan to the Coast
Guard ship. The small craft was dragged out of the area
toward Honolulu, where it would be impounded in a basin at
the Ala Moana Tower in downtown Honolulu—along with
many other confiscated Japanese fishing vessels. I'd been
amazed the previous week, when we were going to the
Hawaii Speaks program, by the many unmanned fishing sam-
pans sequestered there. The Coast Guardsmen took no evident action to expose the pictures taken. Perhaps that would
happen later.

When the battleship *Tennessee* issued forth from the channel, the *Roe* in accordance with previous instructions, left her
patrol station and moved to five hundred yards abreast of the
Tennessee to act as her antisubmarine screen until she joined
the fleet's formation. Once at the battleship rendezvous area,
the *Roe* moved to her designated station in the inner antisubmarine screen of the battle line—joining the other destroyers
of Division 17.

Each time the battleships shifted as fleet maneuvers were
practiced, the *Roe* had to answer the flag hoists run up on the
Tennessee and double-time to her new position on a reoriented
battle line. During these maneuvers, several U.S. submarines
that had been injected into the battle problem as "the enemy"
sneaked through the fleet's screens without being detected and
sent up green smoke bombs to indicate the simulated firing of
torpedoes at various battleship targets. On one occasion, a *Roe*
lookout spotted a sub's periscope and reported it to the
Tennessee. This caused the battle line to make an emergency
turn away from the submarine.

At night, Division 17 was sent to take up outer-screen picket
positions. At this, I breathed a sigh of relief because with total
darkness most of the night, at least the separation of ships in
the *Roe*'s vicinity would make my ten-hour OOD watch easier
to handle. When all units of the fleet were at "darkened ship,"
the Captain, as usual, felt that for the safety of *his* ship he had
to use me, with my superior night vision, as the deck watch
officer.

After midnight, a sonarman held a good sound contact on a
submarine and reported hearing the sub ping-ranging on her
sound projector. The *Roe*'s contact report to the commander
of the battle line caused him to wheel the force, changing its

axis and base course. Since all radio messages were being encoded, my communicators had to work like a bunch of beavers to keep the Captain informed of fleet actions.

At daylight on Tuesday, a red fleet, comprised of heavy cruisers and six destroyers, was scheduled to make an evening gun attack on the blue fleet with its battle line. Consequently, Division 17 was returned to its inner-screen stations for the battle wagons. To set up the exercise situation, a large flow of messages by flag hoists and radio was generated. The encrypted radio broadcasts kept Blatz and me busy all day doing the decoding work. But from time to time I'd have to dash to the signal bridge to ensure that my signal gang members were keeping peace with the Captain by doing things efficiently. Since they were, I would spend only a moment on the bridge, then go below to continue the decoding of messages.

On one such trip to the signal bridge, I was utterly amazed to see a Secret copy of *Gunnery Instructions* lying on the rail of the starboard flag bag. My first reaction was to hand it to someone to stow safely somewhere on the bridge. But all the signalmen were busy on the port side with flag hoists. Impulsively, I hurried below with the Secret publication to put it in my safe until I could identify who had signed for it. Nobody had seen me carry it below and then lock it in the safe. Blatz had fortunately left the wardroom for a quick snooze. And wonder of wonders, its identification number—according to my classified publication control log—indicated that it had been issued to *the captain*! And he still had custody of it!

This was *it*. It was the big opportunity to get the Captain off my back. Earlier I'd seen him reading a copy of *Gunnery Instructions* to bone up on the best way to handle the imminent attack of eight-inch gun cruisers. I broke out in a cold sweat and my hands shook badly as I thought of how I could capitalize on this stroke of luck.

The Old Man had designed a fool-proof system for ensuring the accountability for all classified publications carried on the *Roe*. Now I could capitalize on his paranoia of ruining his career by losing a classified publication. What I needed to do immediately was to hide it so well that it couldn't be found. That would be tough with a Captain who was expert in inspecting his ship so thoroughly that he'd never let even a pin go unfound. To drop it overboard—as someone probably had done with a partially eaten gallon of chocolate ice cream— was out of the question. The reason was that although the Captain would be nailed for its inexplicable loss, as custodian of classified publications I would be thoroughly investigated for the manner in which I'd handled classified documents in the past. Unfortunately, there were enough warts on my performance over the last six months in the handling of classified publications that I would probably suffer even more than the Captain for the loss of the *Gunnery Instructions*.

The solution was to keep it hidden long enough to worry the Captain silly. Then it had to be discovered in such a manner that the Captain would never know for sure who had orchestrated this lost/found, despicable, dastardly deed.

I contemplated—as I faked decoding a message on the wardroom table—several options for securely hiding the Captain's *Gunnery Instructions*. I made sure that no one passing through the wardroom could possibly guess what I was up to.

I recalled a Sherlock Holmes case where a disguised purloined letter was cleverly and for a long time mixed in with the correspondence of the suspected thief in his own quarters. Since the Captain would probably make me his prime suspect, he'd rapidly zero in on my stateroom as the most likely hiding place for his missing publication. So that's where I should hide it. When he failed to find it there, I would be in control of the situation and not suffer any of the consequences for his dereliction. Later the secret document could be accidentally found. Thus, he could never be quite sure that I had taken it in the first place. From then on, the fear of anything like this happening again should make the Captain think twice about leveling the boom on me. To me, this all made good sense.

So I went into action with heart pounding and an animal-like alertness for anyone passing by who could expose my ploy. Studying my stateroom to see where I could hide the book well enough to foil the Captain's search, I rejected all hiding places until my eye settled on the ventilation piping. It ran aft alongside the outer bulkhead above the porthole, then bent upward, flattened out and bent inward along the after bulkhead to pass through the inner bulkhead and out into the passageway. When I broke the connecting coupling, it seemed evident that a book placed deep into the piping that led the air athwartships could not be seen, because no one could fit his head between the break in the piping and the outer bulkhead. Also, it could be placed so far into the piping that the Captain's groping hand—even reaching in at full arm's length—wouldn't feel it. The trick then was to replace the connecting joint so well that the Captain could not detect that the piping had been recently broken.

The plan seemed sound. So with my heart racing and with a bristling feeling at the back of my neck, I inserted the book deep into the piping and pushed it a little deeper into the tube with a ruler. I then carefully returned the connecting sleeve to its precise original position. Even on close inspection, the Captain would have a hard time determining whether it had been tampered with.

Throughout this operation, I'd listened carefully for the footfalls of anyone passing my stateroom. But no one came forward to hazard the secrecy of my activity.

When I went to the bridge with a decoded message, the Captain, in a matter-of-fact way, said, "Ruhe, issue me a copy of *Gunnery Instructions*. I need it right away."

Dumbfounded, I blurted, "Aye, aye, Sir" and hurried below—playing out the charade—only to return in a few minutes to report: "You've got a copy of *Gunnery Instructions*, Captain. My log showed that you were issued a copy on February 25th and that you've still got it since you never signed for its return to my custody."

The Captain gave me a long, hard, icy stare and then snarled, "Dammit, Ruhe, I know I returned it to you on the same day. You just forgot to check it off."

"But Sir," I cautiously ventured, "Your system makes sure that on the return of a classified publication the person to whom it was issued initials that it was returned to me. Unfortunately your initials to validate the book's return are not in my log."

"Don't get smart with me, Ruhe," the Captain yelled. "I know that I returned it. So you just go and find it in your safe and bring it up here to me."

Again I went through the charade of going below and returning to deliver the bad news: "There's no copy of the instructions in my safe, Captain. All three of the *Roe*'s copies are issued—one to Mr. Norvell, one to Mr. Parish, and one to you, Sir."

The Captain, who was in the chart house rummaging through the chart desk's drawers, began jumping up and down and muttering some curses when he heard my report. He also opened his mouth to say that he didn't have the instructions, but then thought better of that. Quietly and resignedly, he said, "We'll just have to find my copy. So let's get started."

When I looked helplessly at him, as though I didn't have the foggiest notion as to where to start searching, he snapped, "It might have been mislaid somewhere up here. Get all your people looking for it. And be thorough!" So I got Roger and Chason and Kirk going through the flag bag stowages. Then they thoroughly checked all drawers; scrutinized every inch of the pilothouse, signal bridge, and chart room; and then rechecked on the possibility that its hiding place was so obvious that where the book had come to rest might have been overlooked. Still, nothing was found. And it was so reported.

"Okay. We're going below," the Captain growled. "Parish, you take the deck and keep me informed of all changes in the fleet's disposition and the action we're taking." Leaving the bridge in the middle of ship maneuvers showed that the Captain was really at his wit's end. He was so worried that his seniors would learn about his losing a classified publication that he'd risk having the *Roe* look bad in changing stations.

The Captain and I went directly to the wardroom where he insisted on seeing my log to verify that he hadn't checked his *Gunnery Instructions* back to me. He only casually glanced at the log entries, however; more to the point, he groped among the piles of publications on several shelves of my safe for the missing document. As he did so, he said, "Get B.D. and Sheehy to help me look around this ship. You keep working on your decoding of the operational messages."

Then when he'd gathered his "search team," all three men started forward. First they went into B.D.'s room. Then they went into Blatz's room. Then they hit my room—with lots of noise as though my room was being torn apart. And that's what the Captain was up to, as B.D. explained to me later on. He pulled all the drawers completely out of my dresser to see if the book was hidden behind them. He removed the mattress from my bed, overturned the springs, and prodded the metal confining slabs to see if one was loose and something hidden behind it. The loud wrenching metallic sound I heard in the wardroom was from the Captain tearing the ventilation line's coupling apart. B.D. said that he'd reached as far as he could into both parts of the piping without luck—and showed it by a disgusted look on his face.

Then the search team came out of my room and swept forward. Soon they were hurrying back through the wardroom, moving aft. They said nothing as they passed.

Half an hour later, I heard the Captain's heavy footsteps as he climbed to the bridge. I followed him up with a decoded message in my hand, curious as to how the Old Man was taking this lost document business. His face was drained of color and large beads of sweat shone on his forehead. "Parish," I heard him snarl, "I'll take the deck. . . .You put out to the whole ship on the 1 MC that a copy of *Gunnery Instructions* has been mislaid and must be found immediately . . . and brought to the bridge. . . . All hands turn to and search their compartments and watch stations . . . and do it thoroughly. This is a serious matter!"

When this word was passed, I looked around at the men on the bridge. All faces, including Mr. Parish's, had tight little smirks. They were enjoying the Captain's discomfort.

"Captain," I reminded, "You've got to promptly report the loss of a classified publication to your immediate superior in command and give the circumstances of how you believe it was lost."

The Captain's frown deepened and his shoulders shivered as though he'd experienced a sudden chill. "Don't be smart, Ruhe," he growled. "It will be found. . . . Don't worry." But he was the one doing all the worrying. He looked sick and tense as though he was ready to have a heart attack. The whole business was getting to him—more than I'd expected. It gave me a tinge of concern that I might have carried things too far. Yet I thought, "Let him sweat it out a bit longer until he's so worried he'll never forget this bitter lesson."

After half an hour of pacing the deck and with no one reporting the finding of a *Gunnery Instructions*, his face began to redden and the veins in his neck swelled noticeably. He was getting furious about the way things were going. He'd been glaring at me intently, but finding me with only a blank face, he frustratedly snapped at me, "You take the deck. I'm going below to find out who hid my book." Then as an afterthought, "Get Mr. Parish up here to relieve you as quickly as possible." The Old Man was going to question people all over the ship as to whether they'd seen some officer—and particularly me—in the past two hours somewhere where he wasn't expected to be. Luckily, I'd stayed exclusively between the wardroom and the bridge.

When Mr. Parish relieved me as OOD he quietly counseled, "He's not going to give up on finding the book. He'll just get madder and madder and he'll take out his anger on all of us." The nasty black look Mr. Parish gave me while saying this seemed to indicate that he thought I'd carried my vendetta against the Captain too far. But why was he fingering me?

In an hour, the Captain was back on the bridge, looking as mean as a snake. When he saw the quartermaster's entry in the ship's log: The Captain held a ship's inspection to locate a lost classified document, he ranted and raved about making false assumptions. Then he yelled at the first-class signalman who was blinking a message to the *Buck*: "Chason. Stop sending your private messages between ships. This is no time for socializing."

Again I reminded the Captain of the need to report the loss of a classified document to higher authorities immediately.

At this he blew up. "Get off my back, Ruhe," he screamed. "I'll do that when I'm satisfied that it is really lost." His voice faded into an ugly croak. He added in a whisper, "Until then, I'm not giving up." Old Scruggs was a fighter. And was frantic. His smooth, self-confident exterior was crumbling as he apparently visualized himself as "the interested party" in a court martial for a security violation. Such fantasizing, I began to fear, would give him a heart attack.

Mr. Parish, noting the devastating effect on the Captain from his lost publication, whispered to me, "Give up, Ruhe. The Old Man's in a bad way and can't stand much more of this torment." Then Bill Norvell, who had been hovering around the back of the pilothouse, suggested in a low tone that I "allow the book to be found. And just stop this sadistic business." Sadistic? Soon, B.D. sidled up to me and quietly said, "I'll help you make the book reappear so the skipper will never know who hid it." Why was everyone so certain that I was behind this whole affair—particularly Bill Norvell, who'd been in hack and gotten several unsat fitness reports from the Captain? Convincingly, he had added, "The Old Man's no harder on you than the rest of us. It's just his way of running this tin can."

Consequently, when I went off watch and when no one was around my stateroom, I rebroke the joint in the ventilation piping and retrieved the *Gunnery Instructions*. Then I hid the book inside my three-combination safe.

Unfortunately, I couldn't make the book reappear until I was back on watch and beyond suspicion. So it wasn't until my four o'clock watch on the following morning that I carried the book to the bridge under the jacket that I would wear while on watch.

The Captain hadn't slept a wink and was weaving noticeably while pacing back and forth across the pilothouse. My cheerful, "Good morning, Captain," received only a surly grunt from the Old Man. I recognized that it would be stupid to needle him any further. He would also make dog meat out of me if the book reappeared in a manner that would center his suspicion as to its "loss" on me. The stakes were high.

Thus, when the Captain was out on the wing of the bridge having a blinked message from the *Morris* read to him by

Chason the signalman, I placed the *Gunnery Instructions* in the lowest drawer of the chart desk under a copy of the general signal book. Then I waited for the fireworks when someone found it lying there innocuously.

Well into the watch, Chason was digging around the chart desk to get the general signal book. His "Oh my God!" was a dead giveaway. Without further thought he ingenuously held up a book and said, "Here's the Captain's *Gunnery Instructions*." At which, the Captain, overhearing Chason's amazed discovery, charged back into the pilothouse and yelled, "Where was it found?" as he grabbed the instructions from Chason.

Chason, unflustered, cooly said, "In the bottom of the chart desk, Sir."

"You didn't search your station thoroughly, Chason, when I ordered all of you to find that book," the Captain roared. Then he turned to me and said, "Get Mr. Parish up here right away."

My "Aye, aye, Sir" was one of relief, not of resignation. Plainly, the Captain was playing out a charade, using Chason as the guilty party. The Old Man was clever to save face this way. He *knew* that his *Gunnery Instructions* wasn't in that drawer earlier!

I had some qualms about letting the wrong man take it on the chin from the Captain. Indeed, that's what it amounted to when the Captain told Mr. Parish, "Transfer this man," pointing at Chason, "off this ship as soon as we get back to port. The *Gunnery Instructions* were in the chart desk all the time and he failed to find them."

Mr. Parish shrugged slightly and raised his eyebrows skyward while a small, relieved smile spread across his face.

It was all over. And the Old Man hadn't gotten a heart attack.

I still felt bad about old Chason being treated so badly. He was my crustiest and best signalman. So after being relieved of the OOD watch, I located Chason lounging by the twenty-four inch searchlight. I was just about to commiserate with him about the dirty deal he was getting when he blurted, "Gee, thanks, Mr. Ruhe, for getting me kicked off this crazy ship." He obviously meant it. "It was a neat way to get me sprung from this job. And don't worry about me. Every destroyer needs a good signalman. So I'll pick me a happy ship for my next duty."

I was going to miss old Chason. And I felt that Captain Scruggs would end up putting in a good word for Chason with skippers of other destroyers.

At daylight the fleet changed its axis, forcing the *Roe* to dash at twenty-five knots to her new position in the inner antisubmarine screen. It was great fun having a free hand as OOD to conn the *Roe* between battleships, cut off destroyers, and adjust course and speed to slide into a new position. The Captain stayed in the pilothouse, quietly reclining in his bridge chair. With downcast eyes, he continuously massaged his forehead as though trying to rub off some skin. Even though bombing attacks were laid on as a finale to the war games, the Captain, wearing his helmet at general quarters, ignored what was going on. For the time being he was drained of all vigor and animation.

But not for long. Just after the *Roe* left her escort station abreast of the *Arizona* and I had ordered nine knots speed to fall into our division's column, the Captain ordered, "Ten knots." It was too much speed, so the *Roe* got too close to the *Morris* before I bit the bullet and ordered, "Eight knots." The Captain didn't protest that, but when we tied up to the *Morris* in Pearl Harbor at nine-thirty, the Captain was back to normal, cursing, calling for more speed-bells than necessary, and dashing all around the bridge. Yet he made a good landing.

As soon as the *Roe* was secured in her nest, I lay on my bunk and with all of my clothes on fell asleep. When a messenger was sent to have me arrange for the transfer of our eight torpedoes to the base, he couldn't wake me. Bill Norvell then sympathetically told the messenger to "let him sleep" and took care of the torpedo transfer himself. He evidently felt I deserved something for the Captain's denouement.

During the rest of the week I dashed around the base chasing letters for the Captain, correcting publications, getting ready for a "surprise" inspection on the following Monday, and readying reissued torpedoes for the battle torpedo attack (BTPA) firings soon to be held. After work I headed each day to Waikiki, where I took a surfboard out to the Queen's surf to master the technique of catching big waves and riding them in to the shore standing up. Near the end of the week, a dark-brown beach boy who was lying on a board close by me as we waited for a big wave to start breaking said that I was only the second *haole* (non-Polynesian man from the mainland) whom he'd ever seen riding the Queen's surf. The other *haole* he described as a red-headed merchant marine sailor who came through Hawaii periodically. And he was pretty good at it.

On 10 March, the *Roe* was issued one hundred gallons of paint to change her exterior completely to a gray-blue color—a new shade of camouflage paint to be tested for its visibility under varying light conditions. Hence we conducted more visibility tests comparing the *Roe* to the customary Navy gray-painted destroyers.

On Tuesday, the division commander called for a drill that entailed decoding fifteen messages in one hour or less. Blatz and I did the job with ten minutes to spare and got a "Well done" for our efforts. Then Blatz quietly left the *Roe* with orders to Sub School in hand and without saying goodbye to the Captain. He was so eager to leave the *Roe* that I was happy seeing him go across the gangway. What a lucky guy! But then it was sort of sad because he was the most cheerful person on the *Roe* and provided the best laughs at all times.

At five in the afternoon the *Roe* shoved off for line-patrol duty off the harbor entrance, a hateful routine.

All of the following morning, as the restricted area was being swept for intruding submarines, we conducted many rehearsals for the BTPA firings on the next Sunday. In this battle event, three key officers, Hop Nolan, B.D., and Bill Norvell, were selected to be control officers for the firing of actual torpedoes. One at a time—along with a torpedoman, a signalman, and the Captain—they were sequestered in the chart house to await the commencement of a run against a surface target. On the announcement of "surprise" by an umpire, a firing team would rush out onto the bridge and practice getting off a two-torpedo salvo at a target ship in fifty seconds or less. At fifty seconds, all power would be pulled to the torpedo director and firing circuits for the torpedo tubes. So the control officer had to input rapidly to the torpedo director an estimate of firing range, target angle, and target speed—while maneuvering the *Roe* into a good firing aspect. Each officer in an alerted firing team took his turn at a simulated firing of torpedoes. All in all, by lunchtime the runs had been smoothed out so that a successful firing of two actual torpedoes by each of the three officers was expected on Sunday.

In the afternoon, the *Roe* was ordered to rendezvous with the carrier *Yorktown* for plane-guard duty during aircraft launch and retrieval operations. As expected, when the *Roe* was on station astern of the carrier, I, as the strongest swimmer and wearing only swimming trunks, went to the *Roe*'s bow to do the lifesaving job if a pilot was dumped into the sea. But as luck would have it, nothing happened on takeoffs and landings. I decided that the best insurance the carrier pilots had for safe operations was to have me sitting on the plane guard destroyer's bow counting my toes.

We continued to screen the *Yorktown* through Thursday, with more plane guarding and more uneventful takeoffs and landings. The whole business was boring and the warm tropical breeze almost lulled me to sleep. Earlier, we had ironed out kinks in the method used for our BTPA torpedo drill by only applying an offset to the torpedo remaining questionable. After leaving the Yorktown at dusk, more surprise torpedo attacks were practiced. The results on the actual firing runs would be an important factor in grading the *Roe*'s readiness to employ torpedoes in wartime and would figure in the overall score for a Gunnery "E."

On Friday, with the actual firings close at hand, both B.D. and Bill Norvell were so jittery that they had trouble figuring out how to maneuver the *Roe* for a good firing aspect. On one practice run, when Bill conned the ship so the target ship *Dewey* was thirty degrees on the *Roe*'s starboard bow—perfect for a firing situation—the Captain suddenly ordered, "Left full rudder," and fouled up the run. Nevertheless, he insisted that Bill was wrong in his maneuver. It didn't look that way to me, sitting up in the torpedo director. Only Hop Nolan looked really smooth, cranking out a two-torpedo salvo in thirty-two seconds on his practice run. Because B.D. and Bill Norvell were slow in making decisions, I'd trained the torpedo gang to keep functioning in hand operation beyond the fifty-second cutoff point. This would enable us to salvage a lesser score for the record. Personally, I was doing my part quite flawlessly, except for the accuracy of my estimated target angle.

Late in the afternoon, I supervised the readying of six torpedoes for the firing runs on Sunday. My torpedomen made the final adjustments from descriptions that I read to them from a checkoff list. All was set to go, yet as I tried to go to sleep before midnight, I thought of a hundred reasons why the torpedoes might miss or be lost.

At 0630 on Sunday morning, I was transferred to the destroyer *Dewey* and climbed to her crow's nest to act as an official observer for her torpedo firings at the cruiser *Boise*. I had to evaluate the hits by observing the torpedo wakes relative to the *Boise*'s position during the torpedoes' runs. Each torpedo was set to run at thirty feet of depth, well under the target ship's keel. Although each of the selected *Dewey* officers successively fired two-torpedo salvoes, only one firing run, determined by a roll of the dice, was counted for the "official" score.

On the *Dewey*'s official run, the range to the *Boise* was less than one thousand yards, making the change in bearing so rapid that the gyros in the *Dewey*'s torpedoes didn't appear to catch up. My observation of both torpedo wakes showed clear misses astern, but the pilot of an observation plane taking pictures of each firing run said he'd send the developed pictures to the firing ships on Monday.

When it was the *Roe*'s turn to shoot, Bill Norvell became the control officer for the "official" run. His range at firing was low, but he applied the wrong offset on the first torpedo—which I immediately questioned. Yet the torpedo was launched with his ten-degrees right offset and missed astern. For the second torpedo, I shifted to local control and used torpedoman Stroh's sight angle. That torpedo's wake seemed to pass only inches from the *Boise*'s stern. Sadly, the *Dewey*'s official observer evaluated both of Bill's torpedoes as misses. However, all six of the *Roe*'s torpedoes were recovered and returned to her in good condition. This saved me a lot of work because a lost torpedo required a great deal of paperwork—making excuses for why the torpedo had sunk from sight.

When the *Roe* received the photos of her firing runs, I ascertained that on Bill's official firing runs both wakes had indicated probable misses astern of the *Boise*. The second torpedo, however, had missed so close to the *Boise*'s stern that I pointed out to the Captain that it was actually a hit by the torpedo, running at thirty foot depth. With the gaseous bubbles that cause the wakes rising at six feet per second to the surface, and with the torpedo running at forty-five knots, the torpedo was actually about 130 yards ahead of its wake when it reached the *Boise*'s stern. That meant that the *Roe* should be scored a hit in the last few feet of *Boise*'s stern.

"When we have a breather, Ruhe, later today," the Captain sensibly said, "I'll have you boated over to the *Dewey* so you can show the head of the observing team these pictures and get him to change our BTPA official score—so we'll be back in the running for a gunnery 'E.'"

I did just that, but futilely, because the *Dewey*'s gunnery officer said, "That's the first time I ever heard about that six-feet-a-second business and that a thirty-foot-depth torpedo leads its wake by 130 yards. And I don't believe it." I argued and argued but most of the *Dewey* officers gathered around me shook their heads in disagreement with my "proof" of a hit. The *Dewey*'s captain, a peer of Scruggs but senior by a few numbers, snidely said, "You can know that one of Sailor

Scruggs's boys would pull this kind of crap." It was a lost cause with a bunch of officers who apparently knew very little about torpedoes. So I returned to the *Roe* with the bad news. As I explained what had happened aboard the *Dewey* (leaving out the *Dewey* captain's remark), I watched Captain Scruggs flare up and snap, "Dammit, Ruhe, you didn't put your heart into your assignment." Resignedly, he said, "So there goes our 'E' out the window." However, he made no mention of reflecting this on my next fitness report.

12

Dangerous
Fleet Operations

AFTER ALL FOUR DESTROYERS of Destroyer Division 17 had completed firing their torpedoes at the *Boise*, the recovered torpedoes were delivered back to the firing ships. All six of the *Roe*'s fish were hoisted to the main deck and found to be without damage.

By mid-afternoon of 18 March, the division was off to join the Blue Fleet, which included the carrier *Yorktown*, several battleships, a few cruisers, and a flotilla of destroyers. At high speed and in seas so rough, we could not stuff the big "fish" into their tubes and it became necessary to tie them down on the main deck. Destroyer Division 17 then took screening stations off the heavy cruiser *Chester*'s beam and began closing a Gray Fleet composed of a single battleship (the *California*), several cruisers, and six destroyers. When the enemy Gray Fleet was located, all of the Blue Fleet's destroyers were to attack the enemy battleship *California* with a simultaneous massive salvo of torpedoes from long range.

En route to the blue fleet, I had the signal gang rerig the flag-hoist halyards to speed up the two-blocking of flags and to meet the heavy demands of multiple flag hoists on both sides of the signal yardarm. The signalmen had been acting jittery and unsure of themselves because of the Captain's frequent bawlings out for their erratic execution of flag-hoist signals. Therefore, to improve their morale, I studied the way they were doing things—usually in the established manner— and then looked for changes in the signalmen's routines. The rerig job was probably a better way to make their signal jobs more efficient.

With Blatz gone, decoding help had become critical. So B.D., Chick Sayles, and Doc Brown were drafted into forming a "coding board" to ease the strain created by the fleet's policy of encoding all radio transmissions. The "small boys," the destroyers, had only a few officers to handle the vast number of messages generated by a fleet's operations. Unfortunately, my first "class" for the coding board was interrupted by the commodore's ordering a maneuvering board drill for all four ships.

The Captain assigned the OOD, B.D., and me to solve the maneuvering board problems posed by the division commander. The *Roe*'s first problem was how to go from her present position, three hundred yards astern of the *Morris*, to a station eight thousand yards and forty-five degrees on the *Morris*'s port bow while making five knots more than the *Morris*'s base speed of fifteen knots. We easily solved that by drawing a few relative movement lines on a maneuvering board. As soon as the *Roe*'s solution was blinked over to the commodore he posed a more difficult problem. We ran into snags, however, when the three of us took a long pause to figure out how to draw the relative movement lines. Annoyed by the delay, the Captain started raising hell for our "stalling." Then when we began drawing lines on the maneuvering board, he kibitzed the developing solution, claiming that the lines drawn were wrong. But he had no correct solution to offer. Sadly, being heckled impaired our capability to think "relative." The mental blockage created for all three of us carried over into the next relatively simple problems. So we looked bad on the commodore's drill until the rough seas forced the Captain to go below due to seasickness. From then on our maneuvering board team starred and eventually earned a "well done" from the commodore.

At nightfall Destroyer Division 17 was still running in column formation. The four destroyers took station two thousand yards off the *Chester*'s starboard beam—with the Blue Fleet headed to intercept the Gray Fleet. The waning moon wouldn't rise until two in the morning, so I automatically became the OOD for the duration of total darkness. The Captain wanted it that way. I could see better in the dark than the other *Roe* officers and stood a better chance of spotting a ship in inky blackness and thus preventing a collision. Moreover, for these long sessions as deck officer, I drank a cup of strong black coffee. Because I rarely drank coffee, I received the full benefit of the caffeine's stimulus.

Even though ships painted the customary light Navy gray were difficult to see in total darkness, even at close ranges the luminescence of disturbed water in the tropics made bow and stern wakes easy to see, even at considerable ranges, through binoculars. The stern wakes provided a continuous trail on the sea's surface while one could spot the bow wakes' occasional surge upward and outward at even greater distances. Running in company with the *Chester* a mile to port seemed safe. But overall, the invisibility of destroyers on an extremely dark night made the situation quite dangerous.

When the moon began to rise well after midnight, I was relieved of the watch and went to bed—only to be awakened within an hour to decode a host of messages over which the Doc and Chick Sayles were laboring unsuccessfully. So many messages were badly encoded by battleship "greenhorns" that I had to apply the logic of, "How could a dumb, inexperienced communicator get fouled up?—pick the wrong device for encoding, inadvertently skip a line of text, or have his strips fall out and then put back in their slots improperly!" With that reasoning, I was able to break all the messages—but lost a lot of sleep in the process.

All during the 18th, the Blue Fleet headed westward, making fifteen knots. Contact with the Gray Fleet was expected at about midnight. At three-thirty, the Blue Fleet simulated an attack on an enemy fleet. The Blue Fleet's flotilla of destroyers were directed to make an assumed twenty-five knot launch of torpedoes by divisions at the "capital ships"—the enemy's battleships. Thus, when our division peeled off to attack a theoretical enemy battle line out on our starboard bow, the other two divisions of the flotilla headed for the same objective by cutting across the van of the Blue Fleet's formation. With all tactical maneuvering done by flag hoists, much confusion reigned, and our division almost collided with another division of destroyers that were closing for the long-range torpedo firings. It would have been much simpler to execute this attack with plain-language broadcasts over the tactical voice-radio circuit. But since every radio broadcast was supposed to be encoded for security purposes, even using flag hoists was more practical.

Late in the afternoon, my chief radioman, Feath, heard on a secondary tactical circuit that two *Yorktown* planes had crashed in midair, killing everyone. This virtually obliterated my continuing regret for not being physically qualified for flight duty.

Well after dark, Destroyer Division 17 was ordered to a scouting line twenty miles ahead of the Blue Fleet. With a spacing of four thousand yards between destroyers, I could barely distinguish the wakes of the *Morris* and the *Buck* on either side of the *Roe* through my binoculars. And at times I felt that I was imagining their wakes rather than actually seeing their churned-up trails on the sea's surface. There were no telltale flashes of light shown by the opening of a door to a lighted compartment on a ship, nor were there flare-ups from someone lighting a cigarette out in the open, since these violations had become mast offenses on most of the ships of the fleet.

Shortly after midnight I began seeing the wakes of four ships in column proceeding up and parallel to the *Roe*'s starboard side. Their wakes seemed about a thousand yards off. Evidently, it was a destroyer division making about five knots more speed than the *Roe* and headed in the general direction of where the Gray Fleet was expected to be found. Were they closing for a flotilla torpedo attack? There had been no radioed sighting-reports on the primary tactical circuit to indicate this.

Then, alarmed, I realized that the wakes of the second and third ships in the column seemed dangerously close to each other.

"Captain," I reported, "I can see the stern and bow wakes of four ships in a column out on our starboard beam. And two of the ships are about to collide with each other."

The Captain merely grunted.

Impulsively and without further thought, I moved to the radio telephone and depressed the "talk" switch. "This is a small boy," I blurted. "I hold four small boys in column on my starboard beam fairly close aboard about a thousand yards away. . . ."

Exasperated, the Captain shouted, "Ruhe, you can't send a message like that—in the clear without a proper call-up."

I couldn't think what the call should be for four unidentified ships. But somebody out there had to know that one of the four ships was about to climb up the stern of the ship ahead. I had to emphasize how dangerous the situation was. So I continued, "The bow wake of the third ship in column is within fifty yards of the stern of the second ship."

"Stop transmitting, Ruhe, until you can do it right," the Captain screamed. "You're making me the laughingstock of the whole fleet."

Whether I was or whether I wasn't, I felt that saving two ships from a collision came first. So I pressed the talk switch and transmitted, "The third ship in column should slow his screws . . . now."

At this, the Captain clamped his hand over mine to prevent me from sending any more messages. "This is crazy, Ruhe," he growled, "You don't know what you're doing. . . . Stop it!" But he wasn't kicking me off the bridge. "Ruhe," he added, "You've got to learn proper voice procedures. You're the communications officer and should know better. But no one would ever know it to hear you on our 'PriTac' circuit."

By this time, the luminescent wakes had moved out of sight beyond the *Roe*'s starboard bow, so I reported that I could no longer see the wakes of the four ships.

"Ruhe," the Captain disgustedly muttered, "You're no help on this bridge."

Within ten minutes there was startlingly a brilliant shower of sparks in the direction of the disappeared wakes. Then all sorts of excited reports flowed on the primary tactical circuit—all in plain language. The destroyer *Somers* had climbed up the stern of the *Warrington* in a disastrous collision. The skipper of the *Warrington* was first on the air, reporting, "My depth charges are all set on safe. I'm dead in the water. My after steering room is flooded, but flooding is under control. There are no serious personnel casualties." Then the *Somers*'s skipper said, "I'm stopped. And flooding in my bow is under control. Only a few people are hurt." Soon the skippers of other ships reported that they'd called away their fire and rescue parties and were "on the way," to go to the help of the *Somers* and the *Warrington*. Though there were no fires and neither ship was in danger of sinking, the whole business was a thorough mess.

Promptly, the admiral in charge of the Blue Fleet announced over the PriTac circuit, "Cease present exercises. Light ship."

When the ships turned on their masthead and running lights, I was pleased to note that the destroyers of Destroyer Division 17 were where they were supposed to be. But I was surprised to see many ships far closer to the *Roe* than I'd imagined. The few tiny lights visible far out on the horizon were undoubtedly those of the Gray Fleet.

His pent-up anxieties were released by the termination of the night torpedo attack exercise, and the Captain almost gratefully said, "We kept out of trouble, Ruhe. Didn't we? But you sure have to do some quick learning of voice procedures before any more of these exercises are held."

This time I said, "Aye, aye, Sir," and resignedly awaited an "instruction session" from the Captain, who was "only trying to be helpful." My unstated question was: "Are procedures more important than the safety of ships?" Perhaps they were for the advancement of one's career. But I couldn't believe that. Doing good for the sake of the Navy had to be more important than promoting one's own welfare.

Because all the ships were lighted, I was allowed to be relieved of the watch and hence was able to turn in to my bunk. After only two hours of sleep I was back on the bridge for a regular watch. But it was a pleasant one, even though the ships were once more darkened and running at high speed while zigzagging: The Captain had turned in for a nap.

At seven o'clock all hands were sent to general quarters. This time the Blue Fleet's flotilla of destroyers launched a real torpedo attack against the Gray Fleet's battle line—putting twenty-seven torpedoes simultaneously into the water at about ten thousand yards range to the battleship *California*. Three columns of destroyers had been maneuvered efficiently to the right—a most satisfying thing to watch. Each of the destroyers, making thirty knots, fired two torpedoes set on low speed at the battleship target. The wakes were easy to follow all the way to where most of them seemed to indicate hits on the *California*. It was a stirring, if not confusing, moment, with destroyers disentangling themselves after their attack; planes whipping around overhead, and ships in the Gray Fleet turning radically to evade the wakes of the torpedoes.

We spent the remainder of the day picking up torpedoes. They were easy to locate since their yellow exercise heads stuck well out of water after they'd blown themselves dry at the end of their run. Each torpedo was identified by its serial number and returned to the firing ships by the motor whaleboats of several of the destroyers. The *Roe*'s two torpedoes showed large dents in their exercise heads—a product of having been fired on the beam and then tumbling when they hit the water. They did run hot and true. The Captain gloated that the *Roe* "should get a good score for that firing!"

When moonless darkness had again settled in after sunset, I was once more back on the bridge. Moonrise wasn't until two-forty on 20 March, so I had a good eight hours of uninterrupted OOD duties to look forward to. Such a long watch was hard on my feet and very tiring, but I felt buoyed by the thought that the fleet would end all its battle problems and return to port by mid-morning.

The Captain had returned to the bridge at the start of the night battle problem. Condition two was set and the Blue Fleet was making twenty-five knots. Again, the *Roe* was back in a division column trailing the *Morris* at three hundred yards. For some dumb reason I was actually pleased to be directing the *Roe* in the inky darkness with ships rushing all over the place at high speed. Moreover, I was spotting wakes that I judged were six thousand yards or more away. My intermittent reports of wake sightings were so reassuring to the Captain that he stayed in his bridge chair. He was also less caustic in his corrections of the turns I added or subtracted from the *Roe*'s props to maintain station. Even his cursing was muted. It seemed for the time being the Captain and I were getting along much better.

Then far off I spotted the wakes of two ships that appeared to be converging dangerously. Spontaneously I sprang to the radio telephone, and without thought of my "procedures" lesson earlier in the day, I depressed the "talk" switch and blurted, "This is a small boy. I hold two wakes of small boys about six thousand yards ahead of the big boys. They seem to be on a collision course with each other. . . ." Forewarned, the OOD of one of those ships might by intense peering through his binoculars be able to see the ghostlike shape of a closing destroyer near at hand. By immediately backing full on his engines he could thus avert disaster. I had to be more urgent on my next broadcast. But the Captain jumped out of his chair and moved my hand away from the talk switch. With some nasty oaths he made it clear that there'd be no more of this "trying to be helpful" business.

"Dammit, Ruhe," he growled, "that's a helluva way to call up unknown ships. . . .You're making this ship a worst example of bad communications. . . . Do it if you think it's necessary to avoid a collision . . . but do it *right!*"

At least I wasn't being relieved of the deck watch. Yet I felt guilty for not having looked up the call for "unknown ships" ahead of time.

I was still trying to remember the "proper procedures" for this situation when we received word over the tactical radio "CEASE PRESENT EXERCISES. LIGHT ALL SHIPS." Then, additional words were heard: "The *Farragut* and *Aylwin* have collided. All ships stand by to render assistance."

Searchlights on several ships—far out ahead of the *Roe*—illuminated the damaged destroyers. Flames shot skyward from the burning forward part of one of the ships and the crumpled bows of both tin cans were easily visible in the red light of the raging fire on one of the destroyers. Both were dead in the water but didn't seem to be sinking. Yet one of the destroyer's bows was well down in the water.

I suddenly recalled that the *Aylwin* was commanded by Lieutenant Commander "Speed" Rogers, who'd been the first lieutenant on the cruiser *Trenton* when I went aboard her after graduation from the Naval Academy. He had said in a fatherly way, "You're wasting your time, Ruhe, on a cruiser. Get destroyer duty. That's where you'll learn to be a real naval officer." He had also mercilessly heckled all of us "fresh-caught ensigns" to be "good naval officers." But without much success. The cruiser, with her many officers, was not conducive to an ensign's professional development.

The radio telephone broadcast message after message: "*Philadelphia* [a cruiser] is standing by to render assistance." "My [no ship identified] fire and rescue team is en route in whaleboat to *Aylwin*," "Heavy fires on the *Aylwin* are raging up forward. Will need help to contain the fire." "*Farragut* has heavy flooding forward of the wardroom. But all bulkheads aft of the wardroom appear undamaged." "We've only a few men hurt by the collision [ship not identified]."

Later in the night we learned that the *Aylwin* had burned as far back as the wardroom. Only the closing of the wardroom door had prevented the flames from spreading further through the ship. Several men were reported to be badly hurt and one man was dead. It seemed that cables without armor had burned briskly and carried the fire along. The *Philadelphia*'s fire and rescue team were the deciding factor in stopping the fire from spreading aft and had saved the *Aylwin*. Poor Speed Rogers. He tried so hard to keep the *Trenton* "shiny and clean" despite the indifferent performance of "his" ensigns. He'd never make it now. Destroyers sure ruined the careers of lots of good officers.

When the word was passed, "SECURE THE BATTLE PROBLEM," a feeling of elation rose in the air. It was all over! Even Mr. Parish was certain of that—appearing on the bridge in his best white service uniform in anticipation of being back in port shortly and going ashore to be with his wife.

Then as the fleet's entry into Pearl Harbor began, the *Roe* was ordered to a patrol line off Diamond Head. The message to the *Roe* indicated no duration for this "security patrol." It looked as though the *Roe* wouldn't go back in to Pearl for the next couple of weeks. But that was destroyer life. A life for dogs, with everyone dog-tired.

On the third day of patrol off Diamond Head, the Captain received permission to leave station for some machine gun practice in the firing area south of Molokai. There, a plane towed a white sleeve just above the water and a few hundred yards away—while the *Roe*'s machine guns chattered. No ammo had arrived in timely fashion at the guns, which meant that we missed several practice runs. On the run "for the record," however, Bill Norvell's gunners got four hits in the sleeve. That was very good shooting and would help toward getting the gunnery "E."

On the fourth day, the *Wainwright* and the *Buck* joined the *Roe* for a simulated division firing of torpedoes. Without the *Morris*, however, the exercise seemed futile. At one point, Captain Scruggs, the senior skipper and thus in charge of the exercise, acted confused and ordered the three destroyers to "fire torpedoes" when the ships were overlapping each other. Thus actual torpedoes, had they been fired, would have hit our own destroyers. Mr. Parish overheard me criticizing the incompetence of the Captain to Chason the signalman. At this, the exec's face clouded over and he angrily dressed me down—in an uncharacteristic manner—for being disloyal to the Captain and doing it before a member of the crew. "Ruhe," he snapped, "you're getting too critical of everything our Captain does. Just stop it or I'll transfer you off this tin can."

Making Mr. Parish upset meant that I had carried things too far. Hence, I vowed not to say another derogatory word against the Captain, regardless of what I felt were his stupidities. That should sweeten my disposition since hating the Old Man had made me pretty much of a sourpuss.

Later, when we assumed that the *Roe* would shortly return to Pearl Harbor, she was ordered to continue her patrol off Diamond Head. Although darkness had settled in, B.D. relieved me of the deck watch with the Captain reclining in his bridge chair. So I headed for the wardroom to read official mail. I was certain that any ships encountered would have running lights and could be tracked easily and avoided, despite the blackness of the night.

An intelligence report told of British submarine actions over the past few months. It was amazing to read about the number of times they were discovered by enemy antisubmarine units and heavily depth-charged. The U.S. submarines wouldn't operate in the sort of restricted waters that the British encountered. Another report predicted that war for the United States would start in April 1941. In fact, Walter

Winchell on a Sunday night broadcast had said, "There'll be war in sixteen days."

Then I heard a long, four-second blast on the *Roe*'s whistle. That was a signal to some ship close by that the *Roe* was turning to starboard. This was followed by two short blasts from the *Roe*, indicating that she was passing the ship port to port— an unusual maneuver with a strange ship. So I dashed to the bridge to see what was happening.

The *Roe* had been on an easterly course near the end of her patrol line when it became evident that a ship coming up from the southeast would cut across her patrol line and come close to the *Roe*. The Captain was excitedly pacing back and forth, muttering, "Why is the damned fool turning away when he's the privileged vessel?" The Captain also berated B.D. for steadying on a course that barely cleared the invisible ship's stern light. The ship was also showing a red running light and two white masthead lights, one over the other.

"The lights say she's a towing ship and is not free to maneuver," the Captain reminded B.D. But B.D. was sufficiently nervous at the Captain's interference and foul mood—a carryover from the earlier division maneuvers—that he might not have assessed the situation correctly. But neither had the Captain.

"There's a tiny white light close to the water and well astern of the towing ship that would indicate that a tug is towing something," I offered. "The small light's on what is being towed." At this, the Captain roared, "Silence on the bridge. I'm handling this."

Then the tug gave many short quick toots on his whistle. It was an emergency warning that the *Roe* was about to collide with him or cut his tow line.

I could visualize what was happening. The tug, by turning hard to starboard, was forming a long half-circle catenary in the towing line back to the object being towed. And B.D. was steering the *Roe* between the tug and its tow.

When the *Roe* was well past the tug, the tug played a searchlight on its tow. It was a sled carrying a large rectangular canvas target used for gunnery exercises. It had a tiny white light mounted on its after end. Moreover, the sled was dead in the water and falling farther and farther astern of the retreating tug.

"The tug must have dropped his tow line," I optimistically suggested.

"I want silence on the bridge," the Captain snarled. "Ruhe, why don't you just shut up?"

B.D. was probably saying a prayer that he hadn't cut the tow line. If he had, he'd really catch hell from all directions.

Without offering to help retrieve the sled-target, the Captain had B.D. swing the *Roe* around and head back for her patrol line off Diamond Head. And shortly, the Captain went below.

"If you've cut the tow line," I whispered to B.D., "that tug guy will put us on report and there'll be an investigation and a lot of apologies to make."

As though guessing what I'd said to B.D., the Captain called me to his sea cabin and said, "Ruhe, when we get back in I want you to go over to that fleet tug and apologize to her skipper for me for causing trouble with his tow. You might also find out whether or not we cut his tow line. If we did, offer to do something to put us in the clear. And by all means discourage him from putting in an official report about the incident. It would give the *Roe* another black eye and we've had enough dumb things from you and Wood already to put us at the bottom of the division commander's list."

The next morning the *Roe* was allowed to return to Pearl. Shortly, my visit with the tug's skipper confirmed that the *Roe* had indeed cut his tow line, but he said that he wouldn't put in an official report on the matter and that there was nothing to be done to rectify the situation. He said that he had already spliced his towing wire and was "ready to have it cut again by another damned-fool destroyer."

13

Hawaiian Charms

WHEN THE *ROE* ENTERED Pearl Harbor late on the morning of 26 March, she followed the *Morris* to a destroyer nest alongside the destroyer tender *Dobbin*. The *Morris*, first to tie up, was conned to the *Dobbin*'s starboard side by the division commander. He managed to crack the jackstaff of the *Morris* against the *Dobbin*'s side in the process. Later he guiltily explained that he was fully responsible for this botched-up landing and that he'd maneuvered the *Morris* "just to keep my hand in," meaning that he didn't want to lose his seamanship skills, which evidently needed "honing." That word still bothered me. So why not apply it to a vaunted senior officer just as it had been to a greenhorn ensign "under instruction."

After the *Roe* was moored to the *Morris*, the *Dobbin*'s repair people came aboard to discuss the work requests submitted for the *Roe*'s fourteen-day refit. It was pleasant to contemplate that finally I'd have two straight weeks to see what Hawaii was all about. I wondered if it had the magical charm that was much sung about in ukelele-accompanied sensuous songs of the islands. I had an itchy, urgent feeling to get ashore and experience the delights described: the lovely hula hands, *huki-laus*, swirling winds over the Pali, the sweet brown maidens in their little grass skirts, the beach at Waikiki, pikake leis, rainbows over the valleys, and particularly, what "aloha" really meant.

But my anticipation of the fourteen days ahead was dimmed when I received no mail after the *Roe*'s long operations at sea. Nothing from Lucrece! Several days previously I'd dreamed about a vague image I felt was Lucrece. In the dream she was so sweet and perfect that I had awakened with a pleasant warm glow, only to have this flush of love quickly changed to one of feeling blue and rotten as the reality of not having heard from Lucrece sank in.

Another dampener to my plans was the Captain's scheduling of me and four of my torpedomen to go to the base torpedo school for the next two weeks. It was a morning and afternoon affair. That made for a murderous routine of school and then trying to get all my other work finished and still have some time left over to spend ashore.

Fortunately, Ensign Ken Steen reported aboard to be my assistant and eventually to relieve me so I could go to Sub School. Ken was a tall, broad-shouldered football player with an easy smile for everything. Criticisms from Scruggs rolled off him like water off a duck's back. Training him to be a good communications officer, however, would take a lot of work. But at least he could now stand in for me when I wanted to enjoy Hawaii.

Over the weekend, and after turning in the *Roe*'s torpedoes to the base torpedo shop for rework, I went to Waikiki to do some surfboarding. This time I was able to catch a few of the big waves and ride them standing up. Then, when exhausted, I withdrew to a spot in the sands under the overhang of the Outrigger Canoe Club. There, I sat listening to brown beach boys strumming ukeleles and softly singing in high-pitched voices such songs as: "Beyond the Reef," "To You Sweetheart . . . Aloha," and, "The Song of Old Hawaii." Later when I went to the Southwicks'—he was the skipper of the *Chester*—both to see his daughter Jean and to play some piano duets with "Bud," the "Old Hawaii" song became particularly pertinent. Two of Bud Southwick's friends who had dropped in and listened to our duets insisted that "Slim Beecher" be rounded up. And so the writer of "The Song of Old Hawaii," Lieutenant Commander William Gordon Beecher, arrived with his guitar and the fun really began. He was easily coaxed into singing some of his best songs, the funniest of which were "Three Thousand Years Ago," and "Nuts to Nihau." "The Song of Old Hawaii" was deferred for more sentimental moments. The long-winded, loud, crazy gang singing that was generated almost ruined any further welcome for me at the Southwicks'. At one point, I thought I heard someone whisper, "You'd just know that one of Sailor Scruggs's boys would act like this when away from his skipper."

Despite a late evening and a miserable open-liberty-launch ride through a drenching downpour, I laid plans for a Sunday of painting in the lush green countryside beyond the *Roe*.

Before noon, I was carrying my water colors through fields of sugarcane. I was looking for a scene of slat-board houses almost hidden in the high stalks of sugarcane with shadowed purple mountains in the background. A few scattered fires burning off the tops of the sugarcane would provide interesting patches of red against the masses of green. En route to the hills, I ate lots of sugarcane; it was a good sort of candy. I noticed that every shack had a shiny, modern automobile parked in the front yard and that the men wore colorful aloha shirts while the women wore ankle-length, shapeless muumuus. All were barefooted. I was amazed to see much cactus. The fields were farmed using contours, which made for a complex irrigation system of tanks and canals to keep the sugarcane well watered. When I dropped into a village store to buy a Coke, I was surprised to find that half the items on the shelves were of Japanese origin. Finally settling on a scene to paint, I had to wait for a rainstorm to pass. Then I did some frantic brushwork before the next shower hit. Just before a fifth deluge of rain, a strong gust of wind blew my painting across a newly ploughed field. When I retrieved it, it was a bit muddied, so I just said, "The hell with it," and took it back to the *Roe* to finish in my room at my leisure. For my part, I looked as if I'd been mud wrestling and I was burned black by the relentless sun. But that was the price one paid for trying to paint the beauties of Hawaii. Soon I was off to a Scruggs cocktail party at the base Officers' Club. The Captain as host was effusively pleasant and introduced me to his friends as "one of my very fine officers." I even danced with the stiff and tentative Louise Scruggs . But who wouldn't be, having to dance most of the time with a husband who was shorter than she was by a couple of inches? She graciously excused her "rustiness" and seemed pleased to be dancing with one of the Captain's "boys." It was also pleasant to see Bill Norvell and Mr. Parish at the party enjoying themselves, with their wives continuously smiling at the Captain's good spirits. This produced an unexpected feeling of camaraderie among the *Roe* officers. Then Louise introduced me to her very attractive, dear friend Mrs. Nina Burne. A little later, Louise casually said that "Mrs. Burne would love to go dancing with you some evening. She watched us dancing and felt that she'd like to try following some of your trick steps. She's a fabulous dancer and you'll enjoy her very much." Another Navy wife promoting a "best friend" with an unmarried ensign? It was a plague that I was suffering through. But enjoying.

Monday I was off to torpedo school, but not before B.D. delivered the bad news that the wardroom mess bill for March was thirty-three dollars—a new high at a time when I needed additional money to do what I hoped to do on my spare time in Hawaii. At that time, five dollars meant a lot to my budget. When I was free to go on liberty, I was stopped at the head of the gangway by the OOD who said, "CinCPac [Commander-in-Chief Pacific Fleet] has ordered that hereafter all officers will go ashore properly dressed." I was wearing an aloha shirt and slacks, and that wasn't "proper." The OOD explained that "CincPac's order means wearing hats, neckties, coats, and shined leather shoes. . . . No sandals allowed."

It was a simple matter to change into "proper civilian dress," but I had never owned a civilian hat in my life. So I borrowed an old, beat-up, gray felt hat from Hop Nolan. It was in such bad condition that Hop told me "just keep it. I'll never wear it again." I could see why, because the front of the hat at its peak had been creased so often that it had developed a small, unattractive hole. By carefully pressing the hole together I was able to pass the OOD's inspection of my "proper dress" for going ashore. When out of the naval base, I folded the felt hat and stuffed it into my back pocket. CinCPac had said "when going ashore," not "while ashore." So I decided to risk that no one else would care whether I had a hat on my head or not. And I steered clear of where CinCPac was likely to be around Honolulu. That was easy to do because my liberty beat was certainly not that of the high and mighty admiral.

Later, after a refreshing swim at Fort de Russy, where I could see Diamond Head down the beach, I returned to the Outrigger Canoe Club for some instructions on playing a uke. The Polynesian beach boys could finger a melody while chording the number. It was something I had to learn. One of the boys suggested that I buy myself a Martin uke at the base PX. "They don't cost much and they're the best."

The next afternoon, after a day of tearing apart a torpedo piece by piece and learning all about its "mysterious innards," I bought a Martin uke and was dumbfounded to discover that it was made in Nazareth, Pennsylvania, only a few miles from my home in Allentown. The beach boys at the Canoe Club, were delighted that I now had my own uke, and they devoted much time showing me how to finger "Aloha-oe," an easy one to start with.

With time on my hands, I decided to honor my commitment to Louise Scruggs to take her "dear friend" Mrs. Nina Burne out dancing. I called Nina for a date that evening—with some concern for what I was doing. What had happened to her husband? I also recognized that the Captain had been overly attentive toward the beauteous ash-blond Mrs. Burne at his cocktail party on the previous Sunday. I felt that he might get envious and ornery if I became too involved with Louise's "dear friend." Yet taking Nina to Lau Yee Chai's restaurant—near where she was staying—was worth the risk. Dining and dancing with this delectable woman proved to be sheer delight. When I danced with her to the slow number "Moonglow," she laid her soft cheek against mine and pressed her full-blown body closely against me, literally taking my breath away. Effortlessly, she synchronized her body to follow my trick dance steps in featherlike fashion. Then, when back at our table on the edge of the dance floor, classmate after classmate sidled up to be introduced and to sit with us—and to take turns dancing with the lovely and exciting Mrs. Burne. At one point, Nina irritatedly scolded me for introducing her as "Mrs. Burne." I got the message. She didn't want to be identified as either a divorcée or a widow. Or was she possibly a married woman on the loose? At any rate, she wanted to be just "Nina Burne."

During this byplay with a woman whom the Captain seemed interested in, I'd noticed a lone young fellow at a table on the far side of the dance floor who kept staring over at us through the gloom of the low lights as he sipped a drink. He seemed to be much taken by Nina's exceptional good looks. So finally, with uncertain steps, he crossed the dance floor and confronted us. But it was me that he'd been staring at. He studied me closely and then said embarrassedly, "You aren't Dave Ruhe. I was sure you were Dave Ruhe, as soon as I spotted you. . . . I'm sorry to have bothered you."

He turned to go back to his table but I stopped him with: "I'm Dave Ruhe's younger brother, Bill . . . and this mistake is made pretty often wherever I travel . . . Come on and sit down with us so I can bring you up to date on what Dave's doing." I glanced at Nina to get her approval. But I didn't need her consent because the pleased smile on her face showed that she was eager to know this tall, rangy, gray-eyed stranger.

Jack Newkirk introduced himself and I carefully introduced "Nina Burne." After telling Jack about Dave's recent marriage and his joining the Public Health Service as an officer, I got Jack to explain how he knew Dave and why he was in Honolulu. "Dave and I went to school together in New York, at St. John's Cathedral Choir School." (Three of my brothers had sung in the cathedral's choir, but I'd been rejected.) "We played a lot of sports together. I also took him up for some airplane rides after I'd gotten my civilian pilot's license." There was more.

But then Jack switched to why he was at Lau Yee Chai's spending an evening alone. "I arrived from San Francisco this morning and tomorrow am connecting with a bunch of American volunteer flyers who are on their way to Kunming, China, to join General Chennault's Flying Tigers. Out there we'll fight with the Chinese against the Japs. We'll be paid $750 a month as squadron commanders and get a bonus of $500 for every Japanese bomber or fighter we shoot down. Chennault, I understand, is himself a helluva fine pilot and tactician—who'll make us the best fighting pilots in the business. And flying P-40s, we should do pretty well and make a bundle of money in a short time."

(From that evening on, I carefully perused the daily Allentown *Morning Call*s, mailed regularly to me by my father, for stories about the Flying Tigers. The Japanese invasion of Burma in December 1941 saw lots of air activity for the Flying Tigers—and lots of kills of Japanese aircraft. Jack Newkirk by Christmas was an "Ace" having destroyed five planes; more kills quickly followed. But then I read a story telling of Jack Newkirk's death in March of '42, when he was shot down while attacking a heavily armed railroad train. I never heard where the bundle of money he'd amassed went.)

Jack danced too much with Nina and Nina gave him the close-to-the-body treatment. My disapproving stares caused Nina to pat me on the leg after she'd finished a dance with him. She whispered in my ear: "He's off to the wars tomorrow so don't envy him. He needs a little bucking up." Nina was really very special!

When it got real late, I paid a ridiculously low restaurant bill. Nina had ordered only a single Coke and had had a low-cost ham sandwich—a good indication that she wanted me to take her out dancing again. When we strolled hand in hand up along the Ala Wai Canal to where she was staying, there was a touch of real magic about this moment with her. The very clear blue night, the warm breeze whispering through the palm trees, the sweet scent of tropical flowers, and the beautiful quietness under a bright full moon, made this truly "a paradise for two." I decided not to ask her about her marital status. It might ruin this very special evening.

I missed the last liberty launch at two in the morning to get back to the *Roe* and had to sleep on a hard wooden bench until the six o'clock milk run. I felt chastened for not being true to my Lucrece. Still, I wasn't getting any letters from her. And it had been a wonderful evening.

When back on the *Roe* at six-thirty, I discovered a message that called for an immediate "stripping of the ship." This meant getting rid of everything we'd illegally held onto after the first "strip ship" effort was put into effect. It meant that the wardroom would be reduced to looking like a barn—no curtains, no rugs, no stuffed furniture, no pictures on the walls. It meant getting rid of torpedo exercise heads as well. War must definitely be imminent. Or so the high command seemed to think.

The next morning, after crating the strip-ship stuff I was responsible for and getting it off the *Roe*, I presented two new job orders for the Captain to sign—ones that I had just received from the chief radioman. For a few minutes the Captain ranted at "such sloppy work" and that I should be kept aboard for not having foreseen the need for the repairs. Eventually he grudgingly signed the job orders. But when I handed him one for a torpedo training gear, he refused to sign it, saying, "You figure out how to get that gear for your torpedo repaired. I'm not helping you on this one."

When Bill Norvell heard about this, he conspiratorily whispered, "I'll get my chief to draw one from another destroyer. . . . Don't tell the Captain. It will just make him mad." Bill knew only too well how balky the Captain could get about little things like repairing the gears of a torpedo.

In the evening with my work caught up, I went to Southwick's "Locker Club"—the new name for his home—to retrieve my swimming trunks and hopefully to remeet Slim Beecher. But no one was home, and I decided to visit the Wileys, who had entertained me frequently and graciously at the Naval Academy. Lieutenant Commander "Doc" Wiley, senior to Scruggs, had been a language professor and a heroic figure with great stories to tell his classes of midshipmen. A lighter-than-air dirigible pilot, he'd gone down with the *Shenandoah* when she'd been struck by lightning and he'd been a survivor of the *Akron* airship disaster. When I arrived at the Wiley home, Doc's wife, Blossom, greeted me warmly and urged me to stay for dinner. She sadly reported that Doc had been transferred to the China Station and that when she could pull up stakes in Waikiki she'd follow him out as far as Manila. So we were a twosome at supper and Blossom took this opportunity to counsel me about "choosing an intelligent, adaptable girl for a Navy wife." She knew that my two years of waiting to get married were up on 1 June and, like most of my classmates, I might be planning nuptials shortly thereafter. And she took it for granted that I wanted to make the Navy my career. Thus, she dished out her philosophy about what made a wife who would make my career successful and self-satisfying. She did this in a motherly, empathetic fashion.

"A good Navy wife," she sagely observed, "should be energetic, make friends easily, and be adventurous." She studied my face to see if I was interested in her advice. I was. So she continued, "She can't be a homebody because she'd just be miserable being uprooted every year or so and she can't be a worrier about her possessions. It's heart wrenching to see what the Navy transportation people can do to a beautiful cherry-top table. And then she has to be frugal to make do with the meager salary a naval officer gets." To make sure that I'd take her advice to heart, she added, "If you insist on marrying a girl who doesn't fit the pattern I've just described, as soon as you're married she'll start agitating to get you out of the Navy—and settle down in some backwater town where she'll feel secure and domestic in her unimaginative way. But you'll be bored as hell staying in the same place all the time. I wouldn't trade my life as a Navy wife with that of one with a prosperous banker . . . or a dentist . . . or a college professor . . . or whoever—despite the long separations and depression when one moves into a dingy place on the next change of duty."

Through all of her recitation, I watched her face closely to gauge her actual feelings about being a Navy wife. Her eyes sparkled. A continual smile kept the corners of her mouth upturned. And the flushed coloring of her face showed that her words reflected her great pleasure in going with her husband wherever he went. She saw herself as a great asset in furthering his career.

Mrs. Wiley's talk made me realize that I actually knew very little about Lucrece. Perhaps she lacked some of the characteristics of a good Navy wife. If she'd only write more frequently and at greater length, I could better judge whether a passion developed over a few days could stand up under the adverse circumstances suggested by Mrs. Wiley. But no letters at all had me almost licked.

On Friday, before and after torpedo school, I had all my men photographed on the *Dobbin* for use in hometown public affairs stories. Then I had them checked out on a gas defense over on the base. Tear gas was used to make sure that they had properly donned gas masks. And all were conscientious. By five in the afternoon I was free, and so with a standing invitation to make myself at home at Slim Beecher's, I went there for a session of jamming and singing. He promptly called in two of his guitar-playing friends and we made an evening of it. I was pleased to hear Slim sing "Up and at 'Em Navy" and "Gangway for the Navy Blue," two songs that he'd written that were favorite fight songs of mine at the Naval Academy. I did a couple of my own songs, which the fellows liked. When I played "Coney Island Washboard Blues," we really hit our stride. Slim was so enthused by the music we were making that he proposed setting up a big jam session at the home of "Dr. Faust" on Sunday night. So I promised to round up a bunch of guys who'd want to join us and we could make it a really big affair.

Before the Sunday session, I went painting with Marjorie Webster, a wealthy California girl who'd come to Hawaii to be where the action was. We chose a spot near Rabbit Island to do some sea scenes. On the way back to the *Roe* for supper, we picked up Johnny Harper—one of my best friends at the Naval Academy. He was going to Sub School in July and reported that he'd just seen my name in an ALNAV that listed those officers ordered to the July class, along with his own name. Also, during the meal on the *Roe*, he told about his intent to marry Emmie Leila Savell of Forest Hills, Long Island, before going to Sub School and that he wanted me to be best man at the wedding. The date was 20 June. "You'll be on your way to New London then and should be able to make it. . . . Just be sure your skipper detaches you in plenty of time." Apparently he'd heard some bad things about Scruggs and had doubts that I was a sure thing to be best man at the church wedding. Then he emphasized, "Emmie's friend, a Powers model—and the girl I think you should marry—will be one of the bridesmaids." It was more matchmaking, but this time by a classmate.

After Marjorie and Johnny left the ship, I read a letter from my father telling of a visit to our home by Blatz Helm and my Academy roommate, Rollo Miller. Both were en route to Sub School, the April class. "They both were exuberantly happy about leaving surface ships to go into submarines," my dad reported. "When I asked them, 'Aren't you worried about having to fight the Japanese real soon?' Blatz answered, 'Mr. Ruhe, if they're dumb enough to start a war against us in the Pacific, we'll sink their fleet in a couple of weeks and it will be all over!' Rollo nodded his head in agreement." Doubtfully, my dad had also asked, "Do you fellows actually believe that defeating the Japanese at sea can be that easy?" For my own

part, I couldn't tell one way or the other. But senior Navy people seemed to think that the fleet's battle line would quickly
win a big fleet battle as decisively as Nelson had done at
Trafalgar.

On Easter Sunday, 12 April, I took communion at the
church service on the *Dobbin* and felt slightly cleansed. Of
what? Seething anger toward Old Scruggs? Or the disgusted
feeling toward all communicators? Whatever. On leaving the
church, I was handed a small, white, leather-covered Bible. It
gave me a touch of guilt. I was getting too much for nothing.

After a quick swim at de Russy, I went with Slim Beecher to
Dr. Faust's home in Waialai. The house was a perfect replica of
a Japanese home, with its sliding doors, rice-paper panels and
windows, and woven-grass mats on the floors. And we had to
walk in our stocking feet after entering. The music-jammers
arrived en masse just after we got there. Alex Anderson, the
celebrity songwriter of the "Cockeyed Mayor" and "Lovely
Hula Hands" had brought his ukelele. A personable little fellow by the name of Cook had flown over from Maui with his
clarinet—to join three more clarinet players. "Freckles," a
great guitar player—even better than Slim Beecher—was the
best musician on hand and was always deferred to by the other
three guitarists. A bass fiddle player and me on the piano
rounded out "the ensemble."

The jam session started slowly, inhibited by the too many
deadbeat friends whom Dr. Faust had invited to be our audience. Missing from our music was the carefree wildness that
we'd had on Friday night at Slim's house. At one point, Doris
Duke arrived with her two big Polynesian boyfriends. Or were
they her bodyguards? You name it. The heavily muscled, dark-
skinned men looked more like Chicago gangster hoods. And
Doris Duke, with her shadowed eyes and sharp, sharklike fea-
tures, was easily recognizable from her pictures in the tabloids. When there was a break in the music, one of Doris
Duke's escorts sidled up to the piano and asked my name and
why I was in Honolulu. I gave him the information, and when
I saw him report what I'd said back to Doris Duke, she nodded her head in a disquieting fashion. Then she whispered
something to him as I swung into "From Monday On" in order
to pep up the music. That did it. The music got really hot.

Later, Dr. Faust suggested that all of us adjourn for a recess
and sit on the tatami mat flooring for a meal of borscht. But
Slim said, "Let's call it a day and get going. We can get a ham-
burger at Kau Kau Corner on the way back to my house." The
rest of the musicians were happy about calling it quits. Four

straight hours of playing inventive variations of contemporary songs was a bit much for a Sunday afternoon. Before leaving, one of Doris Duke's boyfriends asked me to go home with the three of them "to get something to eat." But Slim Beecher's deep frown and slight disapproving shake of his head indicated, "No way." So I gave my regrets to the boyfriend and followed Slim out of Dr. Faust's home before Doris Duke could waylay me and make things sticky. So much for "the wealthiest woman in the Islands."

On Monday, the refit work was completed, so the *Roe* left the *Dobbin*'s side and shifted to a mooring buoy near West Loch—a ten-minute longer run for the liberty launch. In fact, going on liberty had become so difficult what with having to wear "full civilian dress including hats," two hours lost in just getting there and back, and having to suffer through downpours in open boats, that I decided to stay aboard and write letters. But on Tuesday after torpedo school, where we studied depth engines and gyros, I went ashore by two o'clock to try a painting from the Pali—looking toward Kaneohe Bay on the north side of Oahu.

The Pali, at the divide in the mountain behind Honolulu, fronted on a precipice overlooking the northern part of the island. It was there that King Kamehameha, with his army from the big island of Hawaii, pushed the Oahu army off the Pali to their death in the valley far below.

Painting a watercolor between deluges of rain while anchoring my painting against the swirling winds over the Pali was a frustrating experience. Every time drops of rain began splattering my painting, I'd duck under an overhang in the mountain's side and wait until the rain had blown over. A sudden gust of strong wind finally finished off my first attempt to record the glorious Kaneohe Bay scene. My painting was ripped out of my hands and sailed out into the valley below. I hastily attempted a second painting until I got to the point where I said, "To hell with it, I'll finish it back on the *Roe*." And left.

Wednesday, I was ashore early to ride the surf at Waikiki and then to get a few more ukelele instructions. By prearranged plan, Johnny Harper joined me at Waikiki and, after getting a snack at Marjorie Webster's place, we took the three Webster sisters to hear the highly venerated Arthur Rubinstein in a piano recital at Roosevelt High School's auditorium. His playing of Chopin's "Dance Polonaise" was very expressive. His furious pounding of the keys on Stravinsky's "Firebird Suite" was exciting, and his final rendition of "Liebestraum" was corny, but sweet. All in all, with the tickets costing only two dollars per person, it was a highly rewarding evening. But Alli, a younger Webster sister, said, "The old guy got pretty sloppy in spots and missed on some of his fingering." That was true, for Rubinstein didn't sound as masterful as he did on records produced earlier.

On the way back to the fleet landing, Johnny reminded me: "Be sure to get to my wedding. You'll be hooked on Carol Vermilye, the bridesmaid, as soon as you meet her."

Torpedo school ended the next day. After showering and getting slicked up, I went to Captain Scruggs's party at the Royal Hawaiian Hotel. Nina Burne was there and we had some nifty, smooth dances together. I urged her to leave the party to go on to Lau Yee Chai's for dinner. To persuade her I told her the *Roe* was leaving next morning for fleet operations and that it might be a long time until I'd be back to take her dancing again. Still, she refused. I suppose she didn't want to hurt the Captain, who kept hovering around her—despite the icy looks of Louise. The mellowing drinks and Nina's delectableness as we fluidly glided around the dance floor gave me the courage to tug her gently out onto a balcony overlooking the starlit Waikiki surf. There, with an arm around her waist, I held her close. This was Hawaii as I'd dreamed it to be.

14

The O-Club Caper

ON 18 APRIL THE *ROE* was under way at eight
o'clock from Pearl, following the battlewagons to sea for a few
days of fleet maneuvers. Hawaii was a great place to be, but I
was elated to be going to sea—to be part of the big time. The
plans for the fleet exercises were drawn up better than in the
past so I was able to develop a good frequency plan for the
Roe's radio communications. Hence we flawlessly executed
our responses in exercise after exercise. We neither missed
messages nor misunderstood any messages. My signal force
was functioning just as nicely. They ran up correct flag hoists
and then without delay executed smartly. The *Roe*'s antiair
shoot at a towed sleeve also went well. Our division maneuvering as the fleet changed its dispositions proved a snap. And
a shore-bombardment exercise off Lahaina Roads, Maui, using
graphs, grids of gun emplacements, and locations of landing
force concentrations had the Captain smiling. The *Roe*, moreover, obtained hit after hit in the designated shore defenses
without hazarding the troops ashore.

The night fleet exercise lasted only two hours; "light ship"
was ordered at nine-thirty. This indicated that the fleet commander was getting cold feet from running his ships around in
the pitch blackness. The *Roe*, as part of an attacking enemy
force of destroyers had during the exercise sifted through the
battle line screens and simulated the launching of her torpedoes before a cruiser belatedly shone a searchlight on the *Roe*.
"We did it right this time," the Captain gloated. Demonstrating
the efficiency of his fleet destroyer made this moment a high
point in his career.

All day Sunday sixteen destroyers made torpedo attacks in
flotilla formation against the battleships. The coordinated

offensive maneuvers were thrilling to see. And the *Roe* was continually in her correct position relative to the *Morris*. The division commander flashed no hate-messages at the *Roe*. Only the cruiser *Raleigh*, after a destroyer attack, was seen to send a flashing light message to the *Morris* saying: "Destroyer Division 17's answering of flag hoist signals has been deplorable." However, Commander Swenson didn't follow this up with a nasty message to the *Roe*. He had no reason to indict my signal gang. Perhaps the other destroyers of Destroyer Division 17 had had trouble with their flag hoists, but not the *Roe*.

On Monday, after much fleet maneuvering and antiair gun practice for the destroyers, the fleet went back into Pearl Harbor while Destroyer Division 17 proceeded to the gunnery range off the island of Oahu. The gunnery and torpedo exercises were relatively easy compared to fleet problems. In addition, radio communications continued to be carried out smoothly. I was keeping my fingers crossed against the next bust. The coding board was now performing so well that I had time on my hands and felt a bit lost. I was like a man who looks eagerly for retirement and then, when it happens, doesn't know what to do with himself. So why not get back to reading a good book?—a luxury I'd been deprived of on the *Roe* due to the workload piled on me. The book I picked up and read quickly was Lin Yutang's inspirational *The Importance of Living*, which made me want to write something serious as soon as I could get started on it.

Tuesday's short-range, five-inch gun shoots progressed in a high-scoring, no-casualties fashion. By three o'clock, to show his appreciation for the crew's excellent performances, the Captain had "swim call" announced on the 1 MC system. In a matter of minutes, many of the crew, including me, came top-side in our swimming trunks and dove over the *Roe*'s sides into the cool, deep-blue water. The swells lifted the swimmers up high and then dropped us hard into the troughs. But it was fun. Diving off the bridge from forty feet above the water was just showing off on my part. Yet the crew clapped and shouted their approval when I reappeared on the sea's surface.

All the days of April were balmy and pleasantly warm. It felt truly good to be alive and accomplishing things well in the naval environment. This life seemed to have been made just for me.

Wednesday's exercises proved unusually successful. After an early rehearsal run, the *Roe*, making thirty knots, started firing her big guns at a sled target. All five of the *Roe*'s five-inch guns pumped out twelve salvoes each in measured fire. Fourteen shells went through the canvas target within the circumscribed circle. And many more holes could be seen outside the circle, which meant additional "zone hits." But despite the success of his guns, Bill Norvell had to raise hell with the Captain when he countermanded an OOD order to the helm that would have put Bill's guns into a better aspect for shooting. At this, the Captain snarled, "Watch your step, Norvell." It was a threat with dire consequences to follow.

The score for the gunnery shoot would be high when finally calculated and should place the *Roe* among the top tin cans of the fleet in the fleet gunnery competition.

The afternoon's antiaircraft gun shoot against a red silk target-sleeve, which was streamed well aft of the towing aircraft, proved equally satisfying. Each five-inch gun was allowed five salvoes. Within seconds after "open fire," the sleeve was torn to shreds and almost simultaneously a shell severed the nylon tow-line just forward of the sleeve. This caused the red silk target to flutter slowly down to the ocean. With much good spirit, crew members fished the tattered target out of the ocean and displayed it on the *Roe*'s main deck. There were lots of profane "Jeez-uhhses" and "Christs" as the crew surveyed the damaged sleeve. This kind of shooting appeared to be a new thing for the *Roe*. Maybe the Captain's angry leadership was paying off. The *Roe* was on a roll.

The day's gunnery successes put the Captain into an unaccustomed good mood. Thus at four o'clock, he had the *Roe* conned in close to Barber's Point, where the anchor was dropped. The *Roe* lay only a half mile from the Barber's Point Officers' Club. Mr. Parish took a round of anchorage bearings, then another round, and still another. All three plots placed the *Roe* in the same spot—with ninety feet of water under foot. The exec's three identical positions made the Captain "feel confident that a thorough job has been done in ascertaining the *Roe*'s true position."

After glancing at the *Roe*'s location on the chart, Captain Scruggs ordered the quartermaster of the watch to call away the ship's motor whaleboat. "We're going ashore to have a drink at the O Club" he told Mr. Parish—with an uncommonly warm, mischievous smile. Then he directed Mr. Parish to notify Ruhe, Wood, and Norvell that they were going with him to the O Club "to have a cocktail before the evening meal." The Captain was getting some sort of malicious pleasure by adding Bill Norvell to his landing party. Possibly, the Captain was hoping that Bill would learn a little respect for him when he, the Captain, who was a strong swimmer, went through the breaking surf easily while Bill would find the surf trouble-some. Actually, going ashore that way was necessary. A glance at the Officer's Club showed that there was no pier to land at. The shoreline was a continuous stretch of white sand, while the surf in front of the O-Club broke heavily only a few yards offshore.

As OOD on anchoring, I was still in my summer whites, with open-necked shirt, long white trousers, and recently touched-up white shoes. "Your outfit's okay, but you'll have to wear your cap, Ruhe," Mr. Parish counseled. "The Captain wants his landing party to be in full uniform for their visit to the Naval Air Station O Club." A look through binoculars showed that an outdoor patio facing the ocean was crammed with tables at which many women in muumuus and gay-colored cotton prints plus men in aloha shirts were having an afternoon drink.

"You fellows will have to swim in through the surf," Mr. Parish noted with a chuckle as the Captain's landing party was assembled on the quarterdeck. "Good luck!"

I knew that I was selected for the swimming job because I'd been a top-flight hundred-yard-dash swimmer at the Naval Academy. And B.D. had been selected because he was in good athletic shape and was so wholesome to look at that the Captain would be proud to display him as "a *Roe* officer." But why Norvell? Was the Captain trying to get even with Bill for his criticism of the Captain during the gunnery runs?

At this point, all of the officers on the *Roe* were feeling quite fatalistic about their futures under Scruggs. Hence, Bill Norvell, wearing a small amused smile, acted indifferent to the challenge offered by the four-foot waves sweeping into the beach.

When the motor whaleboat was brought alongside the gang-way, all four officers including the Captain, stolidly walked down the stairs of the gangway with their white caps firmly in place. As the Captain stepped to the rear of the boat, the three of us stood at attention until he'd seated himself.

It was evident that the Captain wanted to show off his virile swimming prowess, gained as a rough-housing water polo player at the Naval Academy. The light-blue surf building up to a threatening height before breaking into a crashing, foaming jumble of pale-green water would be a considerable challenge to a strong swimmer. Seas that would tumble me onto the rough coral bottom swirled ominously in the shallows close to the beach. I was good at body surfing, but going through a breaking wave in full uniform was another matter. It was also evident that we could not take the boat through the waves because its bottom would stove in when it crashed at the edge of the beach.

So we brought the boat to a stop a few feet outside of where the waves broke. There, we dropped anchors to form a span that held the boat from moving any further toward the shore. The boat, however, rose and fell with each successive wave that built up and then curved over and broke.

Before ordering us to disembark, the Captain studied the people at the tables on the O Club patio. He was making sure that most were looking in our direction and were aware of the boatload of officers in gleaming white uniforms readying to dive into the sea. The Captain wanted to be certain that his cocktail-hour screwball caper would be long talked about in the fleet.

Satisfied that his expedition had gained enough attention, the Captain ordered: "Ruhe, you lead the way. And don't make it look foolish." I was the guinea pig—admonished to get ashore in a dignified way. The Captain wanted to see what the problems might be, in order better to impress the audience with his skill as a swimmer.

I teetered on a seat of the whaleboat as it rose and fell, and then I suddenly dove recklessly into the back of a breaking wave and through it. I expected to body surf the wave into the beach once I was in the clear. But the wave caught me with its full force. It picked me up and then ground me down onto the sand and coral bottom. My cap was gone. But after scrambling to my feet in the shallows, I spotted it floating ahead of me. Three other caps were floating behind mine. So I didn't have to look back to know that the other three were having as rough a time as I'd had getting through the breaking waves. Perhaps they needed help?

I spotted B.D.'s head above the churning water. Then Bill's head appeared. B.D. looked fine but Bill was choking and coughing up sea water in an agonized fashion. Behind Bill came the Captain. He was shooting out of a wave and then swimming strongly. But the turbulence caught him, twisted him around awkwardly—definitely *not* in a dignified manner—and slammed him onto the hard coral bottom. It seemed that of all us swimmers, the Captain had looked the most foolish coming ashore.

As all four of us plodded out of the water, I handed the others their water-soaked caps. I put mine back on and the water dripped down over my face. I felt silly as hell. But the Captain had counseled us to "look casual and unconcerned as you approach the O Club patio. The Navy flyers will observe us destroyermen critically." So, despite sand all over my whites, and a scratched face, I toughed it out—meaning that I acted nonchalant while approaching the patio tables.

When we sat down at an empty table on the seaward side of the patio, the Captain hissed, "Act natural."

I took out my handkerchief to wipe my face dry and free of sand, forgetting that the handkerchief had become a soggy mess. Then I pulled out my wallet, dumped the water out of it and laid several soaked dollar bills on the table to dry. I realized that each officer would have to pay for his own drinks, even though this was a command performance instigated by the Captain. He called it his "afternoon adventure."

Expansively happy, the Captain signaled a waiter to the table to take our order for drinks. He joked with the waiter about "needing a bath after working hard all day." Then he began discussing with us the *Roe*'s successful gun shoots earlier in the day. "A few more high scores in the rest of the gunnery exercises and we'll be painting the white gunnery 'E' on the side of the *Roe*'s stack," the Captain gloated. "And I'd like that." He made no mention of a red "E" also being painted on the stack. As Hop Nolan had explained it, "We can't win an engineering 'E' because the Captain insists upon always operating with a 'clear stack.' And we can't have efficient use of fuel that way. Brown-haze stack gases produce the high scores in the engineering competition. But the Captain is more obsessed about the appearance of his ship than about saving the Navy money for the *Roe*'s fuel bill."

For the moment, Bill Norvell, who was smiling at the Captain's show of good will, felt that the Captain was regarding him favorably. In fact, we all felt like celebrating. Then the Captain became aware that the four of us were being watched closely by the patio audience, so he flashed a grin toward the spectators, indicating that his officers were great fun to be with.

Since the Captain seemed to be in a good mood, I suggested that tomorrow's fleet destroyer torpedo attack should be a winner for the *Roe* and put her even higher in the overall fleet competition.

"Stop talking shop," the Captain mumbled. "I want light-hearted cocktail-hour talk at this table." This he emphasized with a *savoir faire* gesture. "We're *not* by-the-numbers tin-can sailors. Wait until these people see us go back to our boat through that surf. They'll remember that for a long time to come."

At this, I decided to sip my drink slowly; I realized that swimming back through the surf was a rotten idea and I might require a clear head to avert disaster. One of us could even drown.

A look at B.D.'s drawn, unsmiling face showed how grimly he regarded the conclusion to this senseless farce. Bill Norvell's deadpan face, on the other hand, indicated that he considered this foolishness just something else he had to accept while serving under Captain Scruggs.

When the Captain had downed his drink, he signaled to us to drink up. Then shortly, "Let's get going."

Since I was the junior officer at the table, I had to, by *Roe* custom, pay the bill. I expected to be reimbursed later by the others for their drinks, but that was a bit optimistic based on previous experiences. Luckily I had just enough money to cover the bill, but not enough for a satisfactory tip, which got me a dirty look from the waiter. Then I hurried down the beach to catch up with the Captain, Bill, and B.D., who had begun striding into the water. Clearheaded, I fastened the chin strap of my cap under my jaw. It should keep my hat firmly on my head while I battled my way back to the *Roe*'s anchored boat. I took a running start, splashed through the shallow waters, and dove into the middle of the next breaking wave. My dive carried me right through the mountain of water, and with a few strong strokes, I was at the side of the *Roe*'s boat. A helping hand from the coxswain, who had remained behind, helped me to climb aboard. The whole business was far easier to accomplish than I'd contemplated.

When I turned to see how the others were doing, however, I could only see Bill's head, which was mostly underwater. Luckily, it was but a few feet from the bow of the boat. Bill was the one who was supposed to have all the trouble, yet he was making it without too much difficulty. His arms were thrashing strongly to get him clear of the pull from the next breaking wave. When his head bobbed out of the water, I yelled, "Here," and tossed him the boat's life preserver attached to a line, which I held onto. I almost scored a ringer, since the life preserver bounced off the side of Bill's head. But he was able to grab it and let me tow him to the side of the boat where the coxswain and I hauled him aboard. While pulling Bill into the boat, I saw B.D. floundering around. He was frantically stroking to prevent being sucked backward by

each succeeding wave. He badly needed help. So again I
yelled, "Here," and tossed the life ring to B.D., who grabbed it
gratefully. With a broad grin he yelled, "I'm saved!"

But what about the Captain?

I climbed onto a seat to peer over the waves. First I noted
that on the O Club's patio many people were on their feet;
some were standing on chairs. They were all staring out to sea,
watching our dramatic return to the *Roe's* boat. Then, after a
few seconds I saw the Old Man in the churning water. He was
flailing his arms weakly and only occasionally gasping a breath
of air. Wave after wave broke over him and tossed him around.
By sheer determination, however, he was managing to inch
himself toward the boat, pulling himself clear of the waves
despite his seeming totally exhausted. It was reassuring to see
that he was still in full uniform with his hat firmly on his
head—held there by the chin-strap around his jaw.

As his head appeared briefly on the near side of a breaking
wave, he muttered something, but the words were lost in agonized gurgling grunts. The Captain was in trouble. And that
was a surprise, because he had made it to a few feet from the
boat's stern. I would have expected him to have gotten a jag at
getting so close to the boat.

Just as I was about to toss the life preserver to the Captain,
Bill, trying to be helpful, threw a heavy coil of the boat's one-
inch mooring line toward the Captain's head. "Here you go,
Captain," Bill yelled in good Boy Scout fashion. But when the
mass of rope landed on the Captain's head it sank him from
sight. Moreover, he'd been too weak to grab the rope when it
hit him. Now, I was *sure* the Captain badly needed my help.

After counting a few seconds and seeing no sign of his head
reappearing, I dove from the gunwhale and headed under
water to his inert body. When I grabbed him around the hips
he was limp. This made it easy to bring him to the surface and
to tow him with a cross-chest carry to the side of the boat. The
Captain had offered no resistance to my lifesaving effort and
his slack body proved easy to haul aboard. Further, it didn't
appear that he needed resuscitation since his breathing was
regular—if only in hissing gasps. But when I laid him on the
bottom of the boat, his eyes were open and glared at me in a
malevolent and unforgiving way. He spoke not a word. The
anger in his stare was unnerving and eerie. What could he be
mad about?

Then he snarled at me, "Ruhe, you shouldn't have done that.
You embarrassed the hell out of me in front of all those people
with your big hero act . . . I could have made it on my own."

Perhaps.

When the whaleboat arrived back at the *Roe*'s gangway, the Captain, unassisted, climbed out of the boat and staggered up the stairs of the gangway. He smartly saluted the colors aft when he reached the top of the gangway and then stumbled to his stateroom.

Again the Captain said nothing.

But at the evening meal, after long minutes during which everyone stared silently at their plates, the Captain menacingly growled, "Ruhe, you showed bad judgment interfering with my return to the motor whaleboat. I could have made it on my own. You humiliated me out there," and his head swung in the direction of the O Club, "and I'm not going to forget this at fitness report time."

All of the other officers, when they were sure that the Captain wasn't looking, gave me small, pitying smiles. I kept mum—not even mentioning that "you still owe me a dollar, Captain, for the drink you had at the O Club." Again I'd learned a lesson the hard way: I should have realized that one can't risk publicly embarrassing a senior officer no matter how well intentioned one's actions might be. My *maturing* as an ensign continued to be painful.

The next day the *Roe* returned to her position, running three hundred yards behind the *Morris*. The division was again screening the fleet battle line for a few days of fleet exercises. The Captain was in a particularly foul mood. He stayed on the bridge at all times and he incessantly changed the OOD's orders to the helm. He also kept insisting on adding or subtracting a turn or two on the propellers when he felt that the *Roe* was closer to the *Morris* than she should be.

On the morning watch he told the OOD, Chick Sayles, to call for his relief. Chick had argued that the three turns added unilaterally by the Captain would have gotten the *Roe* dangerously close to the *Morris*.

There was a brief period when B.D., Chick's relief, didn't have any of his orders to the helm countermanded by the Captain. But when the division started to turn, I heard the Captain yell, "Put the helm over now!" That made the *Roe* swing to starboard too soon and B.D., to save the situation, ordered "Helm amidship." At this, the Captain relieved B.D. of the watch and sent the messenger to look for me as B.D.'s relief.

When I arrived on the bridge, B.D., without looking at me, said, "You can relieve the Captain. He's got the deck now." When I smartly said to the Captain, "Sir, I'm ready to relieve you," he snapped at me, "You've got the deck, Ruhe. But don't let your attention wander. The whole fleet is watching how well this tin can carries out its maneuvers."

By intensely concentrating on the OOD job, I lasted more than an hour without the Captain butting in. When I saw the Captain using the stadimeter to check the distance to the *Morris*, however, I knew I was in trouble. "We're at only 240 yards, Ruhe. Dammit. Get the hell off this bridge and get a competent OOD relief up here on the double."

All I could say was, "Aye, aye, Sir." Then I hurried below and looked for another victim to take the OOD watch. But who was left who was free to stand a four-hour watch? Only Mr. Parish appeared to be available. So I explained my dilemma. Mr. Parish was much amused at the suggestion that he take the deck. Still, he lazily ambled toward the ladder leading to the bridge and climbed upward in a resigned fashion.

I don't know how long Mr. Parish lasted as OOD but later at lunch in the wardrom he didn't appear rattled or disagreeable. His calmness was a good sign that the OOD problem had been resolved satisfactorily.

When the Captain arrived for lunch and sat down at the head of the wardroom table, all the officers put on forced smiles. The meal started on a light note, as the Captain observed that the *Roe* had not been singled out by the flagship *New Mexico*'s query of "station?" at any time. This meant that the *Roe* was always where she should be. As the meal progressed, the portholes on the starboard side of the officer's wardroom mess allowed bright beams of sunlight to bathe the wardroom in a warm, cheerful, subdued light. It produced a friendly atmosphere. But suddenly the light through the portholes dimmed and plunged the wardroom into a gray darkness. The Captain swung his chair around to see what was blocking off the sunlight. To his horror, he saw a large warship was passing up *Roe*'s starboard side and so close aboard that a collision between the two ships seemed inevitable.

"Who's got the deck?" the Captain screamed.

We all looked at each other and noted that *all* of the *Roe*'s officers were seated around the table. Only Norvell had the guts to say it like it was. In a low, sarcastic tone he muttered, "You do, Captain."

The Captain was out of his seat like a shot and raced up the ladder to the bridge—to relieve himself as OOD.

15

Aloha oe
(Farewell to Thee)

THE *ROE* SCREENED THE BATTLESHIP *Arizona* while she transferred fuel oil to the destroyer *Morris*. This indicated that the *Morris* was not returning to port with the rest of the fleet on the morrow. Shortly she joined the *Roe* on a north-south patrol line off Diamond Head—with the *Morris* fifteen thousand yards south of the *Roe*. Both tin cans conducted antisubmarine patrols to detect unfriendly submarines that might thread their way to the entrance to Pearl Harbor, where they could observe the procedures for entry into the port. It was doubtful that we could distinguish echo returns from snooping submarines from the great number of false echoes from wrecks on the bottom off Oahu. Yet the *Roe*'s sonar continually picked up the pinging of the *Morris*.

No letter or dispatch explaining the fleet's termination of exercises had been routed to the Captain or me by Ken Steen, who had already relieved me of my letter and message-control duties. Perhaps he'd doped off. Still, I'd have to read all incoming mail to ensure that every bit of necessary information was getting to the pertinent officers.

In the afternoon I took my communications gang on tours of the *Roe* to qualify them to meet the minimal requirements for knowing their ship. This was someone's brilliant idea. But frankly, in conducting these ship tours I was discovering how much about the *Roe* I wasn't familiar with. And yet if the *Roe* was damaged by collision, grounding, or shellfire in wartime, we would all sure have to know her thoroughly to provide the proper damage control.

The *Roe* returned to Pearl the next day after the battlewag-ons had settled into their berths in the harbor. A north wind was blowing strongly as the Captain and B.D. tried to tie up to the *Morris*, which was moored to a buoy in the center of the harbor. In the process, the *Morris* parted her heavy hawser to her mooring buoy and the *Roe* was forced to break free from the *Morris*. As usual, I was on the bridge to watch the mooring evolution. I silently made my judgments as to how the job should be done correctly. Then I checked my seamanship ideas against what actually happened. I felt that when the *Roe* had been snubbed tightly to the *Morris* all engines should have been immediately stopped. But evidently B.D. (or was it the Captain?) left a backing bell on too long. I had heard the Captain shouting, "Wood. Don't part the *Morris*'s hawser." At any rate, after both ships drifted around a bit, the *Morris* put a new line over to her buoy and the *Roe* tied up to the next avail-able buoy. But this was only after much quack quack between our Captain and Beanie Jarrett, the skipper of the *Morris*.

Mail came aboard and with it a long and anxiously awaited letter from Lucrece. After nervously tearing open the enve-lope, my eyes blurred and my legs were suddenly weak. I read:

> I feel terrible about this. But I must tell you that I married a lonely, compassionate German, Arthur Baur. He is here with the occupation forces. He badly needs me. . . .

I read no further. Lucrece, my Lucrece, married? I was stunned. My life was in tatters. Had she gone mad? Or did she have an innate desire to torture herself by marrying a Nazi? Perhaps she was finding some sort of self-gratification in being miserable. Or did my adorable Lucrece have a Dr. Jeckyll–Mr. Hyde character that I hadn't discovered in the very short time that we'd been together? What she'd done defied all logic.

I returned to the letter to comprehend why she had elimi-nated all hope of our ever having a married life together. The letter continued:

> He's so concerned with the well-being of our Dutch people that I love him even more than I might have believed when he first came into my life. He wants so much to ensure that the Dutch have enough food to make their lives bearable. I wish you could know my Arthur so you could appreciate how mar-rying this lovely man is worth the great difficulties which he's

brought into my life. It's caused everyone to hate me. Even
my old friends call me a collaborator and all sorts of other
vile names. I've had terrible things shouted at me countless
times and my clothes have been ripped by vengeful Dutch
women. They even threw me to the ground and chopped off
most of my hair until I was almost bald. But worst of all is the
silent censure I get from many sides. And that includes my
sister, Manon, who thinks I've gone crazy. The only safe place
for me is locked inside my apartment. What have the
Germans done to my people? Why have they become such
monsters?

It was signed "Lucrece." Nothing more.

Were there hidden meanings that I should surmise by reading between the lines of this tragic letter? Or was Lucrece
actually reveling in her self-inflicted misery? I searched her
distressing letter for clues that would indicate that her marriage to a German was more meaningful than appeared on the
surface. Yet I found no such clues. So I decided to forget the
whole business with Lucrece and get on with my life. I could
change nothing! Little did I suspect that many years later I
would learn the truth about this strange love affair.

After the Saturday morning skipper's inspection of the ship,
all the junior officers hurried ashore. Out to Waikiki I dashed,
to rent a surfboard and develop more skill in riding the waves.
This time my board was one of the new, hollow variety—
much lighter, shorter, and far easier to paddle out to the big
Queen's surf far offshore. Catching a six-foot wave and then
standing on the board all the way in to the shallows had
become a breeze. The exhilaration and sheer joy I felt in riding the waves were better than skiing. But perhaps my feelings
of well-being were enhanced by just being freed from my
doomed love affair and the depressing environment of a "taut"
ship.

After a couple of hours catching many waves, I found that
my waterlogged body was still strong enough to haul the
board out of the water and carry it back to the Outrigger
Canoe Club. Then I joined a group of '39ers—classmates—at
Trader Vic's drinking den. But moving an evening along by
one drink after another made such little sense and was so
costly that I decided it was far better to return early to the *Roe*
for a decent meal and to prepare for a good liberty on Sunday.

The service next day at the First Union Church in Punahou
promised to be a spiritual treat, since the minister was
reportedly the best preacher on the island. His sermon did

prove full of arm waving, yet his message was virtually unintelligible to me. But the glass on all four sides of the church allowed the glorious outdoors of flowers, acacia trees, and distant colorful vistas into the church. Marjorie Webster and her two sisters were there. So we later went to a horse show. It was at a spot where the jagged volcano in the background and the swaying palm trees made a delightful setting for excellent horse jumping—with the Army team running away with all the honors.

The Webster girls, having other plans, dropped me off at Waikiki. Confronted with an unplanned evening and being well fed up with this catch-as-catch-can way of putting together a meaningful liberty ashore, I almost couldn't bother trying to find a fun way to spend the next couple of hours. Erratic destroyer operations made this sort of social life most unsettling. I tried calling Slim Beecher for an evening of music together. He wasn't home. I tried the Southwick home. No better luck. Then the Wileys. But they were away at some cocktail party. Reluctantly, I called Nina Burne to go with me to Lau Yee Chai's for supper and dancing. When she put me off with a "Wait 'til I think," I felt I'd made a mistake in believing that our evening dancing together had been something special. Then there was an overly long pause with total quiet at her end of the line. Finally she whispered, "Yes." Hesitantly, in a barely audible voice, she told me to pick her up at her father's home.

Nina's reluctance to go dancing became clear on arrival there. Her father had many friends in for cocktails and they regarded me in a cold and unfriendly fashion. Quite obviously they didn't think that it was proper for "the commander's daughter" to be dating a bachelor ensign.

In a taxi headed for Lau Yee Chai's, I finally bit the bullet and asked Nina why her father's friends regarded me so antagonistically. I had originally believed that the "Mrs. Burne" meant that she was either a widow or a divorcée. That could make her worth pursuing as a key person in my future. But she eliminated that illusion with a dull thud. "None of my father's friends approve of me running around with a man while I'm out here. You know I have a husband back on the mainland—thirty-seven-hundred miles from here—who is nothing but a playboy loafer. I needed a change from his sort of life so that's why I'm staying with my daddy. But his best friends don't understand that part of the picture. I should have met you somewhere else and saved you this embarrassment." She said this with a tense seriousness that accented the discomfort she was feeling for exposing me to the problems of a married woman.

The evening had started badly. I had to admit that trotting around with a married woman on the loose was not my style. Yet Nina was so special and delightful that I'd stopped thinking clearly. It was now a matter of making us more of a twosome and to hell with the risks involved.

At Lau Yee Chai's we joined Johnny Harper and his slim, attractive date, Jo Steele. Johnny, with a marriage in Forest Hills, New York, pending, looked a bit too smugly pleased with his new girlfriend to make it certain that I'd be best man at his wedding two months hence. However, he greeted Nina unsmilingly and gave me a dirty look as he introduced Nina to Jo. Apparently, he believed that the bridesmaid I'd meet at his wedding was The Girl for me to marry. He was signaling that I wasn't supposed to get too friendly with Nina.

Very rapidly, classmate after classmate and other ensigns with dates flocked to our table for six—which was quickly expanded by a waiter to a table where in short order twentysix people were chattering noisily, exchanging dances. and picking at bits of food. The management, with broad smiles, appeared much pleased that the young Navy people were making Lau Yee Chai's their official hangout. Moreover, I didn't have to feel furtive about having Nina as a date. She'd become part of the gang and a great addition to the bachelorensigns' social group.

When it was time to call it quits, Johnny discovered to his embarrassment that he had no money to pay the bill. Fortunately, I'd brought along enough money, so we didn't have to ask the girls to chip in in order to get us sprung from the place. Nina even let me kiss her on the way back to her father's house. That was all. But that made it much easier to accept a thorough soaking from a sudden downpour in the open liberty launch that ferried me back to the *Roe*. I didn't even mind having to wear my badly creased, dripping felt hat as I arrived at the *Roe*'s quarterdeck. I felt that "being in proper dress" when going and coming to a ship of the fleet was a foolish deviation from Navy good sense. Yet I recognized that it was just another aberration in the greening of a tin-can ensign.

On 1 May, Mr. Parish received orders to command the destroyer *Gilmer* on the West Coast "without delay." His evident happiness at being freed from the *Roe*'s rat race made everyone equally pleased for his sake. There'd be no stopping him now, I felt. The many warm congratulations from the

officers for his getting a good destroyer to command, and the
many trips to his cabin by most of the crew to wish him well,
showed his great popularity with everyone on the *Roe*. His
leaving the ship proved more of a cause for celebration than a
wake. That's how much this exec was liked. Then within two
days his name appeared on an ALNAV indicating that he'd
been promoted to the rank of lieutenant commander. It had
taken sixteen years for him to move up from the rank of lieutenant! Again, as Mr. Parish had predicted, the Captain's bad
fitness reports on Mr. Parish didn't mean much in a Navy
preparing for a big sea war.

Hop Nolan became the executive officer with Mr. Parish's
departure and Bill Norvell took over the duties of ship's navigator. The Captain did not seem to react to these changes. He
made no snide comments about the future of Mr. Parish after
he was separated from the Captain's ever-present helping
hand. The crew wondered who would now provide our relief
from Scruggs's unrelenting "help."

Over the next weekend, I was able to do several good watercolors. The first was near Nanakuli, where the sailors had
their outing camp. When I was driving there in a borrowed
jalopy, I was surprised by the abrupt change from fertile land
around Pearl Harbor to the extremely arid land a few miles to
the west. The reason for this great variation in climate was
evidently due to the funneling through the mountains of rain
clouds that had formed in the center of the island. I saw several rainbows above the well-sprinkled green valleys and
included them in my painting of deep-blue mountains and
bright green fields.

On Sunday, Marjorie Webster took me sightseeing around
the island and together we finally painted scenes in Wahiawa,
where rice-paper red carp streamed from bamboo poles in
celebration of Sons Day, a Japanese holiday. The main feature
of my painting was a gnarled old tree done in a delicate and
flowing Japanese style. That made the people of the village
like my work. En route, we had stopped at an outdoor luau
where a large pig was being roasted under steaming palm
leaves and over a bed of red, fiery coals. We ate lunch on a
spread-out mat in a luxuriant, fragrantly blossoming mountain forest.

With torpedo school consuming five mornings of the week
and with much extra work being continuously piled on, my
liberties ashore didn't allow enough time for me to keep in
good physical shape. But I did have time for some tennis,
swimming, and surf riding.

The school was interesting. Monday, we learned about the magnetic exploder feature in the Mark-14 torpedo's warhead. Breaking the back of an enemy ship by having the torpedo triggered off a few feet below its keel sounded great. But would it work as advertised?

It was clear to me that the *Roe*'s officers had little interest in her weapons. In fact, the Captain had never raised a question about the readiness of our torpedoes nor had he shown any concern about shells jamming in a five-inch gun's barrel during a firing run. Consequently, I had to insist noisily that the *Roe* be taken over to the ammunition depot in West Loch on Wednesday to have our five-inch shell cases gauged to ensure that they actually fit into the barrels of our guns. The Captain said that he thought this was a waste of time, but he okayed the trip.

When we arrived at the depot, as duty officer I had to act like Simon Legree. I had to roust the crew out of their bunks and hiding places to join an "all hands evolution" of passing shells onto the dock. There the shell cases were gauged by the depot's experts. A few of the shells were rejected as nonfits. The rest were restowed in their magazines. When the job was finished at five in the afternoon, the *Roe* steamed back to the center of the harbor and tied up in a nest of destroyers alongside the tender *Dobbin*. Then, at full speed, the Captain left the ship without commenting on our success in finding some trouble-making shells. Dead tired, I turned into my bunk right after supper. But as nest duty officer, I was awakened at one o'clock in the morning to move the *Roe* so the inboard *Wainwright* could back her way out of the nest.

On Thursday after torpedo school, I had to process a lot of new classified coding material. This meant reading all coding instructions thoroughly, separating the strips of the various strip ciphers and properly stowing all mechanical elements. Finally, I thought I'd get a good night's sleep—only to learn that the *Roe* was going to sea at eleven o'clock to plane guard the *Lexington* during her flight operations next day. Another destroyer had been assigned this job, but she'd limped back into Pearl with engine trouble earlier in the day.

During the plane-guarding operation, the *Roe* was on station five hundred yards off the *Lexington*'s quarter. At all other times the *Roe* stayed one thousand yards dead ahead of the carrier. The *Lexington*'s putting sixty planes into the air in a short period of time and then seeing them land with great ease heightened my regard for the usefulness of carrier aircraft in a sea war. Their bomb loads seemed to make them more deadly in fleet engagements than the battleships, with their limited-range big shells. As usual, I was in my swimming trunks sitting on the *Roe*'s bow and nothing adverse was happening. No aircraft missed the carrier's deck when landing. I was surprised to see some of the planes on landing drop at least ten feet to the carrier's deck without any evident damage to the planes. The carrier aircraft were far more rugged than I'd guessed.

On Saturday, the *Roe*'s division officers were told to inspect the sea bags of their men in order to be certain they had the specified amount of clothing. Emphasis was placed on ensuring that they all had heavy winter underclothing. This made it look as if the *Roe* was about to go somewhere where it was real cold. The Aleutians? Or the North Atlantic? I'd noted that another Pearl Harbor–based division of destroyers had left early in the month to go to Trinidad in the Atlantic. They'd need cold-weather clothing there? It all seemed like more fleet nonsense.

In the afternoon a triangulation party from the carrier *Lexington* came aboard the *Roe* to score the *Lex*'s eight-inch gun shoot. Their third salvo produced a beautiful straddle of a towed target and from then on they continued to be on target—in range and deflection. As OOD for this evolution, I had a rough time with the Captain's countermanding every order I gave to the helmsman or to the man on the engineroom annunciators.

On Sunday the other destroyers of Destroyer Division 17 joined up with the *Lexington* and soon the division commander was in a plane testing the visibility of his four ships with their different colors. The *Roe* was still painted a gray blue. In addition, he maneuvered his four tin cans by PriTac radio—responding to the *Lex*'s turns made during her flight operations. On one maneuver, the Captain took too literally one of the commodore's orders and cut the *Roe* across the bow of the *Lex*, leaving only about two hundred yards between the two ships. It was a dangerous situation for which I caught hell from the Captain for taking the *Roe* "too close to the carrier." The lesson here was always obey the general prudential rule, which calls for the responsible person to play it safe as far as the ship is concerned even if a senior officer wants to put your ship in danger. As the OOD, I was the responsible person. Thus I learned to act first and then argue about it later!

On Monday, the commodore again tested visibility, but this time from a submerged submarine, looking through a periscope to make his comparisons. At one point in the tests, our Captain conned the *Roe* at the sub's periscope, forcing the submarine to go deep and earning us a growl from the division commander. Captain Scruggs then claimed, in answer to Commander Swenson's criticism, that the helmsman had steered a course other than that ordered. And that was that.

Starting on Tuesday, 13 May, the *Roe* went into a one-week refit alongside the destroyer tender *Dobbin*. This provided me with the opportunity to have a game of tennis in the afternoon, do some surf riding later on, and then go to Lau Yee Chai's to join a lot of ensigns who were whooping things up. It wasn't, however, until Wednesday that I got a dubious, whispered, "yes" from Nina, agreeing to a date.

Earlier, when I paddled my surfboard out to the Queen's surf, I had noted many beach boys sitting on their boards beyond the breaking waves. They were gathered around a brown-skinned, dead-looking surfrider lying on a board. There was much excited chattering about how the fellow had broken his neck trying to catch an exceptionally big wave and that he'd been found lying face down in the churned-up water. Then he'd been hauled clear and nobody seemed to know what to do about the dead man. So I caught a wave and rode it in to the beach and got a couple of lifeguards to go out and bring the man's body back to the beach. I was increasingly a man of action!

Later, when I picked up Nina, her mother and father gave me fish-eye glares and acidly advised, "Come home early, Nina." It was evident that they did not like the idea of their married daughter going out with the likes of me. Undeterred, however, we had a great time together. When we entered Lau Yee Chai's I bought Nina a pikake lei. But she wouldn't follow the custom of kissing me through the lei before I draped it around her neck. Again, our table expanded and expanded as more and more ensigns and their dates arrived. Soon about twenty people sat around the table. So I ordered ten different Chinese dishes for the whole crowd. When the food was put on the table it looked and tasted unappetizing. I only picked at the stuff, but Nina piled right into the many dishes, much to everyone's amusement. Her dancing was equally uninhibited. And her conversation was so mature and sparkling that I wondered how a girl who had so much on the ball could have a husband who stayed thousands of miles away from her—and for more than a few days.

Thursday, the commodore came aboard to ask me to play tennis with him that afternoon at Ford Island. We were to play against Captain Latimer, the *Dobbin*'s skipper, whose doubles partner was "the best tennis player on my tender." Obviously, Commander Swenson thought that I was the best player in his division since he mentioned, "This is a grudge match and I've put some money on the outcome. . . . So play up to your potential, Ruhe." That sounded very much like an order. So I played alertly and placed my shots carefully. At times, however, the commodore would knit his brows tightly and harrumph when the ball went out. But I held him up well and we won. At this he expansively said, "I'm paying for the drinks, Ruhe." This hadn't been a pleasant game for me, because the *Dobbin*'s skipper was senior to Commander Swenson. I had to really watch my step when I slammed a put-away in Captain Latimer's direction. I was discovering that senior officers didn't like to lose or be humiliated. Thus this kind of tennis was risky business for an ensign.

On 13 May the ports on the *Roe* were welded shut. Then the glass of each porthole was painted black. The wardroom looked like a funeral parlor. The logic for this supposed wartime measure escaped me—unless it was certain that the *Roe* would shortly be committed to a real war.

By Saturday I was so dead tired that I laid down on the wardroom transom after lunch and couldn't get up until six that evening, despite the fact that I was the duty officer. As the watch crew whipped in and out of the wardroom all afternoon making their reports to me, I could barely crack open the lids of my eyes. And my answers were almost inaudible. Luckily, even though it was payday, not a single sailor required my attention for any infraction ashore. The *Roe* would have to go back to sea just so I could get some rest.

In this state of exhaustion, I received a letter from Holland. It wasn't addressed in Lucrece's handwriting however. It was from Lucrece's friend, Vivienne. And what she wrote was not surprising:

> I know that Lucrece has written to you about her marrying a Nazi. And I'm certain that you, like the rest of her great loves, are heartbroken at the news. But you shouldn't be. You're too nice a person to have fallen under Lucrece's spell in the short time you were together. So I feel compelled to tell you about the two sides of her personality. You saw her only as a lovable, exceptionally beautiful woman who led you to become infatuated with her. She's done this to other nice men. But she always finds some crazy excuse for a parting of the ways. This leaves her men desolate. She does this to feed her obsessive

desire to be miserable. And she dotes on the concern which people feel for her disillusionment with life.

Marrying Arthur Baur is another of her tragic acts being played out. Herr Baur is a spare, much older man with short-cropped hair. He's a recluse and spends most of his time immersed in his books. He definitely is not a blond Aryan of the Master Race. Nor does he strut in public like most of the arrogant Germans who are here. Marrying him has been a disaster for Lucrece. The women of Amsterdam—she's moved there—have treated her badly, making her cry bitterly for being humiliated by their cruelty. It's obvious, however, that she does not discourage the bad treatment she's getting. The poor thing. The war has made her its victim. You can feel lucky if you've broken free of her. I'd say, "just forget her."

Sincerely, Vivienne

Vivienne's letter certainly eliminated from my mind the thought that Lucrece would in time recognize the mistake she'd made in marrying the Baur fellow and would sooner or later free herself from the albatross she'd tied around her neck. Thus I was now free to promote new options for a girl to marry when the two-year ban was lifted. Yet, though there were plenty of girls for a young ensign to select from, none was as dazzling as Lucrece. She'd made all other girls seem commonplace. Except, perhaps, Nina.

Although there was a rumor that more of the Pearl Harbor ships were going to be transferred to the Atlantic, we heard nothing about the *Roe*'s going to the East Coast. According to the newspapers, President Roosevelt was giving additional support to the English, who were losing merchant ships to U-boats at a dreadful rate. In March and April 1941, a news article estimated that eighty-four ships of about five hundred thousand tons of shipping had been sunk by the Nazis' submarines. It was beginning to be nip and tuck with the British. In addition, German battleships and armed raiders were at sea destroying many more Allied ships. Unquestionably, the U.S. Atlantic fleet needed beefing up in order to provide significant help.

On Monday night I called Nina for a date. She hesitatingly said, "We've got to make it Wednesday . . . and I'll meet you at Lau Yee Chai's after eight o'clock. . . . And please don't call me at my home." This sounded ominous, but was some sort of progress for me.

When back on the *Roe*, I was told that we were getting under way at seven-twenty-two next morning. That seven-twenty-two was disturbing. It was too precise for just another deployment for a fleet exercise. Moreover, this movement was all a big secret.

After daylight, the *Morris*, the *Roe*, and the *Buck* pulled out of their nest alongside the *Dobbin* in succession and joined the *Enterprise* off the sea buoy. Before we reached screening stations, the *Morris* went close to the carrier and received some mail from her—passed over by a line. Shortly thereafter the *Morris* passed some mail to the *Buck* and then the *Buck* delivered a mysterious brown envelope that was marked, "For Lieutenant Commander Scruggs's eyes only." Meanwhile, the admiral on the *Enterprise* directed the three destroyers of Destroyer Division 17 to shift screening stations to the battleship *New Mexico*, which had sortied from Pearl Harbor close behind the *Buck*. Following the *New Mex* was the cruiser *Nashville*, and shortly all five ships settled on a course of 147 degrees true at fourteen knots speed. In the interim, the Captain had torn open the brown envelope, read its two-page enclosure, and quietly—but loud enough to be overheard by those in the pilothouse—said, "We're going to the Atlantic."

It was aloha oe, "Farewell to thee" to Hawaii for the *Roe* and her crew.

16

Adieu to the *Roe*

FAR ASTERN OF THE *NEW MEXICO*'S group of warships, the battleship *Idaho* and her screening ships were visible. Beyond them, we could make out only the tops of the battleship *Mississippi*. By midmorning on 20 May all three battleships were in a column, and the carrier *Enterprise* followed to the rear. And all were on a course of 147 degrees true (heading southeast) and making fourteen knots. The *New Mexico*, the flagship of this battle force, was the lead ship of the battle line.

And three cruisers and ten destroyers were in screening stations for this cruising formation of ships. All were headed for the Atlantic. But I was perplexed that the course of 147 degrees true headed the force for Cape Horn at the southern tip of South America. That would be a tough, many-weeks route to get into the Atlantic. Thinking what that meant depressed me. Going around the Horn would make it impossible to get to Johnny Harper's wedding in Forest Hills—I'd be lucky to get to Sub School by the fifth of July.

One thing was certain: we were not going to return to Pearl Harbor. And that was bad news. For the *Roe*'s officers, it meant losing a lot of whites that were still on the *Dobbin* being laundered. For others it was even worse. Bill Norvell revealed that he'd left his wife, Elva, with no money. On hearing this, however, the Captain said, "Louise has plenty of money and she'll take care of Elva. Don't worry about it." Page and Sheehy gloomily mentioned that their wives were arriving at Honolulu the next day. And B.D.'s pregnant wife was en route to Hawaii on the *Lurline* and couldn't be reached to tell her to go back home. As for Nina, that chapter in my book seemed finished.

193

After the *Roe* arrived at her station fifteen hundred yards on the starboard bow of the *New Mex*, the Captain assembled on the fantail all men except those on watch. He then emphasized that even if the United States wasn't at actual war with the Germans, that operations in the Atlantic would involve "the real stuff." He explained that President Roosevelt had on 24 April 1941 committed U.S. naval forces to protect allied shipping west of thirty degrees west longitude. "Hence," as he noted, "battle drills and emergency drills will be conducted to count from now on." For the many men who had loved ones ashore in Hawaii, the Captain had only bad news. "There won't be any opportunity until the *Roe* arrives in Norfolk to send personal messages to your wives or sweethearts. We're sailing under a total communication blackout." Then he gravely added, "Even *I* am unable to get word to my wife that we've left Hawaii for good."

I had thought that at fourteen knots the *Roe* might get to Norfolk by 11 June if our force of ships went through the Panama Canal and not around Cape Horn. That still seemed possible, but I realized that I was going to miss a lot of travel money from the West Coast to New London and a lot of per-diem money as well. In fact, it meant that I'd be so short of money on arrival at Norfolk that I would only be able to afford an old wreck of a car—which hopefully I could keep running until the end of Sub School.

On the next day at sea, the crew dashed around: going to general quarters, reacting to simulated shell hits from a German surface raider, rendering first aid to the simulated injured personnel, acting out a response to a severe oil fire in the engine room, and playing a *Roe* attack on an enemy U-boat. The morning of drills proved extremely confusing, what with the Captain scurrying from the scene of one drill to another and irritably criticizing the men's performance. He was like a horsefly buzzing from one person to another and taking a nip out of each one's flesh. He indicated that the *Roe* had little time left until she'd be under actual attack by German warships, aircraft, or submarines.

Finally, after six hours of relentless drilling of the crew, he charitably declared a "Rope Yarn Sunday"—a free afternoon for the crew. That meant no work for men not on watch. The *Roe*'s sailors of the new Navy spent the afternoon loafing. A few read magazines and a few played cribbage or wrote letters. But for the most part they just lay out on deck sunning themselves. They weren't like the old salts I'd observed on my midshipman cruises in the '30s who put tiny models of ships into narrow-necked glass bottles, wood-carved big-breasted women, or wove antimacassars out of twine to be put on the arms of their living room chairs. Moreover, the *Roe*'s sailors seemed to get tired faster than the old breed.

On Friday, Chief Radioman Feath handed me a coded message and conspiratorially said, "This might be of interest to us. I picked it up on ComFifteen's broadcast frequency." I recognized that Feath was a snooper. He continually listened in on a host of radio circuits unrelated to the *Roe*'s operations. He was always curious about things that were transpiring—everywhere. "Perhaps we ought to decode it," he suggested. "It doesn't have an addressee. Yet it might say something we should know." Feath's sharp, pale-white face made him look like an inquisitive elf who had just emerged from a cave into the daylight. And his expression was alight with anticipation.

I wasn't against Feath's snooping. But I knew the Captain would be furious if he knew that several off-duty radiomen were listening in on half a dozen radio circuits because of Feath's curiosity. I felt that monitoring ComFifteen's Panama business was carrying things a bit too far. But a coded message without an addressee? That caused me to pull a strip cipher out of my safe and convert the enciphered message to plain language. The message when decoded was for the commander of our force of ships. In effect, it said: "Your latest movement report indicates a nonreceipt of my 220810Z which calls for transit of the Panama Canal by your ships on 6 June commencing at 1900 local time. Acknowledge."

What did the message suggest?

When I checked the *Roe*'s present position it appeared evident that remaining on course 147 degrees true was making it difficult for our force to get to Panama by 6 June. In fact, when I heard the crew talking about crossing the Equator on Sunday, I realized we'd be far off the course for going through the Canal. I also measured the distance to Panama from our present position and noted that our entire force would have to speed up a couple of knots to make it to the Canal by 6 June. But if I showed the message to the Captain, he'd blow his top "for listening in on an unauthorized circuit."

I dallied and dallied. Then I finally took the message to the bridge to show to the Captain. He read it and reread it. His scowl deepened. With a pained expression on his face he asked, "Where did you get this thing, Ruhe? And why are you showing it to me?"

"Perhaps we're the only one who received this message," I ventured defensively. I was edgy and uncomfortable, sensing that the Captain would make the delayed delivery of this critical dispatch all my fault.

The Captain shifted his feet nervously. He wanted no part in this communication snafu. Yet he recognized that a failure to get the "6 June" information to "the flag" could have dire consequences. Wearily, he asked, "Why the hell did you pick up and decode this thing?" The Old Man wanted the whole matter forgotten. "On second thought," he added, "why are we monitoring ComFifteen's circuit on this ship?"

I was forced to admit that perhaps we shouldn't have been listening in on ComFifteen's broadcasts. But since we were, a no-addressee dispatch was too irregular to be left undecoded.

"That's a helluva'n excuse, Ruhe. . . . You've put me into a real bind because now we'll have to deliver it to 'the flag' on the chance that over there they've not received it." After a long pause, the Captain finally snapped, "Deliver it in plain language. It shouldn't be delayed a second longer."

That was too gross a violation of communication security to be risked. So I begged the Captain to have the message sent to "the flag" as Feath had received it—encoded. That would cause additional delay in getting the plain-language decoded version to the admiral on the *New Mexico*, but that would be a lesser offense on our part.

The Captain's lips were edged with white as he muttered, "Dammit, Ruhe, send the coded version. . . . And you wait for the ax to fall."

The message was blinked over to the *New Mex*. After a silent wait of many minutes, there was a flurry of blinked messages that changed the course of the force to eighty-two degrees true.

We increased speed to sixteen knots. Doing sixteen knots would push the upper speed limits of the battleships but the new course would head us for the Panama Canal and we'd be off the Canal by the evening of 6 June.

After settling on the new course and at the new speed, there was an agonizingly long wait for the reaction of the admiral on the *New Mexico* to this communication fiasco.

I was reminded several times by Captain Scruggs, as he paced back and forth across the pilothouse, that I'd shown poor judgment in allowing such snooping on radio circuits which we had no business monitoring. "This will be reflected in your fitness report, Ruhe," he caustically reminded. Not for one second would he admit that Feath's curiosity and my helping hand should be appreciated for what it achieved—i.e., saving the force commander a great deal of embarrassment. The Captain was only concerned with the possibility that he'd be censored by the admiral for mishandling this important message. He worried that the admiral would ask, "How did the *Roe* receive this dispatch?" And even worse, "Why was it decoded?"

A furious blinking of a searchlight on the *New Mex*—directed at the *Roe*—broke the silence on the bridge.

"Here we go, Ruhe," the Captain tartly noted. "Stand by for a ram."

I'd been on tenterhooks waiting for a blast from the admiral. Then, his message, "Explain your failure to promptly deliver this important message from ComFifteen to my command," left little doubt that he was much displeased with the *Roe* for its Little Miss Muffett helpfulness.

The admiral didn't ask on which frequency the dispatch had been received. Only the delay between the *Roe*'s receipt of the dispatch and the time it was finally read by the admiral seemed at issue. At least two hours of delay had been involved. Understandably, my foot-dragging before facing the Captain with the decoded version of the dispatch was at fault. In fact, only the evident importance of this secret dispatch had steeled me to face the Old Man's wrath. It was a "damned if you do, damned if you don't" business.

"Okay, Ruhe, you blew it," the Captain growled. "Now you explain to the admiral over there"—pointing toward the *New Mex*—"why it took *you* so long to do something about it." After pausing for many seconds, the Captain added, "Thank God I'm getting rid of you as soon as we get to the East Coast. You're nothing but trouble."

How does one explain to an admiral a reluctance to get into a pissing contest with a martinet like the Captain?

It wasn't possible to draw up an answer that would fully mollify the admiral. Yet I painstakingly spelled out an evasive, chicken-shit explanation: "ComFifteen's encoded dispatch was received with no addressee. On the chance that it might be needed by the force commander it was decided to decode it. Its import was immediately recognized and there was no further delay in its transmission to you."

The frown on the Captain's face as he read my reply was like a black storm cloud, ready to dump a torrent of rain on my head. "I should put you in hack again to keep this ship out of trouble," he threatened. But then he told Jones, the new chief signalman: "Send Ruhe's answer out just as it is. . . . And we'll hope the admiral doesn't get any madder."

Shortly, Chief Feath showed me a plain-language broadcast message that told of the British battlecruiser *Hood* being sunk on 24 May 1941 by the German super-battleship *Bismarck* in the Atlantic. It was a bad day all around. It made more pressing the need to get our three battleships into the Atlantic to help the British in their sea war. Fortunately, there was no answer from the admiral!

That ended a bad day for me. I would just have to watch my step for the next couple of weeks. Then I'd be in the clear.

As our force of ships sailed east, the drills continued. And the Captain settled down a bit. He treated me in a friendly and fatherly manner, only being marginally upset when there was a mishandling of a communication drill. Then he had called for a repeat of the drill, stating "We have to iron out all of our kinks before we get involved in the real thing." The Captain was a purist and a hard worker. He was also intent on making the *Roe* the best fighting ship in the Atlantic Fleet. I wondered if he really knew something about our apparent drift toward war.

I began to whistle happy tunes. The *Roe* would go through the Canal on 6 June and get to Hampton Roads in plenty of time for me to be best man at Johnny Harper's wedding. My optimism was so great that I asked Hop Nolan to prepare a letter detaching me from the *Roe* "on arrival at a U.S. port" to carry out the orders I had in hand to attend Sub School—the class convening on 5 July 1941.

The Captain actually signed this paper with, according to Hop Nolan, a good-riddance gesture. So I went to work inventorying all classified publications, ciphers, and communication department Title B equipment. I was laying the groundwork for my final relief by Ensign Ken Steen just after the *Roe*'s arrival in the Atlantic. In short order I was able to determine that everything was okay in all respects.

On the 27th of May, Chief Feath routed a news item telling of the sinking of the *Bismarck* by the British. I let out a loud whoop on reading about this major setback to the German Navy. There were more cheers heard as the news was passed around the ship. The *Roe* was joining a shooting war against the Germans and each Allied victory in the Atlantic was now a triumph for *our* side. Then President Roosevelt declared an "Unlimited Emergency." This definitely placed the U.S. Navy on a war footing.

For the next week all went smoothly. The Captain acted kindly toward me. He called me "Bill" and asked pleasantly if all was going well with my being relieved by Ken Steen. I assured him that the communication department was now in great shape—the best on all destroyers. He smiled in a proud, tolerant way at that.

On 4 June the *Roe* took on forty-eight thousand gallons of bunker oil from the *New Mexico* and at the same time received twenty gallons of chocolate ice cream, courtesy of the admiral. Was this a show of gratitude? At any rate, the Captain, on being made aware of this gift for the *Roe*'s wardroom mess, called Steen, who was the mess treasurer to the bridge. "I don't want a repeat of the missing ice cream business like back in February. If you don't know what I'm talking about, ask Ruhe. It was his problem then." The Captain evidently saw this gift as a potential source of trouble.

All in all, I was beginning to feel that destroyers were the finest part of the Navy for my career and that perhaps I'd made a mistake opting to go into submarines.

On the morning of 6 June 1941, Feath picked up another one of those damned, no-addressee coded dispatches on ComFifteen's circuit. I thought that I'd told Feath to stick only to the circuits that were in the *Roe*'s communication plan. Thus, my immediate reaction when he showed the dispatch to me was to mutter, "The hell with it. I'd be crazy to decode this thing." I was like Lady Macbeth muttering, "Away foul spot." So I stowed it in my safe and decided to forget about it.

But the thought that perhaps the admiral on the *New Mex* might not have seen this message kept bugging me. The possibility that this message might affect our force's transit of the Canal haunted me. Perhaps there'd been some sabotage of the locks that would delay the transit or perhaps covertly laid mines had been discovered off the entrance to the Canal. The possibilities seemed many and made me finally decipher the dispatch—just to stop my unbridled guessing.

The message said in effect: "Order of ships transiting Canal commencing at 1900 will be *New Mexico*, destroyers of DesDiv 17, *Nashville*, etc., . . . Encourage high-speed transit of Gatun Lake to minimize transit time of all your ships. . . . Ensure total secrecy during your passage across the isthmus."

That message didn't sound very important so I put the coded and decoded versions of the dispatch back into my safe and went to my bunk. Going through the Canal would be an all-night affair and I'd be on the bridge most of the time so it seemed wise to get a little shut-eye while it was available. But like the "foul spot" I kept thinking that having the *New Mexico* go through first might be critical and that the admiral might have to be advised of that.

It was three in the afternoon—there were four more hours until the start of the Canal transit. There was enough time to figure out whether something actually needed to be done by the admiral if he'd missed this message. So I went to the bridge and studied the force of ships through my binoculars. Though the hull numbers and names of all the ships were painted-out it was easy to distinguish the key ships by their top hamper. The *Idaho* and *Mississippi*, I noted, were now out ahead of the *New Mexico*, suggesting that they were oriented for a different order of entry into the first lock just beyond Panama City, the Miraflores one. The ships were obviously in the wrong order, and the *New Mex* had evidently *not* received the latest ComFifteen message. Of that I was certain.

Reluctantly, I carried the decoded version to the bridge to show the Captain. I expected a torrent of abuse and I got it. "Dammit, Ruhe. Don't you understand that this message makes the admiral and his staff look even dumber than the last time?" The Captain's shoulders sagged and there was a sorrowful look on his face. Sending this message, he seemed to feel, would be the last straw in wrecking his status with the admiral. "You're going to get an unsat fitness report on your detachment. You know that, don't you?" This was the Captain's reprisal for my hazarding of his career.

All I could say was, "Yes, Sir." My neck and palms felt clammy but I was sure there was no alternative. I had to alert the admiral to the need for reorienting his ships to conform to the Canal transit plan. So I stood my ground, noting that: "The admiral needs this information, Sir."

The Captain's jaw clenched tight and there was fire in his eyes before he ordered: "Send out the coded version and let them decode the bad news."

After many long, anxious minutes, the flagship *New Mexico* began running up a series of flag hoists to both sides of her signal yardarm until the cross-tree was chock-a-block with signal flags. At the same time, signal lights were blinked at the *Enterprise* and the other two battleships, calling for a reorientation of the force of ships.

The *New Mex* continued steaming steadily on the base course while the big warships with their accompanying screens maneuvered to fall in astern of her so she would be the first ship to enter the first lock of the canal.

This took a good deal of time. And perhaps because the admiral was overly busy carrying out ComFifteen's instruction, this time there was no chastising of the *Roe* for her slipshod communication performance. Hence, when the *New Mex*

entered the Miraflores lock there were no blinked messages to
the *Roe*. Flag hoists, however, ordered Destroyer Division 17
to fall in astern of the *New Mex*, with the *Morris* and *Roe*
entering the first lock after the *New Mex* had floated free of it.

The totally secret movement through the Canal proved to be
a burlesque act as the line handlers on the dock yelled at the
men topside on the battleship: "On the *New Mex*. . . . Have
your men stand clear. . . . We're tossing over the heaving
lines." The huge, iron monkey fists used by the Canal people in
getting lines across to ships in the lock would really spoil
one's day if they hit you. The bolo-delivered, cannon-type balls
on the end of the heaving lines could either cripple a person
or kill him outright.

Shortly, after the *Roe* and the *Morris* had entered the first
lock, a dungaree-clad Canal worker down on the dock shouted
up at the *Roe*, "Tell Sheehy to come topside. I've got a message
for him from his wife in Hawaii."

So much for total secrecy!

As the Miraflores locks were flooded to float the *Morris* and
the *Roe* up to the level of the Pedro Miguel locks, I had the
chance to reflect on the whole business of being a Boy Scout
doing good deeds. They were apparently not appreciated one
bit by this Navy I was in and could be detrimental to one's
career. And yet, I wasn't sure I could stop myself from doing
what seemed right.

Once free of the Pedro Miguel locks, the *Roe* hurried
through the Gaillard Cut and then dashed across Gatun Lake
at twenty-six knots. The dim light of a half moon was sufficient
to spot and avoid the small islands in the lake. It was too dark
to see alligators scrambling down into the water as the *Roe*'s
heavy wake swept up over the mud shores. Shrill, excited par-
rot squawks protested the *Roe*'s rapid movement—their rau-
cous calls seeming to indicate that even the wild parrots knew
of the *Roe*'s passage across the Isthmus.

The *Roe* had gone through the cuts at only fifteen knots, yet
she completed her transit of the Canal in four hours and twenty-five minutes. A record of sorts.

As she later lay stopped in Limón Bay off Cristobal of the
Canal Zone, while waiting for the passage of the remainder of
the Atlantic-bound force of warships, a gentle swell from the
Atlantic caused the *Roe* to pitch slowly in a soothing manner.
There was a pleasantness in standing on a destroyer's undulat-
ing deck that was lost when one went ashore to firm ground.
Destroyers were actually seductive things. Yet I knew that
when the *Roe* moved to the North Atlantic, the furious waves

there would challenge a man's true grit. The Atlantic was an
unfriendly ocean compared to the Pacific.

On the morning of 7 June and just before the force steamed
out of Limón Bay and headed north, Captain Scruggs in a sly,
offhand aside to me said, "We're going to Guantánamo Bay,
Ruhe. And then you're on your own."

My heart sank into my shoes. With a quivering voice I
asked, "And then we go to Norfolk?"

"No!"

"Does that mean that when we get to Guantánamo I'll get
detached from the *Roe* to carry out my orders to proceed to
Sub School?"

"Of course."

"Then how do I get from there to the United States?"

"That's up to you, Ruhe." The Captain was smilingly pleasant without a touch of vindictiveness. I noted, however, that
he'd stopped calling me "Bill" and that I'd apprehensively
exhaled until I was out of breath.

En route to Guantánamo, the *Morris* punched a hole in her
bow as she closed the *New Mexico* to receive mail. The *New
Mex*, with her thick side armor, had only a scratch to show for
her being rammed by a destroyer. But I had the chilling
thought that Captain Scruggs might do much the same thing
while I was the OOD and then I'd get tied up in a court of
inquiry for several weeks and my plans would go up in smoke.

All my belongings had been packed in an old battered suitcase and two metal cruise boxes—there being no wood to
make me the traditional wooden cruise box. All wood, as flam-
mable, had been removed from the *Roe* when she was
"stripped." Thus I was ready to depart the *Roe* at a moment's
notice. Now all that was needed was the word, "Go." But
Captain Scruggs maintained a closed-lips secrecy about the
Roe's destination after Guantánamo. He did, however, knowing of my great concern about getting to Forest Hills, tell me
out of the hearing of anyone else that the *Roe* was going to
Bermuda to relieve the destroyer squadron leader *Sampson*—
and wasn't going to the East Coast. The Captain also explained
that Destroyer Division 17 was being dissolved and all of her
destroyers would become leaders of Atlantic Fleet destroyer
squadrons.

Our seventeen warships anchored in Guantánamo Bay on
10 June, among a horde of other ships. I was frantic to get
ashore and find out from my friends if their ships were shortly
going to sail to the East Coast. But like Captain Scruggs, it

was unlikely that their seniors would breach the secrecy of their ship movements.

Tuesday was sticky hot and the sun bore down relentlessly. Only the Officers' Club, with its rotating overhead fans, seemed bearable in my overwrought condition. The club was crowded when I arrived there in the afternoon; no one there knew anything about what was going to happen next. Or they wouldn't tell me.

Frustrated, I quickly downed a Tom Collins and went for a swim in the Bay. But the water was lukewarm and muddy and was thus no help for my depression.

When back aboard the *Roe* I asked for permission to use the *Roe*'s motor whaleboat the next day to visit other ships anchored in the harbor. I also asked to be detached from the *Roe* before cruising around the bay to find a sympathetic skipper who'd help me get to the East Coast. If I found one, I'd be able to transfer my belongings to his departing ship without delay. I didn't want to miss a chance that one might be sailing shortly. Thus, early on Wednesday morning I had the *Roe*'s whaleboat coxswain pull up to the gangway of ship after ship. I'd then dash up the gangway to the quarterdeck, tell the OOD that I had to get to Sub School soon and that I needed a ride to an East Coast port in order to carry out my orders. Plaintively I'd ask: "Are you leaving soon for Norfolk . . . or some place like that?"

Each OOD I encountered in this fashion claimed he had no knowledge of his ship's departure plans. Each seemed mystified as to why I thought his ship might be a means to carry out my orders. When I went aboard the *Morris* and repeated the same request I got a negative answer. But I noticed two wooden cruise boxes on the quarterdeck. When asked about the cruise boxes the OOD said, "They're the Division Commander's and are being delivered to the *Winslow*." Commander Swenson was leaving for another assignment? In the States? A ray of sunshine had broken through my gray cloud of pessimism. My next stop was obviously the destroyer *Winslow*.

I ran up to the top of the *Winslow*'s gangway, my heart very much upbeat. The OOD, Neal Almgren, was an Academy classmate. He listened to my plea for a ride. Then he said, "Wait 'til I ask my Captain," and disappeared up the ladder leading to his skipper's cabin.

Neal was back shortly with the unequivocal resolution to my problem: "Bring your gear aboard right away." That was all I wanted to hear. So I turned to dash back down to the whaleboat. But Neal stopped me with a word of caution: "I told Captain Dees that you were a good chess player—a member of the Naval Academy's chess team. That proved to be the clincher. Captain Dees," Neal added, "loves to play chess and unfortunately there's no one on board who can offer him a good game. . . . He's looking forward to playing with you. . . . And that means you're likely to have to play with him every waking hour until the completion of this trip." As an aside, he added: "Make sure that he wins a few games so that this tin can remains a happy ship." No problem! I immediately transferred my belongings to the *Winslow*.

The next morning at eight o'clock the *Winslow* got under way and proceeded out of Guantánamo Bay. But she commenced an antisubmarine patrol off the entrance to the bay. In the Atlantic they were worrying about intruding U-boats. Throughout the day as the *Winslow* moved back and forth across the entrance, the tops of the destroyers in the bay were visible. I had quickly spotted the tops of the *Roe* and kept a check on her. She evidently remained at anchor even though other destroyers got under way and exited the bay.

During the day as the *Winslow* patrolled off Guantánamo Bay, I was free of any duties and had the time to reflect on the past ten months on the *Roe*. With the U.S. Navy on the eve of a probable big sea war in the Pacific against the Japanese, the events I observed were indeed sobering. And serving on a "hell ship" with an abusive skipper had helped bring a lot of thoughts into focus.

It seemed that we officers of the U.S. Navy were at a moment in history when we were treated as acceptable persons in all circles of society—even among the most affluent and the most elitist. I might even have been able to promote my Doris Duke connection into a marriage to her or one of her peers because she was actually about my age. But my Naval Academy professor's warning, "If you marry wealth, you'll earn every cent of it," made this a dumb option. Putting aside thoughts about the possibility of getting married soon, I concentrated on what I had learned about the Navy and where it was going.

I recalled that when the *Roe* in 1940 finished the job of transferring decrepit old destroyers to the British, then took part in the phony war in the Atlantic, and finally did Neutrality Patrol duties off Martinique, all the emphasis was on helping the British in a peripheral and inconsequential way. Virtually no emphasis was placed on the German U-boat threat and the *Roe*'s capability for antisubmarine work. It seemed that direct involvement in the European war was remote. The war would be over before the United States became truly committed to defeating Hitler. "Strip ship" was not treated very seriously nor did we worry much about the reliability of the weapons that might be used.

But when the *Roe* deployed to Hawaii, we clearly were dealing with an approaching sea war in the Pacific. And destroyers would be used in a different fashion, since we'd be fighting an enemy with different objectives than the Axis powers, which emphasized submarines to bring Great Britain to its knees. In the Pacific, the readiness of the *Roe* was gauged by her gunnery and torpedo capability for fighting major surface battles in support of the U.S. fleet. In the Atlantic, her antisubmarine capability was of first importance. Submarine School would reorient my thinking not only about my professional future but also about the importance of submarines in war.

The Tripartite Pact between Japan, Germany, and Italy now began to make good sense. By threatening a war against the Soviets in Siberia, the Japanese encouraged a continuing German U-boat campaign in the Atlantic. This meant that U.S. destroyers were siphoned off from the Pacific Fleet to meet the heavy demands for antisubmarine warships in the Atlantic. Thus a Japanese Pacific sea war against the United States was likely within the next few months—before our "two-ocean navy" program had begun producing destroyers in considerable numbers.

Naval leaders were obviously intent upon readying the fleet for war. And Captain Scruggs had been overly energetic in driving his officers and crew to a state of war readiness. Spit-and-polish had ceased to be the most important activity of the *Roe*. More important were better communications, improved gunnery, coordinated launching of torpedoes by many destroyers at major enemy warships, and maneuvering with the fleet.

Yet antisubmarine preparations had been mainly ignored, despite the threat posed by enemy Japanese submarines to our big warships. The great numbers of British aircraft carriers, battleships, and cruisers either sunk or damaged in 1940 by U-boats should have highlighted the threat that Japanese submarines might pose against the U.S. fleet. When an occasional red fleet submarine had been injected into a Blue Fleet problem, the sub almost invariably penetrated the destroyer screens undetected and made simulated successful attacks against the "heavies." In addition, although it was understood that the main job of U.S. submarines was to be the "eyes of the fleet"—i.e., acting as far-out pickets to warn of the approach of enemy warships—this function had not been practiced by the Pacific Fleet. The scouting function had been usurped by surveillance aircraft catapulted off the heavies—despite the shortcomings of air reconnaissance at night and under low-visibility conditions of fog or rain.

It seemed that for all the stepped-up Pacific Fleet activity against surface warships, destroyers such as the *Roe* were not being adequately prepared for antisubmarine warfare. Scruggs, for example, never called for a depth-charge drill. And exercises using U.S. subs for antisubmarine practice were at a minimum. Submarines in the Pacific were not considered critical to a sea war's outcome. A decisive battle between the U.S. and Japanese fleets was felt to be the key to victory.

Thus, the diluting of the Pacific Fleet by sending the *Roe* and three battleships, an aircraft carrier, three cruisers, and ten destroyers to the Atlantic would make it easier for the Japanese to win their imminent Pacific sea war. Still, in many ways, we were dancing at a slow pace toward war.

My ten months on the *Roe* indeed had been sobering. As the *Roe*'s communication officer, I'd had significant responsibilities. Added to that were the draconian demands made by Captain Scruggs. Although I didn't like the way that I'd been treated, it was the Captain's way of forcing me to become a competent, professional naval officer and to bring my communication department up to a war readiness level. It had been a rough struggle over the past year. Yet, in a perverse way, I owed the Captain a debt of gratitude.

At nightfall the *Winslow* steadied on a northerly course and headed for Norfolk. I said a silent "Adieu" to the *Roe* and had a momentary pang of regret at leaving this fine ship and the very good men who manned her—particularly the chiefs.

Tin cans, I'd come to feel, had provided the best sort of professional maturing for this tin-can ensign new to the Navy.

Epilogue

THE *WINSLOW* ANCHORED OFF the Naval Operating Base, Norfolk, Virginia, on 15 June. When I went ashore I confirmed that most of my classmates were either getting married within a few days or were urgently looking for the right girl to marry. After staying only a day there, I drove to my home outside Allentown, Pennsylvania, in a 1935 black Chevrolet sedan I'd bought for fifty dollars—having gotten an advance on my travel orders of a couple of hundred dollars. The car was pretty much a wreck but proved to be a no trouble car.

On 19 June I went to Forest Hills, New York, for the rehearsal of Johnny Harper's wedding and met "the girl"! Carol Vermilye was a bridesmaid and of New Amsterdam Dutch heritage. She wore a yellow linen dress, had a golden suntan, and was a natural blond (but with a high IQ). She was a Powers model—but not one of the long-legged variety of salon fashion models. An outdoors type, Carol played a good game of tennis and was on the New York Athletic Club's traveling lacrosse team.

At the party after the rehearsal—where Johnny Harper had been nervous as a cat and badly needed my calm, steady support—Carol and I danced to Sammy Kaye's "Music on the Park" (Central Park, New York). The band's hit tune was "Hey Daddy." But the words, "I want a diamond ring, bracelets, everything," didn't apply to this very nifty, down-to-earth girl. At a pause in the music, someone told the bridal party that the submarine *0-9* had gone down off Long Island a few hours earlier with the entire crew lost. That didn't dampen the gaiety of the party, despite the fact that Johnny and I were imminent submariners. With the feeling of immortality of young ensigns, the report of the *0-9*'s loss proved only a momentary distraction.

The next day, Johnny's wedding went off as planned, except that he dropped the ring when I handed it to him.

Three weeks later, on a weekend during Sub School, I suggested to Carol that we get married the day after graduation. Without a pause Carol said, "Yes!" And I've discovered ever since that I'd really taken to heart Blossom Wiley's fine advice as to what made a "good Navy wife."

My old captain, Lieutenant Commander Richard M. Scruggs, became a rear admiral before the end of the war and was in charge of an echelon of amphibious landing ships at the invasion of Okinawa. He won a Silver Star and two Legion of Merit awards for his distinguished war record. My observations of his—at times—incompetence as a peacetime skipper apparently didn't pan out when he changed over to war. Similarly, his abusive and punishing methods of training the officers resulted not in derelicts of the Navy, but in successful warriors. Their war records attest to the wisdom behind the Captain's harsh mistreatment of all of his men. Running a "hell ship" evidently made some sort of good sense.

Mr. Parish took his destroyer *Gilmer* into the war, won a Navy Cross, a Legion of Merit, and a Bronze Star for his war actions and became a rear admiral by the end of the war.

Hop Nolan ended up as a captain and won two Navy Commendation Medals during his World War II destroyer service.

Bill Norvell ended the war as a rear admiral, winning a Legion of Merit and two Navy Commendation Medals for his wartime destroyer actions.

B.D. Wood retired as a captain after having won a Bronze Star and Navy Commendation Medal for his wartime destroyer service. He is presently living in Plano, Texas.

Ozzie Wiseman, the winner of a Navy Cross in early World War II air action, was shot down by Japanese fighters at the Battle of Midway in 1942. He was a Lieutenant (junior grade) at the time of his death.

Charley King, a lieutenant, was lost at sea off the fleet tanker *Chemung* in the North Atlantic in August 1943.

Commander Swenson, the division commander, went down with the cruiser *Juneau* in the Solomon Islands in November 1942. He was a captain at the time.

And Blatz Helm, having made lieutenant, was lost on the submarine *Pickerel* as a result of Japanese antisubmarine action in April 1943. By then he'd won a Silver Star.

All of the above officers, except for B.D. Wood, have passed away.

As for what happened to the author of this story, I learned that my bad record under Scruggs was overlooked when my request for Sub School was processed. Consequently, I served in submarines throughout World War II and ended with command of the submarine *Sturgeon* in late 1944. Like the other Scruggs-trained officers, I was well decorated, with three

Silver Stars and a Navy Unit Commendation for my wartime actions. Over my twenty-eight-year career in the Navy I later had command of the destroyer *Beale* and the guided missile cruiser *Topeka*, held several division commands, and spent much time in the Pentagon. I managed to move my family (which includes six children) twenty-four times—and one of the moves was to Hawaii! After retiring from the Navy in 1967 as a captain, I had a successful seventeen-year career with the major defense contractor General Dynamics, plus an eight-year stint as editor of a magazine, *The Submarine Review*. Three years ago Carol and I celebrated our fiftieth wedding anniversary, but without the presence of Johnny Harper, who went down with the submarine *Shark* in 1944.

Not forgetting Lucrece—my father visited her several years after the war and reported that she was "most attractive, sparkling, with a quick wit and seemed very happy." When he said that he and his newspaper companion on a trip to Europe wished to attend the Netherlands' coronation of the new queen, Lucrece, evidently with good connections high up in the government, readily obtained choice seats for them. My father also noted that Arthur Baur, her husband, was banned from Holland and could return to their home in Amsterdam for only short visits. Then in 1966, my midshipman son Barnaby, after a boomerang contest in France, visited Lucrece and found her "slim, lovely, wistful, and still showing a strong emotional attachment to you, Father." She took him to her study, "which was full of books, and played Brahm's Symphony No. One by candlelight, with the trees outside of her bay-window swaying wildly in a blustery wind—a perfect setting for the music."

In 1983, after winning an international boomerang championship in Germany, my youngest son, Richard, visited Lucrece and reported that she was holding court for several old friends, who were admiring male visitors, one of whom quietly confided: "She was an invaluable person in our underground against the Nazis during the war."

She had at that time a son who was "an electronic wizard and a daughter who was very Dutch. And she was handsome, thin, and with perfect skin and a beautiful complexion."

Lucrece was among the fortunate ones who survived World War II. I consider myself equally lucky. I had joined the fleet during a unique period of American history, just before the war. In that time before the attack on Pearl Harbor, I personally witnessed and participated in America's slow dance toward war. Except for a few senior leaders, America seemed focused on itself and unwilling to recognize the storm clouds and sacrifices that were building on the horizon.

I served on a tin can under a captain whose harsh leadership became the stuff of fiction and screenplays. I had been abused, demeaned, and terrorized for almost a year. But I later survived four intensive and action-packed years of submarine warfare. Upon reflection, I can assure the reader that Captain Scruggs never became my model for naval command. But, in a perverse way, perhaps because he believed that war was coming, he put me through his wringer and made me tough and professional enough to be sitting here in 1995 telling you about the wonders of America and its Navy before World War II.